INTERNATIONAL SOCIETY

Also by Evan Luard

THE BLUNTED SWORD: The Erosion of Military Power in
Modern World Politics (1988)

International Society

Evan Luard

NEW AMSTERDAM
New York

© Evan Luard 1990

All rights reserved.

First published in the United States of America in 1990 by
NEW AMSTERDAM BOOKS
171 Madison Avenue
New York, NY 10016

by arrangement with The Macmillan Press Ltd

Printed in Hong Kong

ISBN 0–941533–80–8

Contents

v

Preface

Over the last few years I have published a trilogy of books, each subtitled "a study in international sociology". The books were based on the belief that the study of international society, including relations between states, is best seen as an aspect of the study of society generally: in other words of sociology.

For many centuries nations have established among themselves societies of states, having many of the characteristics of smaller societies. These, I believed, could be studied by the use of methods and concepts comparable to those employed by social scientists in studying other types of society.

Each of the three books adopted a predominantly historical approach: that is, they compared a number of "international societies" which have existed at different periods in history. The first, *Types of International Society*, described the different characteristics of a succession of historical societies of states, including the various social structures, institutions, prescribed norms of conduct, roles, systems of stratification, motives and means employed within each, and sought to identify the typical "ideology" of each society. The second, *Economic Relationships among States*, examined the different types of economic relationships established between the different members of a number of such societies. The third, *War in International Society*, described the changing character of war over recent centuries, showing how its forms and purposes, the issues over which it has been fought, the assets which it has been used to procure and the beliefs about its legitimacy, have varied from one international society to another according to the interests, goals and "ideology" of the governing élites in each age.

It has been suggested that it might be useful to try to summarise, in a single and briefer volume, the main features of this approach. The purpose is to bring together some of the main findings of the earlier books and to set out the presuppositions which underlay those findings. It is hoped that this may be of some interest to general readers, as well as to specialists in sociology and international relations.

Introduction: The Study of International Society

IS THERE AN INTERNATIONAL SOCIETY?

The first question to be asked in studying international society is: does such a society exist?

At first sight the world as a whole is an entity so vast and amorphous, the links between its parts so tenuous, that it is meaningless to conceive of it as a "society" which can be subjected to systematic scrutiny. Its five billion people, scattered as they are among 160 or so different states, each having its own culture, traditions, economic system and political organisation, appear to possess so little in common, to enjoy so little systematic contact, to have so little knowledge of, let alone any sense of kinship with, fellow members of the society, that the conditions necessary for "social" existence, it may be held, are entirely lacking. The common traditions and institutions, the social cohesion, above all the common system of values, which are sometimes seen as the essence of social existence, do not here exist. On the contrary, the degree of hostility and conflict among the members, the frequency of all-out warfare between them, might seem to make the concept of a single world "society" a nonsensical one.

If we define society in a sufficiently narrow way – to mean a compact, closely integrated community, comparable to the primitive societies mainly studied by social anthropologists, or even the social structure of a village or small town in industrial countries today – then international society clearly could not qualify. Many of the features we associate with social existence of that kind are here lacking: the bonds of mutual dependence, the sense of community, the common loyalties – all important features of social existence in these smaller societies – are almost completely absent. But if the comparison is made with the kind of societies found in modern industrial states, the difference is far less. For there too there are among the members large differences in culture, religion, political

1

belief, race, language (in many cases), speech and way of life that are not much less than those which exist in the wider international society. There too there are major conflicts of interest and purpose: among occupations, classes and regions. There too there exists (and increasingly exists) no commonly accepted system of beliefs and values. Even in terms of size and numbers such states as the US, China and India today, bringing together hundreds of millions of peoples, of many creeds, races, colours, political ideas and ethical beliefs, are far closer in character to the world as a whole than to the small-scale communities traditionally studied by anthropologists (the population of the entire international society is, after all, only five times that of China). For all its diffuseness, its geographical dispersion, its lack of integration, its disharmony of value systems, therefore, world society is not altogether different from the national social systems that have been widely studied.

The differences between the two are anyway rapidly declining. While national societies have grown larger and more diffuse, international society has become less so. Only a century ago or less, sociologists such as Comte and Durkheim could conceive of national societies almost as if they *were* (or should be) closely integrated communities; and assumed they had, or might regain, a common pattern of beliefs and values – "consensus" or "solidarity" – which, though quite different from those in primitive societies, might unite their people in a similar way; though now societies (*Gesellschaften*), they could none the less retain, it was suggested, some of the character of communities (*Gemeinschaften*). Today 'this seems an increasingly unreal assumption. The lack of any genuinely shared religious beliefs, the alienation of large minorities, the existence of a substantial under-class, the wide differences in interests and conditions, way of life, and above all ways of thought, have caused modern national states not only to cease to be "communities", but to be scarcely even "societies" in the sense traditionally understood.

Conversely, the world as a whole, growing smaller, begins to take on some of the features of such a society: if not integrated, at least interdependent and interrelated. Only a century or so ago contacts between states remained relatively marginal. Only a tiny proportion of mankind ever stepped outside the borders of their own countries. Most had little knowledge, and even less *consciousness*, of those living elsewhere. Most of the people of China in 1850 not only knew nothing of the people of the US or of Europe; in many cases they did not know of the latter's existence. Only a little more than a century ago there were no diplomatic links, hardly any trading links, virtually no contacts of any kind between those countries. Where there was no mutual consciousness among peoples there could not be in any meaningful way a society among them. There existed, possibly, some kind of European society, or an inter-American society, even an Asian society of sorts. There was no world society.

Today the situation is altogether different. Almost every inhabitant of every country now has *some* awareness of the world outside their borders. They are likely to buy (or to wish to buy) at least some foreign goods. They will probably see films, newspaper accounts, television programmes, that provide some information about other lands. Postal and telecommunication services link every country in the world. Diplomatic and commercial contacts join almost all of them. More important, the *ideas* that become widespread in one part of the world become known, often widely known, in others. Political creeds spread rapidly across the world; science and technology crosses frontiers quickly and easily; the current fashions – in pop music, clothes, in sport and entertainment – move in a very short time from one country to another.

Finally, and perhaps most important for our purpose, the *actions* taken in one country have a rapid effect elsewhere. The price set for oil by one group of countries, that demanded for capital goods by another, the rate of interest set in New York, the emergence of recession in Western Europe, all of these have a huge and immediate impact, direct or indirect, on millions of people scattered throughout the world. The defence policies adopted by the Soviet Union, the foreign policy adopted by the US, the racial policies adopted by South Africa, the revolutionary policies adopted by Iran or Libya, all of these have repercussions that are quickly felt elsewhere. The result is that the interrelationships – social, cultural, economic, and political – between different parts of the globe are today as close as were those between different parts of Britain only a century or so ago. And they can reasonably be described as establishing a network of mutual influence, a set of complex but defined and understood interrelationships, which in themselves create a "society" of a sort.

The consciousness of interrelatedness is reinforced in many ways. Individuals, in travelling in increasing number to the remotest parts of the world, in absorbing foreign cultures, in undertaking trade with distant territories, or investment in far economies, are made aware of a common world system. Governments, equally, become almost as concerned to influence what happens in other parts of the world as to influence what happens at home: to prevent (or promote) the spread of communism elsewhere, determine what kind of government shall be established in Nicaragua or Afghanistan, to solve the "world debt problem" or the "world hunger problem". The establishment of new organisations to tackle "world" issues – to promote world health, to run world postal services and world telecommunications, to co-ordinate the world's air transport, to protect the world environment, to oversee the world's monetary system, to counter the world trade in narcotics or protect world patents – all these help to establish the image of an international community, having its own institutions, which are designed to promote international purposes, and which increasingly overlay the institutions of states, set up to promote state purposes. Even the phrases in common use – "world population", the "international environment", the "global commons" or "multinational corporations" – all these help to build up the consciousness of an international society. And it is through the creation of such a consciousness that the basis of a society begins to be established.

Is the society we are concerned with that once known as the "society of states"? A society of states undoubtedly exists. It is reflected in diplomatic relationships, in treaties and understandings among governments, and the activities of international organisations (which are controlled by the representatives of states). But the study of international society goes beyond a study of the interactions of states. A large range of transnational relationships are undertaken also by groups and individuals. Together these represent significant inputs into the transactions of international society, and they must be one of the objects of our study.

Over recent years a great deal of attention has been devoted to "transnational relations" and to the activities of "non-state actors".[1] Such studies recognise the role that these informal, non-state relationships play in modern world politics. But in accepting that role, one should not downplay (as some seek to do) the dominant part still played by states. It is not the case, as is often suggested, that an increase in the part played by non-state actors implies a reduction in the role played by states, that is by governments. On the contrary,

1. For example, by J. Nye and R. Keohane, in *Transnational Relations and World Politics* (New York, 1971); R. W. Mansbach, *The Web of World Politics: Non-state Actors in the Global System* (Eaglewood Cliffs, 1976); J. N. Rosenau, *The Study of Global Interdependence, Essays in the Transnationalisation of World Affairs* (New York, 1980); and in Britain particularly by writers of the "world society" school of John Burton.

though the transnational activities of non-state actors have, with improved communications, grown over recent years,[2] this has been accompanied by a similar increase in the scope and intensity of relationships among governments. The power of the latter, both at home and abroad, has indeed probably increased faster than that of non-official actors. To a considerable extent the relations which groups and individuals can undertake – in the field of trade and investment, cultural relations, of migration, even travel and tourism – is more closely controlled by governments in the modern world than in any earlier time. The transfer of resources between states, perhaps the most important way in which international social relationships can be transformed, is supervised and limited by the actions of governments. Governments regulate the affairs of their own people in far more detailed and complex ways than before. Their command over armed power is more absolute than ever (to the extent that in developed states there is now virtually no possibility, as in all earlier times, of armed rebellion). The relationships which individuals can undertake across frontiers depend on the understandings and agreements reached among governments. And the general character of international society at any one time, including its characteristic "ideology", is thus determined by the actions and decisions of states more than by those of individuals or groups. A study of international society which does not recognise this primary role will thus give a misleading picture. And while, therefore, in the present study we shall be concerned with all relationships undertaken within international society, our attention will be focused especially on relationships among states, which remain the dominant (because the most powerful) actors within it.

2. It is arguable, however, that the role played by non state-actors was almost as significant in earlier ages; for example the part played by the pope and the Catholic church generally; by the emperor, by wandering friars and wandering knights, by non-national condottiere and their troops, during the Middle Ages; by transnational religious movements, Calvinist preachers and Jesuit priests, and by mercenary troops and commanders, in the age of religions (1559–1648); by non-national (i.e. foreign) monarchs, intellectuals and writers in the age of sovereignty (1648–1789); and by leaders of national revolutions, bankers, merchants, and cosmopolitan adventurers of various kinds, in the age of nationalism (1789–1914).

HOW DOES IT DIFFER?

If there does exist an international society of a sort, what *kind* of society is it? How does it differ from the other types of society which social scientists have mainly studied in the past?

The first difference is that international society is, more than almost any other, a highly decentralised society. The important point is not that power at the centre is very weak: almost non-existent. This lack of centralised enforcement machinery distinguishes it from most *national* societies where power today is highly centralised. But it does not differ from the situation which exists in many primitive societies, where there is often no central power, and no forcible sanctions against offenders.[3] More important is the fact that power in international society is not only dispersed but highly *concentrated*. Military power and administrative authority alike are monopolised by a relatively small number of power centres: the governments of national states. Each of these usually disposes of its own armed forces; is able to command some loyalty and co-operation from all, or most of, the people coming under its authority; and claims total independence ("sovereignty") from any external power, whether other sovereign states or international authorities. To a considerable extent these national governments *mediate* between their own people and those of other countries; that is, they can to a large extent determine what kind of relations they can enjoy; what travel elsewhere they can undertake; with whom they can trade and under what conditions; whether they shall be at peace or at war. Against them not only international authority but individuals and groups within their own populations are virtually powerless. It is because of this overwhelming power of the national state, and its control over relations of other kinds, that the study of international relations has traditionally been concerned almost exclusively with the relations of states rather than of peoples. And it is for the same reason that in the present study, though we shall be concerned with all relationships within international society, much of our attention will be focused on those that occur between states.[4]

3. For a study of such societies see J. Middleton and D. Tait (eds), *Tribes without Rulers* (London, 1958); Lucy Mair, *Primitive Government* (London, 1962); L. T. Hobhouse, G. C. Wheeler and M. Ginsberg, *The Material Culture and Social Institutions of the Simpler Peoples* (London, undated) pp. 53–61.
4. It is this which distinguishes the approach presented here from the "world

This leads to a second, and closely related, difference between international society and any other. This is that there does not exist at the international level the *formal* structure of relationships which is sometimes seen as the essential characteristic of social existence. In primitive societies this exists, for example, in the clearly defined relations of family, kinship and lineage groups, clans and tribes. In national states it exists in the clearly established structure of authority, expressed in local and national government, and in well-recognised social and institutional relationships. Within international society the links between individuals, scattered among many nations, are more diffuse, tenuous and uncertain; and even the relations that exist between states, through their membership of alliances, regional groupings, functional organisations and world bodies, are far looser and more incoherent than those which exist within most other societies. The authority exercised by international organisations, and the loyalty they can command, is weak and unpredictable. Their membership is not uniform. There is not even a clear structure of authority *between* international organisations, which are frequently in conflict with each other. Though this is not altogether different from the situation which exists in some national states – for example in some developing countries today, where centralised authority is weak and local leaders and organisations often strong – it none the less specially typifies international society, characterised as it is by a fluid structure, without clearly defined relationships, nor any simple hierarchy of power.

There is a third feature of international society related to this. Here, even less than in modern national states, does there exist any sense of community, or even of *solidarity*, sometimes said to be an important or even essential feature of smaller societies: that is, the sense of belonging to a particular group with common traditions and (usually) the belief in a common origin or destiny which marks the group off from others (the "strangers" from other lands or tribes,

---

society" approach of John Burton and his school, who have sought to place the main emphasis on non-governmental relations and to play down the role of the state. It is difficult to resist the conclusion that that approach contains an element of wishful thinking: such writers present the world they would like to see rather than that which they find. As shown above, the state remains more powerful than any other institution of the modern world and realism suggests that in the study of international society primary attention must be given to the relationships of states.

who do not share that common destiny). It is true that this sense of solidarity is also weak in many modern industrial societies. Yet in that case it does usually exist in some form: in the form, for example, of national pride, "patriotism", a sentiment that may be evoked at least at a time of national crisis, when it is most required. At the international level such a sentiment is scarcely to be found at all. Common membership of the human race, common membership of world organisations, common participation in the struggle to promote world peace, world progress or the protection of the global environment, none of these is sufficient to create any very close bond of fellow-feeling between members of one state and those of another. In other words national loyalties far outweigh any embryonic feelings of loyalty to humankind. The differences should not be exaggerated. In any national state today the sense of *hostility* to some fellow-citizens – for example, to those belonging to a different class, different region, different occupation group, different religion or race, or even to a different political persuasion – is often at least as important as the sense of *sharing* a common nationality (and partly accounts for the prevalence of civil war in many countries of the world). Even within a single city the factors that *divide* some from others – the very rich from the very poor, for example – are often as important as those that unite. The lack of solidarity at the world level, therefore, though an undoubted fact, is one that distinguishes it not from the kind of national society most commonly found today, but only from that increasingly rare phenomenon (perhaps always more rare than some anthropologists would have us believe): the closely knit and well-ordered primitive society, in which powerful social pressures have created a strong sense of fellow-feeling within a closely knit and relatively harmonious group. There is, it is true, no international "community", with the *common* values, beliefs and interests that that word implies. But there is an international "society" of a kind.

There is a fourth difference between international society and other societies. In most smaller societies a sense of solidarity, in so far as it exists, stems from an acceptance of the *legitimacy* of the existing social order and the structure of authority that exists there. For whatever reasons, authority is generally felt to be justified and so to be obeyed. That justification may stem from an underlying ideology which permeates the entire society; from social conditioning; from mere inertia (it is usually easier to accept authority than to reject it); or from a rational calculation that existing authority, whether or not it stems from widespread popular consent, at least provides the best available basis for a stable social existence. However derived, this sense of legitimacy helps to sustain the social structure. It is reinforced by rites and traditions, myths and symbols, flags and ceremonies, which strengthen loyalties. At the international level these sentiments scarcely exist for most people. There are a few everywhere, no doubt, who are willing to accord a special authority to world institutions – an authority accepted as transcending that of national states and deserving at least nominal allegiance from them – and who might accept a corresponding duty to comply with their injunctions. But such people are rare exceptions. For the most part citizens do not at present acknowledge such obligations. The myths and symbols that surround international authorities – the UN flag, UN uniforms, the office of the Secretary-General – arouse little response among the mass of people in most countries. In general the obligation the citizen feels to obey national authorities far outweighs any obligation he feels to heed the demands made by international bodies. In almost every case it is the national state which is believed to enjoy the main legitimacy, the primary right to demand obedience.

Finally, international society lacks, even more obviously than these, the common value-system, the *consensus* on the way in which society should be ordered, that is sometimes held to be the condition of a stable social order. Once again the difference is not an absolute one. An absence of consensus is as clearly visible in many national societies – often racked with civil war, with religious divisions, deep economic conflicts and strong political dissension – as it is at the international level. Modern societies in which there exists any genuine and widespread consensus, a common pattern of belief, even on fundamental, ethical or political values, is the exception rather than the rule. But it has to be accepted that social consensus is even *more* lacking within the international community than it is within most smaller societies. And it is above all on the most fundamental questions of social order – what are the obligations owed by one state to another, what are the rules that should govern co-existence between them, in what circumstances are acts of violence legitimate? – that the most glaring differences of belief are visible. Lack of consensus on these, the fundamentals of co-existence, could clearly be a source of continual conflict, possibly even of disintegration, within the world society.

All of these are undoubtedly real differences distinguishing international society from most smaller societies. They make it a different type of society from those which have been mostly studied by political philosophers and social scientists in the past. And those differences need to be kept continually in mind in the analysis we shall undertake. They should not, however, be exaggerated. None of the features we have found wanting in international society is altogether lacking there. International organisations – for example, the International Monetary Fund (IMF) or the World Health Organisation (WHO) – do exercise a minimal degree of authority over national states, even if it is not of the kind that can be enforced by military power. The social structure that exists among states, even if less clear-cut than that which exists between them, is not (as we shall see) totally lacking. A limited degree of solidarity is felt in world society, even between peoples at distant corners of the earth (as is shown, for example, when individuals contribute generously for the relief of disasters in other countries, or when governments provide funds for international aid programmes or contribute to international peace-keeping operations). Some degree of legitimacy is accorded by governments to world-wide bodies, as is reflected in the undertakings they make in accepting the UN Charter and in the contributions they continue to make to a wide range of organisations. Finally, there does exist a small but growing degree of consensus concerning the principles that should underlie relationships within the international society – such as the obligation, generally accepted if not always observed, to refrain from acts of aggression, forcible interventions or threats to the peace, and even the duty, generally acknowledged in theory, to try to protect fundamental human rights: these are weak at present, and the precise form of each obligation sometimes disputed (as are often the corresponding obligations within states), but they none the less exist in some form.

In other words, the differences that exist between international society and other types of society are differences of degree rather than of kind. Though it is a society that is, more than most, lacking in integration, it remains a society of a sort. So long as the differences are taken into account, therefore, it seems reasonable to study it in a similar way to other societies. And it is not unlikely that the type of analysis that has been made of smaller societies may be of some help to us in seeking to understand its working.

1 Social Theory and International Society

FUNCTION AND STRUCTURE IN INTERNATIONAL SOCIETY

If, therefore, there does exist something that can be reasonably described as international society, how should it be studied? How relevant to it are the kinds of theory that have been devised by social scientists in examining smaller-scale societies?

Some of those theories have been highly specific. They have been designed to assist in the study of particular *features* of society (say, marriage or kinship systems); or particular *kinds* of society (for example, an Amerindian tribe or a Samoan village). Such approaches will clearly not be of much assistance to us in examining a society which does not contain those features, and is itself of a very unusual and particular kind. We must therefore expect that it will be the broadest and most general concepts of social theory that will be mainly of relevance to us in the study of international society.

The first question that confronts us in studying any type of society is: should we consider the whole, the entire society, as a unit, or should we rather examine the parts, that is the actions and attitudes of individuals and groups which together make up such a society? When we apply this question to the study of international society it becomes similar to the question that has sometimes been addressed by students of international relations: what is the *level* at which our study should be addressed, that of the society of states as a whole or that of the individual state?[1]

This is a question which in relation to smaller societies has divided social theorists since the study of society began. There has been a wide difference between those who have looked primarily at the functioning of an entire society, seen as an integrated whole, and those who have preferred to look at the actions of individuals and

1. See, for example, the discussions of this problem in K. M. Waltz, *Man, the State and War* (New York, 1959), and David Singer, *The Level of Analysis Problems*, in K. Knorr and S. Verba (eds), *The International System* (Princeton, 1961).

groups within that social context – the actions which, taken together, make up the sum-total of social relationships.

Traditionally much social theory has favoured the former approach. In a sense the whole concept of sociology as the "science of society" inevitably encouraged that framework for analysis. Thus Comte, often considered the founder of the discipline, saw society as a closely interrelated whole, and held that it was impossible to understand particular social phenomena except within their social context. He condemned the "existing philosophical practice of contemplating social elements separately as if they had an independent existence", and held that we should "regard them as in mutual relations and forming a whole which compels us to treat them in combination".[2] Society, he believed, was held together ultimately by social consensus, the body of common ideas that its members shared (a consensus which he hoped would ultimately be provided by "positivist" science): "Every social power, whether called authority or anything else, is constituted by corresponding assent, spontaneous or deliberate, explicit or implicit, of the various individual wills. . . . Thus authority is derived from concurrence, not concurrence from authority."[3] It was this consensus which served to sustain the cohesion of each society.

Herbert Spencer, equally, emphasised the interdependence of a society. He conceived of it as an organism, each part of which contributed to the life of the whole. In his eyes it was above all the division of labour which, like the interdependence of the animal's organs, "makes it a living whole. . . . As it grows its parts become unlike . . . and the mutually dependent parts, living by and from one another, form an aggregate constituted on the same general principles as an individual organism".[4] So, again, emphasis was laid on the unity of society, the parts of which, though increasingly differentiated, at the same time become increasingly mutually dependent. "The unlike parts simultaneously assume activities of unlike kinds. These activities are not simply different but their differences are so related as to make one another possible. The reciprocal aid they give causes mutual dependence of the parts."[5]

2. A. Comte, *The Positive Philosophy* (London, 1896) vol. II, bk VI, iii, p. 219.
3. Ibid., p. 221.
4. Herbert Spencer, *The Principles of Sociology* (New York, 1928) vol. II, Secs 217 and 223.
5. Ibid., sec. 223.

Durkheim followed Herbert Spencer in believing that it was the differences within society that, through functional interdependence, created and cemented its unity. He too felt that the division of labour was the essential bond which held people together in modern societies. In primitive societies this bond was provided by "mechanical solidarity", induced by powerful social conditioning. But mechanical solidarity was "possible only in so far as the individual personality is absorbed into the collective personality". Since this was impossible in modern societies, given the wide scope for free and individual activity, some form of "organic solidarity" needed to be established in its place. But this could exist

> only if each one has a sphere of action which is peculiar to him; that is, a personality. . . . Society becomes more capable of collective movement as each of its elements has more freedom of movement. The unity of the organism becomes greater as the individuation of the parts (through the division of labour) is more marked.[6]

Each of these writers, therefore, while laying stress on the increasingly varied roles played by individuals in modern society, none the less placed their emphasis on the social cohesion which in their view interdependence created.

This type of analysis is clearly directly relevant to the study of international society. Here, even more than in national societies, there exists no "mechanical solidarity", induced by powerful pressures towards conformity such as are exerted within most primitive societies. On the contrary, there exists here, between states as between individuals, an even greater tendency towards autonomous goals and autonomous action. Yet there is, here too, a tendency towards increasing interdependence among the autonomous units, an interdependence brought about by rapidly increasing contacts; even, in the economic field, by something analagous to the division of labour to which Durkheim attached such importance. There is a division of functions of many kinds: for example, between producers of raw materials and producers of capital goods, between oil-exporters and oil-importers, between alliance leaders and alliance followers. In all these ways, and in many others, states have become linked with each other in a series of interlocking relationships. It is thus open to

6. E. Durkheim, *The Division of Labour in Society*, trans. G. Simpson (Glencoe, Ill., 1949) pp. 130–1.

question whether, in this case too, interdependence might perhaps lead to the kind of "organic solidarity" proposed by Durkheim; to the mutual relationship of living parts proposed by Herbert Spencer; even eventually to the social "consensus" seen as the decisive integrating factor by Comte. In other words, the same problem that has caused so much discussion and debate in the case of smaller societies – the problem of *integration* – emerges in still more pressing form within international society as a whole. And it is not impossible that the findings of social scientists on the way integration comes about in the former case may have some relevance to the way it may occur in the latter. At least such findings are worth examination.[7]

Anthropologists too have, almost inevitably, focused their studies on the workings of entire societies. In examining primitive societies they were often particularly struck by the power of custom within such a society, and the role it played in establishing mutually compatible behaviour, and so the conditions for a stable existence. They were inclined to disparage, as Comte had done, any attempt to examine individual institutions of a society in isolation and emphasised that they should only be seen as component parts of a closely interrelated whole. In comparing societies they particularly examined the way in which they seemed able, by establishing socially approved patterns of conduct, to secure a high degree of conformity among their members, and so to establish a highly integrated type of community. They thus in many cases came to think in terms of the "purposes" and "needs" of the society as a whole rather than of the actions and goals of the human beings who were its members.

This attitude is to be seen in many of the writings of early anthropologists discussing the institutions and traditions of simpler societies. But it was made most explicit in the writings of "functionalists", such as Malinowski and Radcliffe-Brown. In rejecting earlier theories that individual culture-traits had been spread from one people to another by diffusion, or that all societies represented different phases of a universal process of social evolution, they demanded that, on the contrary, each society should be considered as a separate, individual and self-sufficient whole that was to be analysed in its own right. Because each institution and culture-trait

---

7. The international relations studies that come closest to such a study are the works of K. W. Deutsch on integration (for example, *Political Community in the North Atlantic Area*, Princeton, N.J., 1957) and those of E. Haas on similar themes, for example, *Beyond the Nation-State* (Stanford, Calif., 1964).

was interrelated with others in a complex way, they could be understood only within their own social context and could not be taken in isolation from it. As Radcliffe-Brown put it:

> Individual human beings . . . are connected by a definite set of social relations into an integrated whole. The continuity of the social structure, like that of the organic structure, is not destroyed by changes in the units. . . . The social life of a community is here defined as the functioning of the social structure. The function of any recurrent activity, such as the punishment of a crime or a funeral ceremony, is the part it plays in the social life as a whole and therefore the contribution which it makes to structural continuity.[8]

Though this approach is now heavily criticised by some, some of its presuppositions remain widely accepted. The "structuralism" of Lévi-Strauss and his followers, though rejecting many aspects of the functionalist approach, maintains a belief in the uniqueness of each individual society, of which the myths, marriage systems, social customs and other traits are held to be linked through a "deep structure", of which the members will (like the user of a language, unconscious of the "absent corpus" of syntactic and semantic rules which govern his sentences) often be unconscious. All forms of social life, according to Lévi-Strauss, "consist of systems of behaviour that represent the projection, on the level of conscious and socialised thought, of universal laws which regulate the unconscious activity of the mind".[9] He suggests that "in order to obtain a principle of interpretation valid for other institutions and other customs", it is necessary to grasp "the unconscious structure underlying each institution and each custom".[10]

This approach too is clearly one that can be fruitfully applied to the study of international society. Here too it is possible to lay stress on the "needs" of the society as a whole, and the functions of various institutions in meeting them, rather than on the self-interested activity of the parts. The assumption can be made that there exists a society of states with conventional patterns of interaction among its members, and that individual institutions within it can be examined to see what

8. A. R. Radcliffe-Brown, *Structure and Function in Primitive Society* (London, 1952) p. 176.
9. C. Lévi-Strauss, *Structural Anthropology* (Harmondsworth, Middx., 1972) p. 59.
10. Ibid., p. 21.

"functions" they perform for the society generally. Thus the system of diplomatic relations can be studied to show how well it performs the function of communication, or of conflict-resolution, for the system as a whole. The institution of "sovereignty" can be examined in terms of its function in establishing clear boundaries to the authority of each state, and in this way reducing intervention by one in the affairs of another and so limiting conflict. The balance of power can be studied as a means of maintaining equilibrium within the society and preventing undue domination by particular powers which may disturb the established social order. Legal procedures, such as mediation and arbitration, can be analysed to show how far they perform the function of authoritatively allocating rights and duties among states, or that of conflict-resolution generally. Even some of the concepts of structuralism might be applied in this way: in the search, for example, for "deep structures", expressed in national mythology and folklore, in the traditions of warfare or patriotic sentiment or in international usage and ceremonies.

The theories of functionalism and structuralism, while first put forward by the anthropologists, have been developed by sociologists in recent times. Talcott Parsons developed a body of ideas about society which he explicitly described as "structural-functionalist". Concerned above all with the "problem of order", he set out a model of society as a social system which maintains itself on a self-adjusting basis. "The most general and fundamental property of a system", he suggests, "is the inter-dependence of parts" establishing "order in the relationships among the components which enter into a system. This order must have a tendency to self-maintenance, which is very generally expressed in the concept of equilibrium."[11] The system is maintained by a series of mechanisms which serve particular functions: for maintaining the "patterns of institutionalised culture" defining the structure of the system ("pattern-maintenance"); for enabling the society to attain its goals effectively ("goal-attainment"); for enabling it to adapt its goals and to make choices between them where resources are inadequate ("adaptation"); and for integrating the system so that units and sub-systems are adjusted to the purpose of the system as a whole ("integration").[12] The system also requires the establishment of specific *norms* laying down the roles to be

11. Talcott Parsons and E. Shils, *Towards a General Theory of Action* (Harvard, Mass., 1951) p. 107.
12. Talcott Parsons, 'An Outline of the Social System', in T. Parsons *et al.* (eds), *Theories of Society* (New York, 1961) pp. 36–70.

performed by individuals in particular situations, and more general *values* influencing final goals. It will need a system for *co-ordination* of responses at times of crisis, together with a feedback, or learning process, for dealing with disturbances when they occur. Together these should maintain the system in a state close to equilibrium. Another sociologist of the same period, R. K. Merton, similarly considered the "functional" role of various social phenomena, such as institutions, roles, social processes, cultural patterns, social norms, social structures and so on, though he at least was willing to recognise that some features of a society could be "dysfunctional".[13] While many modern sociologists reject this approach, a large number have adopted different forms of functional analysis.

Once again these ideas can be applied in the study of international society. That society too can be seen as an organised process of interaction. It can be analysed, like dometic societies, as a mechanical system, with inputs, outputs and built-in mechanisms for maintenance and feedback, allowing it to operate on a self-sustaining and self-adjusting basis. "Systems theory" can be used to show how such factors as the balance of power, bi-polarity or multi-polarity operate according to ascertainable laws to maintain a particular kind of system.[14] "Equilibrium theory" can be employed, on the assumption that international society possesses a natural disposition to re-establish equilibrium once it is disturbed, the disturbances resulting from the actions of some states triggering compensation action by others, so that in time equilibrium will be restored.[15] The concepts of other "structuralist–functionalists" can be applied in the same way. Thus the belief of Merton that social institutions can as easily prove "dysfunctional" as "functional" is especially appropriate to international society, characterised as it is by instability and conflict: thus an analysis could be made of the institutions of world society to consider how far particular institutions – for example, warfare, the alliance system or competition for power generally – were "dysfunctional" in their effect. The operations of the UN could be studied to see how far they performed the role of conflict-resolution,

13. R. K. Merton, *Social Theory and Social Structure* (Glencoe, Ill., 1949) pp. 49–61.
14. Such an approach was adopted in Morton Kaplan's *System and Process in International Politics* (New York, 1957) and in A. M. Scott, *The Functioning of the International Political System* (New York, 1967).
15. This approach has been applied in M. Liska, *International Equilibrium* (Cambridge, Mass., 1957).

"goal-attainment", "adaptation" or the establishment of generally accepted norms of international conduct.

Thus all the types of social theory we have described have a direct relevance to the study of international society. In so far as the latter type of society shares the characteristics of the former, a similar method of analysis should be applicable. But it is important to be aware of the difficulties such theories face in both cases. As we have seen, all make certain assumptions about the nature of society. They presuppose that it represents a closely interrelated whole, not unlike a living organism, held in a kind of unity by the "solidarity" of its members; that it has "needs" and "purposes" of its own, to the achievement of which the institutions of society are functionally related in a semi-automatic way; or that it is a self-contained and self-sustaining "system". Society tends to be conceived as an entity, rather than as the sum of its parts, an entity which is seen as having some independent existence of its own. Whatever the merits of such assumptions when applied to simpler societies – and this itself is questionable – they already become harder to sustain when transferred to modern industrial societies, characterised as they are by much disorder, dislocation and dispute. But they are more dubious still in the case of international society, which is so manifestly unintegrated and racked with conflict. The concepts of "stability" and "equilibrium", though as frequently used about international as about domestic society, are in that case even more question-begging. Even more than in smaller societies, it might be reasonably maintained, *instability* and *dis-equilibrium* are the typical states (so that it might be more reasonable to suppose that it is dis-equilibrium rather than equilibrium which has a tendency to restore itself). And certainly the image of a society operating as a "system" working according to mechanical rules, represents, here, even more than in the case of domestic societies, essentially a flight of fancy, for which no factual evidence exists.

It is not our purpose to pursue these difficulties at this stage. It is enough to make clear that this particular approach, like all other metaphoric theories (theories based on an image), can distort rather than describe. It tends to create assumptions about the nature of social life that at the very least require examination, and which, in the case of international society, it is precisely the purpose of our study to analyse. By creating an image, it prejudges the enquiry. While it may be reasonable, therefore, as we have argued, to assume that there exists a society of states of a kind, we should beware of assuming that it is necessarily one that is "integrated", "self-balancing", "systemic", still less "harmonious", in the way that this particular set of theories might lead us to suppose.

ACTION THEORY IN INTERNATIONAL SOCIETY

Let us turn next to an alternative type of social theory. This places the main emphasis not on the functioning of society as a whole but on the actions of individuals within society.

This so-called "action approach" – the study of social action – is not in contradiction with the one we have just described. The two are complementary. They represent only a difference of focus, and therefore of emphasis. Theories which focus mainly on the wider society of course recognise that this society consists in the actions of individuals; while those that focus on individual social actions recognise that these – by definition – take place within a society of some sort, which will influence the form the actions take. The difference is fundamentally one of attention. Those who adopt the former approach are primarily interested in studying the way the entire aggregate of individuals constituting a "society" operate as a group, how they create social institutions capable of withstanding disruption from within or attack from without, and how they bring individuals to adopt mutually compatible behaviour to that end. Those who have adopted the latter approach are primarily interested in people themselves, in the way individuals conceive the society in which they find themselves and their own place within it, how they react to this social system and in particular how they act to *alter* it. The difference in focus does not *logically* presuppose any difference in conclusion. But in practice the former approach often appears to suggest that it is the social forces which are all-powerful, so that the individual has little chance in withstanding them; while the latter may seem to imply that social influences are less important in moulding individuals than are the actions of individuals in shaping and reshaping their own social situations and social relationships: that it is individual actions that make societies rather than vice versa.

The latter approach certainly has a certain logic to commend it. It is possible, as is sometimes said, that no individual human can exist without society of some kind; that, unsocialised, he or she will not be a human but an animal. What is certain is that no society can exist without individuals. It thus seems logical to begin by considering the actions of individuals which taken together create a society.

So Max Weber, for example, held that sociology was a science which attempted the "interpretive understanding of human action" so as to arrive at a "causal explanation of its course and effects".[16] Actions could be end-rational (that is, directed to the accomplishments of a practical goal); value-rational (directed to the achievement of a value); emotional; or traditional. Action was social in so far as "by virtue of the subjective meaning attached to it by the actor, it takes account of the behaviour of others and is thereby oriented in its course".[17] The meaning to be attached to an action was the subjective meaning attached to it by the actor himself, and so needed to be understood by empathy or "sympathetic participation". But choices of ultimate ends or values could not be explained by any rational arguments, nor necessarily understood by others at all. Some actions, if they could not be related to a known end, would appear irrational or meaningless: in other words we often understand actions only because we understand the reasons why they are taken. Yet the stated motives, or conscious motives, for action, are not necessarily the real ones.

Social *relationships* consist in the probability that a particular response can be expected to a particular social action. The relationship may be temporary or permanent, but will exist so long as the probability remains that certain kinds of action will be taken between the parties. Relationships are not necessarily reciprocal; they may call for entirely different kinds of action by each party. The form of the relationship, that is the action to be expected on both sides, may be embodied in a formal agreement; rest on a promise; or be based only on a tacit understanding. External factors, social or even political, may change the environment and so the nature of the interest each party has in the relationship, so that friendship may be converted into enmity or vice versa.[18]

This approach too is one that is highly relevant to the study of international society. Here too it is possible to focus our attention on the individual members of society rather than the society as a whole; on the actions of individual states and other groups and the relationships they establish. Here too we can direct our concern towards the subjective attitude held by states towards each other, or

16. Max Weber, *The Theory of Social and Economic Organisation* (Glencoe, Ill., 1947) p. 88.
17. Ibid.
18. Ibid., pp. 111–20.

even by individuals to individuals in other states, rather than on "objective" actions. Here too we can examine the actions and attitudes of states and groups with empathetic understanding, in the light of the differing social situation and historic experience of each. A recognition of the differences *between* states and their attitudes and motives may provide a more fruitful and realistic account than the assumption of automatic reactions, based exclusively on social situation, power balances or the needs of equilibrium (as assumed in the last approach we discussed). Here too it will be recognised that state action will not always be "rational", nor necessarily easily understood by others. Here too it may be important to recognise that the underlying motives of states are sometimes different from their conscious, and especially from their declared motives (so they may, for example, proclaim they make war to promote "peace" or "order", or to remedy "injustice", and genuinely believe it, when their underlying motive may be to increase their own power, territory or sense of security). Among states too social relationships are established on the basis of *expected* behaviour; may or may not be reciprocal; may be short term or long term; may suddenly change according to a newly emerging conflict of interests; may or may not be formalised within a treaty or some other formal understanding. And the best way of studying the pattern of these relationships may be by careful study of international history, comparable to the "historical sociology" which Max Weber favoured.[19] In other words, an approach of the kind sketched by Weber for the study of human social behaviour can be applied, almost unchanged, to the study of the behaviour of states in the wider international society.

This conception of "social action" was pursued in the writings of Alfred Schütz. He too was concerned with the subjective intentions and beliefs of individuals in society, rather than their objective actions. He held that the analysis of these intentions and beliefs lay at the heart of sociological enquiry. He distinguished between action directed at a previously conceived goal, "behaviour in accordance with a plan of projected behaviour", and behaviour which was not end-directed at all. Motives could be of the 'in-order-to" type, immediately directed towards a particular goal, so that action and goal were virtually merged; or of the "because" type, that is a motive was attributed to the action after the event. Some action was taken

---

19. Raymond Aron, the French sociologist, much influenced by Weber, favoured this approach to the study of international relations.

to implement immediate projects, only recently conceived; some to implement long-term "plans", including life plans. This did not mean that there was any clear-cut hierarchy of goals: the actor himself would often only be partially conscious of life-plans or a system of life-plans. In order to understand the actions of others we have to understand their "in-order-to" motives. This will enable us to anticipate their actions and to adjust our own behaviour accordingly. If we did this successfully we might not only avoid unnecessarily frustrating the goals of others, but also succeed in maximising our own goals.[20]

These views too have relevance for the study of international relationships. Essential to any satisfactory analysis of these is a study of the way international actors, expecially states, perceive other such actors, how they understand the relationships between them and so frame their actions. Central to this is an analysis of the motives of international actors, above all of states. This can be undertaken by the systematic study of the foreign policy of particular states. But, to comply with Schütz's emphasis on *subjective* motives, it is rather an analysis of foreign policy *formulation*, and the way in which, for example, cabinets, foreign ministers and foreign office officials *see* their foreign policy goals that is required, rather than what they *say* they are in statements of foreign policy. In international society too, the understanding of a state's actions depends on a knowledge of its motives; and here too the state that is most successful in understanding the goals and actions of other states is the most likely to be successful in securing its own goals (so such studies are of direct value to statesmen as well as to scholars). And, here too, a study of the relationships between long-term goals and short-term goals in foreign policy is necessary, including whether or not any systematic hierarchy of goals is established.[21]

20. The most complete statement of Schütz's theories is in his book *The Imaginary Construction of the Social World* (Vienna, 1932). But he set out a great deal of his ideas in his comments on Parsons's *Structure of Social Action* (somewhat resented by Parsons at the time) which were eventually published in 1978 in *The Theory of Social Action* (Bloomington, Ill., 1978).
21. A large number of studies of foreign policy and its formulation have been undertaken by writers on international relations: for example in J. N. Rosenau (ed.), *International Politics and Foreign Policy* (New York, 1961); J. E. Black and K. W. Thompson, *Foreign Policies in a World of Change* (New York, 1963); R. C. Snyder, W. H. Bruck and B. Sapin, *Foreign Policy Decision-Making* (New York, 1962); K. N.

Modern sociologists have pursued the idea of "action theory". Talcott Parsons (much influenced by Max Weber), though as we saw, deeply concerned with the "problem of order" and the way in which a social system maintains itself, started his analysis with a theory of social action.[22] Like Weber he was concerned especially with the relation of the actor to a *situation* and with the "orientation" which he therefore adopted. This orientation was related to the expectations of other actors. All action is relational: adjusted to the situation of the actor and his expectations about other actors. The choice of appropriate action is based not only on the needs, physical and psychological, of the actor, but on his evaluation of his situation, involving the use of standards and norms derived from the social system. The sources of action derive not only from the social system as a whole but from a "plural hierarchy of sub-systems of action", including the actor's "behavioural organism", the personality of the individual, the social system generated by interaction and the "cultural system organised about patterns of meaning".[23]

The French sociologist Alain Touraine has also elaborated a theory of action, though he has been concerned not so much with the sources of action as with its results. Rejecting functionalism as a rationalisation of the status quo, he holds that action is not "just a response to a social situation" but an autonomous force and the source of values. It is concerned above all with "creation and control", and its effect is to transform the actor's situation and his social relationships. But the most important actions are not those of the individual but of the collective group or social movement (for example organised labour): it is this "historical personality" and the emergent "structures" which such forces can create, which are the main source of change within society.[24]

This approach too has its relevance for the study of international society. If the functionalist approach, with its assumption of integration, is especially inappropriate to that study, one that is based on the independent behaviour of individual actors seems particularly

Waltz, *Foreign Policy and Democratic Politics* (Boston, Mass., 1967).
22. For example in his first book, *The Structure of Social Action* (Glencoe, Ill., 1937) and in *Towards a Theory of Action* (written with Edward Shils; Cambridge, Mass., 1951).
23. T. Parsons in *The Social Theories of Talcott Parsons*, ed. Max Black (Englewood Cliffs, N.J., 1961) p. 327.
24. See, for example, "Towards a Sociology of Action", in A. Giddens (ed.), *Positivism and Sociology* (London, 1974).

apt in a society where the most important members, the individual states, declare themselves to be "sovereign" and determined to maintain their independence of social forces. To make the actions of states and other international actors the basic raw material of our enquiry would thus seem a reasonable approach to the subject.

We can, for example, approach it by analysing the situations in which an individual state finds itself, and the relationships which it establishes in consequence. We can examine the "orientations" which they adopt in response to these situations and the pattern of action that results. We can examine the sources of motivation among states; the role, if any, of "norms" and "values"; the influence of "sub-systems", including the governmental system, or the way a foreign ministry operates, on individual decisions in foreign policy. Finally (corresponding perhaps with Touraine's conception of "emergent structures" and collective forces) we could consider the role of *collective* action by states – by alliances, blocs and economic groupings (such as the Group of 77) – in influencing the structure of international society. All of these are approaches directed towards the social action of states and some will be pursued further in the pages that follow.

Once again, therefore, it is not difficult to see the relevance of a theory originally developed in the analysis of smaller societies to the study of international society as a whole and to the actions that are taken within it. An approach which is based on the way members of smaller societies react to their social situation, interpret that situation and adjust their behaviour accordingly, has an obvious relevance in examining the behaviour of autonomous states in international society. Indeed, considering that social pressures within that society are weak, and tendencies towards independent action strong, an approach of this kind seems here to have a special usefulness.

But, as in the previous case we examined, there are problems about the approach which we shall need to keep in mind. Since it depends crucially on social orientation and the way others in society are perceived, we shall need to be always conscious of the special features of the relationships established in international society and the way relationships there are perceived. The actions of states and other collective bodies are clearly so different from those of individuals, and the way they formulate their goals so special, that we shall need to beware of making any exact analogies. The "perceptions" and "motives" of states are derived in quite a different way from those of individuals. We shall therefore need to be clear what we mean when we apply such words to collectivities that have no mind or consciousness (pp. 119 ff. below).

Thus if, as we saw, it is rash to assume that all members of international society are directed and guided in their acts by powerful pressures towards social integration, there may be corresponding dangers in assuming that action in that society is closely analagous to social action in human societies. The analysis of irrational or non-rational action, of the kind undertaken by Pareto and Schütz, based on a consideration of human psychology, may have little relevance in analysis of the behaviour of a state or a trans-national corporation. There are, in other words, substantial differences between the kinds of action taken in the two types of society. If we wish to apply the action approach to international society, we shall need to bear such differences carefully in mind.

STATICS AND DYNAMICS IN INTERNATIONAL SOCIETY

But there is another contrast between types of social theory, of quite a different kind. This is the contrast between theories that are based on a study of society and its operations at any one moment, and those based on a study of society as it evolves over the years; that is, between an approach that is static and one that is dynamic.

Again the contrast is not a rigid one. Those who describe the functioning of a society at a given time are none the less aware of the processes of change within it, whether short term or long term; while those who are especially concerned with changes within a society over time recognise that there are also forces making for stability. Some writers give almost equal weight to both factors: so Comte devoted separate sections of his main work to "social statics" and "social dynamics". Once again, however, the differences in approach create real differences of emphasis.

The first approach, which is that adopted by most anthropologists and many traditional sociologists, seeks to examine the way a society functions *now*, or at least at a certain moment in time. It is concerned with presenting a snapshot rather than a moving picture. Thus it does not record movement or change; cannot compare now and then. It creates, almost imperceptibly, the assumption that a society is integrated not only in place but in time; that today is like yesterday and tomorrow like today. The essential character of social life, it is implied, is ossified in the form which the snapshot records. For this reason society appears fixed and unchanging. Any conflict that may be occurring below the surface will, at any one moment in time, be invisible. As a result the forces of stability are made to appear more powerful than those making for change. The emphasis is on the way that society functions in *normal* times; on the regular rather than the irregular; on the average rather than the extraordinary; on the predictable rather than the accidental.

International society too can be considered either as it exists at a particular moment in time; or as it evolves over a period of history. Here too most writers have favoured the former approach. They have been concerned mainly with a particular international society at a particular moment – usually the contemporary world scene. Being political scientists rather than historians by training, they have not felt willing or competent to undertake detailed comparisons with the international societies of earlier times, and have preferred to concentrate on analysing inter-state relationships within the world they know. They have examined the forces at work – the balance of power, the economic pressures, international institutions, international law – at that time. They have been less concerned with the way each of these, or the entire society, evolves over time. Sentences are typically formed in the present tense; and this creates generalisations – about the motives of states, the demand for "power", the operation of the balance of power system, for example – which, it is implied, hold good of all places and all times. Here too the concern is with the snapshot rather than the moving picture; with the general rather than the accidental; and so, often, with the sources of stability rather than the forces of change over the long term.

This approach to social theory can be contrasted with another, concerned above all with the moving picture rather than with the snapshot; with the changes that take place within society over time rather than the way it operates at any one moment. If a society is examined over a historical period, attention is inevitably focused on the differences between the end of the process and the beginning: that is, on the processes of change which take place during that time. This in turn draws attention to the forces which lie behind change, and especially the *conflicts*, whether between groups, classes or ideas, which are often seen as the main source of change. As a result this dynamic approach often evolves some type of "historicist" theory according to which history is governed, in a semi-automatic way, in a given direction, by the forces that project it, especially by the outcome of a conflict between different social forces. So, Hegel's dialectic – suggesting a universal process of thesis, antithesis and synthesis – emphasised continual change, taking place as a result of continual contradictions. So, equally, Marx's dialectic, which turned that of Hegel on its head (by making the ideal dependent on the material rather than vice versa), also emphasised continual change, also resulting from continual contradictions: this time between the changing forces of production (industrial technology) and the relations of production (relations between owners and workers), and therefore also between classes. Pareto too, rejecting rationality as the basis of many social actions, emphasised the importance of change resulting, in his view, from the changing character of élites, which in time gradually lost their vigour so that, no longer able to conquer or absorb their rivals, they gave way to new élites who established a different type of society. More recent writers, such as those postulating a secular, world-wide transition to an "industrial society" model of social organisation, also imply a predictable pattern of historical evolution.

This approach too is one that could have its place in the study of international society. Here, where fluctuation and change is so rapid, an analysis based on the state of society at a particular moment in time, congealed in the immobility of a snapshot, may seem particularly inappropriate. Here, where political disputes, economic conflicts and continual warfare are the most obvious characteristics of social existence, the assumption of a natural conflict of interests among the members seems more appropriate than the assumption of a natural harmony. The prevalence of conflict not only casts doubt, as we have seen, on the relevance of any model based on the image of society as an integrated or closely interrelated whole; it lends substance to one which takes the universality of conflict for granted.

Emphasis on conflict, seen as the major source of social change, has been maintained by a number of sociologists in recent times. These have stressed conflicts of interest between groups and classes and have strongly rejected theories which assume a harmony of interests between them or a social "consensus". For them the factors that divide citizens, even in apparently democratic societies – social, economic and political inequalities – are far more important than the factors – common citizenship, a theoretical equality of "rights", participation in an apparently "democratic" political process – that may seem to unite them. They have therefore formulated new theories stressing these conflicts of interest: for example between "power élites" and less privileged sections of society;[25] between those groups and individuals possessing authority within any organisation and society and those who do not;[26] between "conflict groups", competing for control of resources, of centres of power and especially of legitimising ideas, so as to hold the balance of power within society;[27] or between social actors, struggling to secure autonomy, and if possible domination, through access to "resources" which are the media through which power is exercised.[28]

In the study of international society it appears even more logical to give primary emphasis to conflictual relationships of this kind. Here it is easy to show the sharp conflicts of interest between individual states and groups of states: between contending great powers, between alliances, between ideological blocs, between rich countries and poor, lenders and debtors, commodity producers and commodity consumers (to mention only a few of the more obvious antagonistic relationships in contemporary world society). Here too international politics can be presented as a continual struggle for power – military, economic and political – between states and groups of states. Study can be focused on wars and warfare, seen perhaps as the most prominent and persistent feature of relations among states, and one which can therefore provide a clue to their most deep-seated ambitions and objectives. Strategic theory, games theory and bargaining techniques can be examined as a guide to understanding the means by which such conflicts are fought out. The proceedings of international organisations can be analysed as evidence of fundamental antagonisms, political and economic, between states and groups of states. Conflicts between rich countries and poor, and the whole range of north–south issues, can be examined as evidence of the most fundamental economic and political divisions of the age. By those methods (all of which have been employed by some students of international politics) the assumption that conflict lies at the heart of international society, as of other societies, can be reflected in the type of analysis undertaken.

It is also possible to base broader "theories" of international society

25. Charles W. Mills, *The Power Elite* (New York, 1967).
26. R. Dahrendorf, *Class and Conflict in an Industrial Society* (London, 1959).
27. J. Rex, *Key Problems of Sociological Theory* (London, 1961) pp. 122–35.
28. A. Giddens, *Profiles in Contemporary Social Theory* (London, 1982) pp. 28–39.

on the same assumption. A number of traditional approaches to international history have been of this kind. The theories of Hobson and Lenin about "imperialism" and its effect in stimulating contradictions between the main European powers, come within this category. So do the ideas of Spengler and Toynbee, postulating regular cycles in international history during which a civilisation goes through a period of emergence, growth, maturity, leading to a time of troubles during which it is often beset by new challenges and conflicts. More recent theories, accounting for the conflicts of interests between rich and poor countries, such as those of Raoul Prebisch, emphasising the division between the industrial powers, at the hub of the world economy, mainly preoccupied with economic relations among each other and concerned with developing countries only as a source of raw materials, and developing countries at the "periphery" controlled mainly by economic forces originating elsewhere and so unable to master their own economic destinies. Some recent writing on political and economic competition among major powers, equally, tends to make an assumption of competitive interaction among states.[29] All of these have been approaches based on the presumption of conflict among states and groups of states; and have often seen this as the main source of change (and sometimes of progress) within international society.

The contrast between these two types of theory is again at root one of attention, and therefore of emphasis. The static theory focuses attention on interrelationships at any one time, and in particular on the way society, through various social institutions, is able to maintain itself in a relatively stable state. The dynamic approach emphasises, on the contrary, the evolution of society over a considerable length of time, and therefore highlights the changes that occur within it. It is perhaps not too great an exaggeration to suggest that it is generally the observers who have most *wanted* change in society who have concentrated their attention on the forces which make for change there; while those who have been more satisfied with the status quo have placed more stress on the forces making for social stability.

In fact there are no good grounds for preferring one approach to the other. In all societies there are forces for stability and forces for

29. To this category belong most writings of the traditional "realist" school – F. L. Schuman's *International Politics* (New York, 1954); G. Schwarzenburger's *Power Politics* (London, 1941); M. Wight's *Power Politics* (London, 1946); and Hans Morgenthan's *Politics among Nations* (New York, 1948).

change. This is as true in the international society as in any other. The important task for the social scientist, whichever type of society he examines, is to *identify* which are the forces that make for stability and which are those that make for change. It is this that must be our task in the analysis of international society in the pages that follow.

KEY CONCEPTS

We have sketched in the preceding sections only a few of the more obvious analogies which can be drawn between traditional social theories and the problems that arise in the study of international society. It is clear that a number of problems which occur in the study of international relations have a considerable similarity to those that arise, and have been extensively studied, in the study of other types of society. It seems not unlikely, therefore, that a comparable method of approach might prove fruitful.

If this is the case, let us consider which particular concepts, traditionally used in the study of smaller societies, may be most usefully applied in the study of the one with which we are here concerned.

In searching for these concepts it is necessary to be selective. Virtually every term that has ever been employed by sociologists in studying domestic societies could be applied, with sufficient ingenuity, in the study of international society as well. But in many cases their use would involve an element of distortion that would largely destroy their usefulness. Even if there were no distortion they might not focus on the most *relevant* factors of the society we are concerned with. In other words we need to keep continually in mind the real differences between the international society and other types of society to which we drew attention in the Introduction.

The intention in the study that follows is to concentrate on ten key concepts which appear to be the most useful and relevant given the known characteristics of world society.

The first is one which, as we saw earlier, has been widely used in recent years in the study of society generally: the idea of social *action*. If we wish to apply this concept to international societies we need first to determine what are the actions – of individuals, groups and states – that are genuinely *international* actions; that enter, that is, into the transactions of international society. The sum-total of actions undertaken within a state which have an impact on those in other states is obviously great. They range from a tourist visit to the signing of a million-pound contract with a foreign government; from the writing of a letter to a son living abroad to a declaration of war. It is thus necessary for us to formulate some taxonomy of international actions that distinguishes them according to their social significance. We need to measure the degree of impact each may have in other states; the degree to which they require or enforce a response; the type of relationships which they may create or presuppose. We need also to consider *how* such actions are taken; the influences that affect them and the groups that are able to exert this. In order to undertake this we shall need to analyse the concepts of *situation*, *relations*, and *decisions* as these apply to actions taken within international society. Such an analysis may assist our understanding of the most basic inputs made within international society: the actions of individuals in one state that affect individuals in another.

Second, we need to look at social transactions from the opposite viewpoint, at what might be called the macro-level: that of *society* as a whole. We need in other words to analyse the social context within which individual actions are undertaken. For a beginning all such actions require at least one partner: another state, or a person or group within another state. We shall thus need to look, first, at the kind of bilateral relationships that are undertaken in this way: the interactions of ego and alter, the state (or group or individual) which acts and that which responds. These bilateral relationships, however, important though they are, are only a part of the social relations into which a state enters. They take place within a wider international environment which itself will influence them and the form they take. That environment will affect the way both parties perceive each other and what they regard as appropriate responses to the actions of the other. It may establish conventional practices, expected patterns of behaviour, which may influence their response; as well as norms of other kinds, customs, rules and laws, which create certain expectations of the actions to be taken. We shall wish to consider how those who undertake international actions acquire their perceptions of this outer social environment. What is the process of socialisation which occurs at the international level; how are norms of conduct and other influences internalised among decision-makers in such a way as to affect their actions? What is the relative importance in this respect of influences from the domestic environment and those from the international society beyond? And how are the choices made between the conflicting instructions which the two often provide? Conversely how are the rules deriving from the wider international society established; and how far can they be said to reflect the purposes or interests of that society generally?

Third, we shall be concerned not only with international society in this general sense, and the way it influences the behaviour of its individual members. We shall be concerned also with social *structure*: that is, the way relationships are organised in particular international societies. Clearly the entire structure of relationships – personal, cultural, economic and political – among all states that are in contact with each other at any one time, is vast and hugely complex. But again our main concern will be with the relationships among states which, as we saw earlier, are the dominant actors if only because they mediate and partly control the relations of individuals. Here the social structure is rather clearer. In the contemporary international society, for example, there exist 160–70 separate states of varying size, power and wealth, all having contact with each other of one sort or another, and joined in a multiplicity of alliances, associations and organisations. The different types of structure of this sort which have existed in different international societies of the past can be analysed. Not only the number of states but the nature and extent of their contacts with each other have differed widely from one age to another. Differing communication systems have brought about differing amounts of personal contact, differing types of commercial relationship, differing degrees of military dominance or subordination. They have affected above all the degree of mutual *concern* within such a society; the degree to which other states have been seen as similar, enjoying similar rights, or altogether different in kind (like "strangers" in many primitive societies). Another structural element, also varying widely from one society to another, has been the system of stratification: the differences in rank and power that are recognised among the members. In one society there may be almost total domination by a single state; in another by only two states; in another by five or six "great powers"; in another by a dozen or so powers of more or less equal rank; while in another there may be a very much larger number of very small states of relatively equal power (see below, pp. 72–6). The structure may be highly decentralised, with minimum contacts between the members, as in ancient China; or highly integrated with maximum contacts, as today. Differences in structure of this sort bring about very different types of international society and there is need to analyse the differences and their social consequences.

A fourth factor to be considered is the role of *ideology* in international society. Some writers have held (for example Comte and Durkheim) that the most important single factor maintaining social cohesion in domestic societies is the existence of a common system of beliefs and values: in a word an ideology. It is the *lack* of such a common pattern of belief that is sometimes held to be the most significant feature of international society, and the reason why no peaceful or stable order can be expected at that level. In examining international society we shall need to consider the truth of such assertions. We shall suggest that there does in fact exist in all international societies some minimum of shared beliefs that will exercise an influence on its members and affect their behaviour and their relationships. The beliefs we are concerned with are those that relate specifically to the international society and relationships within it. Though these may be influenced by beliefs concerning domestic society – political doctrines, social codes or religious creeds – they are distinct from these and comprise only those ideas which concern relationships between states. We shall see that there have been clearly marked differences among the beliefs of this sort which have existed at different periods; and we shall distinguish five international "ideologies" which have existed over the last five or six centuries and their effect on the international society of their day. Each such ideology implies a different type of characteristic behaviour among states. It is thus clearly a factor of special importance in determining the character of international society; and it is a factor to which we shall need to devote special attention in the pages that follow.

Fifth, the character of every society is partly determined by the nature of the *motivations* which predominate among the members. It has been widely recognised that the character of small-scale societies will vary widely according to whether the dominant concern of their members is competitive or co-operative; with winning power or winning wealth; with outward display or inner satisfaction: achievement oriented or status oriented. So too among international societies. These too will vary widely according to whether the dominant goals are the acquisition of territory or the promotion of trade; winning colonies abroad or building industries at home; securing military domination, economic power or cultural influence. In practice, as in smaller societies, no motive is all-consuming for all the members. In each society there exists a variety of motives, though some states will be swayed by some more than others. But there exists always an important variation between the dominant motives in *different* societies. In one foreign conquest will be a dominant goal, while in another it will be relatively unimportant; in one colonial acquisition will be a major objective, in another it will be of no significance; in one the promotion of a particular religious creed will be an important aim, in another the promotion of an ideological faith. Some motives stem directly from the prevailing ideology (thus for example the ideology of dynasticism automatically promoted the search for foreign crowns). But other goals exist independently of the current ideology and often exist in varying degrees in almost every society. One of the things that will most concern us is how far any motives are permanent and unchanging from one age to another; and how far they change from one society to another according to social circumstances or the prevailing ideology.

Sixth, independently of their motives, states undertake certain social *roles*. Just as in smaller societies individuals adopt roles of a number of kinds, based on the expectations that are placed on them by their social partners or by society generally, so too in international societies. And just as some of the individual's roles are specific, that is related to particular situations or partners, and some general, that is performed for society generally, so too states may perform some specific roles – as ally of a particular neighbour, or as mediator in a particular dispute – and some general – as when a state adopts the role of neutral, which then influences all its international relationships. As within states, some roles are reciprocal, that is demand exactly similar behaviour for both parties (for example the obligation to recognise "sovereign equality" undertaken by diplomatic partners); while some demand different and complementary behaviour (for example the roles of great power and client state, block leader and block members, aid-donor and aid-recipient). One question that will be of concern to us is how roles are acquired in the first place; whether they are deliberately adopted or unconsciously assumed. Are they seen in the same light by each party or by all other parties? Is there sometimes conflict between the different roles adopted by the same state? Is there competition among states to perform particular roles? In examining these questions we may get a better idea of the way each state sees its own position within international society.

Seventh, members of international society may be distinguished not only according to their roles but according to the *status* they enjoy. In small-scale societies there almost always exist some differences in status: in the respect accorded to different members (a ranking which is different from stratification by *class*, based on material interests alone). In international societies too there will always exist some ranking system. The criteria adopted vary. Even in the same age states may be measured according to different criteria: military power or economic success, cultural achievement or athletic prowess. More striking, however, are the different types of status accorded in *different* societies. In one age high status is based largely on success at arms (as for Spain or France in the sixteenth century); in another on relative peacefulness (as Switzerland or Sweden may be admired for that reason today). In one it may depend on the extent of territory controlled (as Britain was envied by some for her empire a century ago); in another by the level of economic development (as Japan and West Germany are admired by many today); in one by cultural achievement (as France was respected during the nineteenth century); in another by the social or environmental standards achieved (as Scandinavian countries are respected by many today). As among individuals some forms of status can be *achieved* (as by the country that wins military, cultural or economic or sporting success); other forms are *ascribed* (like the respect afforded to a country for its membership of the Security Council, or its role as peace-keeper). Sometimes there can be conflicting measures of status, each applying to different kinds of states; so one state may be admired by the majority for its contribution to political stability (as Britain was in the nineteenth century, or Norway and the Netherlands are today), another by the minority for its revolutionary fervour (as China was by some twenty or thirty years ago, and as Iran and Libya are by some today). As in smaller societies different status symbols are adopted in different ages (the building of palaces and triumphal arches in one age, the building of large naval vessels in another, the acquisition of nuclear weapons or supersonic fighters in yet another). An examination of the different kinds of status that have been sought in different international societies is clearly an important aspect of the study of international society generally.

Eighth, the character of all societies is determined partly by the nature and degree of *conflict* which occurs there. Given the disorganised nature of international society, this is clearly of special importance in that case. In different ages conflict takes place between different types of group, over different issues and assets. Some types of conflict can be resolved by peaceful means, others only by war. The underlying causes of conflict are likely to be closely related to the dominant ideology: thus in the age of dynasties wars occurred mainly about dynastic succession; in the age of religions mainly about religious questions; in the age of sovereignty mainly about territory and trade, seen as the source of sovereignty and power; in the age of nationalism about national rights, within states as well as between them; and in the age of ideology about conflicting claims of ideological blocs and factions. These changes in the underlying causes of war will bring about corresponding changes in the issues about which they are fought, the assets that may be acquired by them and the beliefs that are generally held about "just" reasons for war. Changes in the character of conflict thus both reflect and influence changes in society as a whole and must therefore be an important subject of our enquiry.

Ninth, a major concern in the study of all societies is with the means evolved for restraining violence and governing behaviour generally. Social scientists studying smaller societies have stressed the importance of *norms* of various kinds – practices, customs, rules and laws – in influencing behaviour, and so bringing about mutually compatible conduct. In international society the same process takes place. Almost always there have existed customary rules of some kind (for example, even in the earliest times there was a general ban on the killing of heralds and other envoys). Over the years these customs have become more firmly established and more widely accepted. There has even emerged a substantial body of "international law" (though this, since it is unenforced and unenforceable, corresponds to custom as it exists in many primitive societies rather than to law in modern states). Treaties are entered into, both bilateral and multilateral, prescribing in great detail the treatment to be accorded by one state to another, or governing its behaviour generally (for example committing it to particular kinds of trading arrangements or to particular forms of disarmament). Together these understandings, implicit or explicit, create a body of norms of behaviour which influence a substantial range of state actions. But they influence behaviour more decisively in some areas than in others; and some states are more willing to conform to them than others. The reason for these differences is one of the matters we will wish to consider in our study. We shall also wish to consider the relationship which exists, if any, between international rules and the value-system which exists *within* states for domestic purposes; and whether a uniform system of international rules is possible among states of which the domestic value-systems differ widely.

Finally, we shall wish to analyse the concept of *authority* as it applies to international society. In small-scale societies the nature of authority has been one of the questions most examined and discussed by political philosophers and social scientists, by sociologists and anthropologists alike. Many of the questions they have raised arise equally in international societies. Indeed that problem occurs there in a form which at first sight is especially acute because in that case authority cannot be imposed by unchallengeable enforcement power. The problem is therefore different from that surrounding authority in modern industrial states (though it is not different from that which has surrounded authority in very many other societies where central government has not been able to command superior force – for example in medieval Europe, where local magnates often exercised effective power in individual regions and recognised central authority only when it suited them, or in some developing countries today where a similar situation exists). In a large number of states, throughout most of human history, authority has not depended on the availability of armed power to the governors (that is why Hume long ago pointed out that power is always in the final resort in the hands of the ruled rather than the ruler). It is for this reason that discussion among social theorists about the nature of authority has so often been concerned with the part played by legitimacy, custom or inertia in securing obedience; or with the normative power of a legal order based on consent; or with the distinction between rational, traditional and charismatic authority. Such distinctions are obviously highly relevant to international society, where authority based on force is so conspicuously lacking. It will thus be necessary for us to consider the ways in which authority is exercised in international society; what kind of legitimacy, without power, international bodies might acquire for themselves; how far the authority already enjoyed by, and willingly accorded to, international functional organisations may spill over to other international bodies; whether use can be made of resort to the law and legal procedures, including procedures for mediation, arbitration and multilateral settlement of disputes, to create the basis of order among states. In considering a society as disorganised and decentralised as this, in which individual members are strongly resistant to all external power, the way in which authority can be effectively exercised is clearly an especially important area of concern.

It is on the basis of these ten concepts that we shall seek to analyse the workings of international society. In considering each, we shall be concerned not only with the relevance they have for the contemporary world scene, but with the way they can be applied to earlier international societies with which this can be compared. For it is above all on the basis of historical *comparison*, we shall argue (as in our earlier studies), that fruitful conclusions about international society must be based. In most of the following chapters, therefore, we shall first consider the way each concept has been applied in the analysis of domestic societies; next test its relevance to a number of historical societies; thirdly seek to apply it to the international society in which we now live; and finally seek to draw general conclusions about the usefulness it may have in the study of international society generally. *

---

* Because of the restricted scale of this book the accounts given below of each factor are necessarily brief and oversimplified: in some cases, therefore, the reader has been referred to earlier works where the ideas have been explored by the author in greater detail.

2 Action

ACTION AND INTERACTION IN INTERNATIONAL SOCIETY

The basic unit of society is the individual social act. Not all action is social. The individual who cleans his teeth, puts on his clothes and takes a stroll in the garden is not undertaking social acts. These do not directly influence the life of any other member of society, still less society as a whole. Only actions which involve direct contact with another member of society can be regarded as social acts.[1]

International society too is made up of individual social acts, and there too not all action is social action. There, even more than in domestic society, many acts are possible – by individuals, groups and states – that are not "social": that do not, that is, represent transactions of international society. Individuals in the greater part of their personal lives, companies in most of their commercial activity, states in most of their actions, operate entirely within the home environment and make no impact on international society. Only when individuals make contact with others outside their own state, only when groups and companies have dealings with groups or individuals in other states, only when states take actions that relate to other states or their inhabitants, does international social action take place. Interaction in this society is international action.

What sort of action does this include? The individual who telephones a friend abroad, who travels on a holiday abroad, who buys a foreign share, who marries a foreigner, who buys foreign goods in the shops, is clearly undertaking international acts of a kind. The enterprise that imports goods made elsewhere or exports to a foreign country, that buys a foreign enterprise or makes use of a foreign currency, is undertaking international actions too. Each of these is a transaction that leaves a mark on international society. But

---

1. Almost every act can be said to involve *indirect* contact with other members of society. In cleaning his teeth an individual uses a toothbrush made by others and creates waste which will be disposed of by others. Weber defined any action "which takes account of the behaviour of others" as social action. Such an action will occur only if there is a *conscious* attention to the behaviour of others, but not if others are only unconsciously assumed to exist, as in the examples just given.

that mark is minimal: none of these actions has sufficient impact on world society to be worth consideration in most analyses of its operation. Usually the actions of individuals and groups become significant international action only when undertaken in *quantity*. If it is not a single individual but a million or two who buy foreign shares, travel abroad, import foreign goods, this can begin to have significant consequences for the wider international society. If it is not a single enterprise which decides to export to a neighbouring state but a large number of them (so perhaps displacing altogether the production of a local industry), if it is not a single shareholder seeking to buy an interest in a firm abroad, but a large number of shareholders or a multinational corporation (so acquiring a substantial part of a local industry or a local market), then it begins to be an international action of consequence.

But it is above all the actions of *states* with which we are concerned in international society. In general these are more far-reaching in their significance than those of individuals and groups. States (which here means the governments of states) can undertake actions that not only add incrementally to the total of social acts undertaken by individuals and groups, but which alter *categorically* the actions that are taken by them. They may not only add to or subtract from the total number of individuals who travel abroad, or the total number of shirts that are imported; they can determine *whether* travel abroad takes place at all, whether *any* shirt can be imported. They cannot only invest in a foreign company, like the enterprises; they can control *all* investment in *all* foreign companies. It is for this reason that a large proportion of the more significant international acts are those of states undertaking their relations with other states; and that the study of international society therefore begins with the study of state actions.

So far we have classified international actions mainly by the types of *actors*: whether they are undertaken by individuals, groups or states. But there are other classifications that can be made. First there is the distinction between positive action and passive action. Not all action takes the form of a positive move: we saw that Weber recognised that a decision *not* to intervene in a situation represented action of a sort. So it is with international action. If a state decides to make no response to a newly imposed immigration control introduced by a foreign state, or tacitly accepts a change in the commercial policy of another state, this still represents an action of a kind: a decision, explicit or implicit, not to respond, not to protest or retaliate. Such *passive* actions are, however, normally less significant in their effect on international society generally than those that are undertaken in the active mood. They will not in themselves bring about any change within international society; and it is those actions that do bring about change which are of greatest significance in the analysis of that society.

Next, action can be distinguished according to whether it is specific and isolated in form, or represents a *general* act which in turn affects a large number of individual actions. If a government stops a particular individual from entering the country from abroad, this is a specific act affecting only that individual. If it passes legislation to prevent any immigration, or any immigration from a particular country, this is a general act affecting the immigration of large numbers of individuals. For the most part it is the latter type of action, having a general effect on many individual cases, which will be of most significance in their effects on international society. But even general acts may vary in their generality, according to the type of acts which they influence and according to the extent of that influence: for example, whether they relate to one other state or many other states; to a particular type of trade or all forms of trade; and so on.

Third, acts can be distinguished according to their *duration*. Whether an act is particular or general, it may last for a short time or a long time. A particular act, such as a decision to seek the friendship of one other foreign state, can be pursued over a long period or a short one. Even a general act, such as a decision to ban all imports of shirts, can be maintained for many years or a few months. Clearly action that is of long duration is likely to be of greater significance for international society than that which lasts only a relatively brief time. An alliance that is maintained for fifty years is of more significance to international social relationships than one that is entered into *ad hoc* for a brief period to meet a particular situation. Trade regulations that are rescinded after three months will affect economic relationships within international society far less than those which are imposed on a semi-permanent basis.

Finally, international actions can of course be distinguished according to the *area* of activity which they affect. Some are concerned with economic relationships, some with political; some with the communication of people, some with the communication of goods; some with cultural affairs, some with sporting relationships. Variations in this dimension too will affect the significance of each kind of action for international society. In general action that affects sporting contact between states will be of less significance than those which affect cultural relations; those which affect cultural relations will be less important than those which affect commercial relations; those that affect commercial relations of less importance than those which affect diplomatic relations; and so on. Actions relating to peace and war will be of the greatest importance of all; and even a particular action in this field will be of more significance than a general action taken in one of the others.

But the significance of an international action does not only depend on the area within which it occurs. It may depend partly on who takes the decision concerned: a private individual, a junior official, a senior minister or a cabinet as a whole. A cabinet's decision about cultural relations may be more important than that of an individual businessman about commerce. Even this is not always the crucial factor. Though the nature of the decision-maker may *affect* the importance of a particular act, it will not determine it. That will depend on the *consequences* of each act (which are not always determined by who takes the decision): on whether these consequences are particular or general; affect one state or all; are short term or long term; affect a more or less significant type of relationship. In other words the act's significance lies finally in its long-term effect on social relationships.

This then is a fairly elementary classification among types of international action. It is one that we shall seek to clarify further in the pages that follow. More important than the distinction among different types of actions is analysis of the different influences which affect them.

SITUATIONS

In international society, as in other societies, there are no isolated actions. Every action occurs in succession to other actions and will in turn be succeeded by still others. In other words it forms part of a continuous network of action that has continued from the time society began and will continue until it ends.

This means that every action occurs within an already existing *situation*. Some parts of that situation will have existed for years and even for centuries: most of the physical environment, much of the tradition and cultural heritage, some of the norms governing conduct and relationships within the particular society concerned. But other parts of the situation will have existed only for seconds: they result from actions immediately preceding and from those parts of the interpersonal relationships thereby influenced. It is these more immediate antecedents which create the need for a response, a threat to be averted, an opportunity to be taken.

In international society, as in domestic society the situation the actor faces derives partly from the distant past, partly from events that have just occurred. The international actor – whether the individual deciding whether to emigrate, the company deciding whether to invest in a foreign state, the government deciding how to respond to a threat emerging from a foreign country – will possess a *long-term* image of society: of big states and small states, of friendly states and hostile states, of a traditional pattern of inter-state relations, political and economic, of immigration rules and customs regulations, of international institutions and diplomatic conventions; an image which remains a relatively unchanging aspect of their situation; which was roughly the same last year and will be not very different next year; and which must be taken account of in any response that is finally made to their situation. But they will also be aware, and more consciously aware, of events which have only recently occurred and which have precipitated the situation in which they find themselves: the invitation from a distant cousin which has stimulated the desire to emigrate, the investment opportunity which has suddenly arisen in a foreign state, the murder of an archduke by an assassin from a neighbouring country. The response that is made to the latter, that is to the most recent aspects of the situation, will be taken in the knowledge of the former, the long-term situation which imposes conditions on any effective action taken.

As in smaller societies, international actors are faced in every situation by both opportunities and constraints; means and conditions; forces of attraction and forces of repulsion. The *opportunities* are the possible alternative ways in which they may secure their immediate objectives: of winning the visa necessary to emigrate to another state, of securing control of the foreign company concerned, of defeating or humiliating the rival state. But they will be aware, equally, of the *constraints* which may qualify their ability to secure their ends: the quota regulations that govern immigration, the rival contenders seeking to acquire control of the foreign firm, the armed forces available to the rival power and the allies which may come to its assistance. The orientation which the actors adopt to the situation, their conception of the best ways of confronting it and the policy that they therefore finally adopt, will take account of their perception of means and conditions, long-term constraints and immediate opportunity.

In international as in domestic society it is of course *beliefs* about that situation (including the attitude of other actors), rather than the reality, which will determine action. Whether the citizen decides to emigrate, the company to invest, the state to declare war, depends not on the facts of international society, but on their beliefs about the facts. And in international society, even more than in domestic society, there may be a substantial gap between belief and reality. The image that is held of that society, the knowledge about its reality – of immigration regulations in a foreign state, economic conditions in a distant economy, the balance of power against a possible contender – is likely to be both vaguer and less accurate than knowledge available to actors reaching comparable decisions within a domestic society. Decisions reached in international society may therefore be (or at least may appear to outside observers) more irrational, less well adapted to the intended objectives, than those that are reached within a small-scale society where relationships are more clearly established. And this will add to the unpredictability of the actions taken, and to the instability of the relationships which result, in the wider international society.

No actor undertaking international action will be totally without knowledge of the other actors with which he deals. That knowledge is often the principal spur to action. The individual contemplating whether to emigrate is influenced not only by knowledge of the situation at home – the level of employment there, the loss of a job, the end of a marriage – but by the international situation as well – the standard of living attainable elsewhere, the immigration laws and employment prospects in the receiving state. The company contemplating investment is influenced not only by is national situation – the unprofitability of available investment in the home economy, the saturation of the market there, the lack of skilled labour and so on – but by knowledge of the international situation – the favourable opportunities in the foreign state concerned, the tax benefits to be had, the flourishing market to be expected. The state that is contemplating war is concerned not only by its perception of the domestic situation – the anger of public opinion at home, the impatience of the armed forces, the incitements of prominent politicians – but even more by international factors – the enhanced security which a victory is thought likely to secure, the prospect of humiliating a rival, the encouragement of allies.

But the *relative* knowledge of the two aspects of the situation may vary greatly and may determine the action taken. The person who knows nothing of any immigration opportunities abroad will not think of emigrating; the company that knows nothing of chances of investment abroad will not undertake it; the state that is totally without knowledge of the actions taken by a foreign state will not consider war against it. On the other hand, if their knowledge had been greater than it was, their actions might be different again: they might have foreseen the difficulty of adjustment in a foreign city, of producing successfully with a foreign work-force, of fighting a successful campaign in an unknown and unfavourable environment.

The inaccuracy of perceptions in international society thus affects the effectiveness of the action taken. The individual who is badly informed about conditions in the state where she plans to emigrate, the company that is badly informed about economic conditions in the state where it plans to invest, the state that receives faulty intelligence about the military capability of a state against which it plans war, is likely to make bad decisions: that is decisions that they will later regret and perhaps seek to reverse. But the *extent* of knowledge may be as important as its accuracy. An individual may have perfect knowledge of the immigration regulations of a foreign state yet make a faulty decision about emigration if she is badly informed about living conditions in the state concerned. A company may have perfect knowledge about economic conditions in a foreign state yet make a faulty investment decision if it has inadequate knowledge about the viability of the enterprise in which it invests (or vice versa). A state may have perfect knowledge about the capability of a foreign power yet make a faulty foreign policy decision if it is badly informed about its intentions (or the intentions of other states that decide to ally with it).

The deficiency in knowledge (or knowledgeability) in international society has other important effects. It often affects the overall direction of *concern* of international actors. In all societies individuals have greater knowledge, greater awareness and greater concern about those members of society who are closest to them: members of their own family, their own community, their own tribe, their own locality. In modern national societies this has become of gradually decreasing importance since mobility has the effect that distances are reduced: in the course of a life-time the individual becomes increasingly remote from immediate family, makes new friends with new jobs, has many neighbours of many different classes and localities, in work and in leisure, so that the focus of concern becomes gradually broadened. But in international society the differential between close and distant social partners is still very great. The political, social, cultural and economic domination of the national state means that the concern of most is heavily concentrated on their own state and its members. Because of this, decision-makers, even when taking decisions about international action, are usually mainly concerned about its effects at home, and only much more marginally about the effects the action may have in other states. The individual contemplating emigration, the company contemplating foreign investment, the government contemplating war, all are primarily concerned about the effects on themselves and their own countries, very little with the effect on the other states where the actions are taken. It is the needs of themselves and their own family, the needs of their home shareholders, the needs of their populations at home, rather than the welfare of the state to which emigration is planned, the economic benefits to the state where investment is to be made, the effects on the population against which war is planned, which is paramount in the minds of the actors concerned.

In other words the wider social situation, that is the international situation, is one that is seen to a large extent through the spectacles of the smaller society. The more distant aspects of the situation – the international aspects – and the more distant people – mainly those inhabiting foreign states – appear only dimly compared to the large figures in the foreground – the needs and aspirations of the family, the company or the state – which appear in far sharper focus. Shrinkage of distance and increasing mobility slowly reduce this contrast, so that awareness of the needs and rights of those who are further off, even of distant foreign states, is gradually enhanced. But for the most part situations in this society are still mainly conceived with the foreground greatly magnified and the background barely visible. This is a major feature of international society, and of the social action taken within it, distinguishing it from much action taken within states.

RELATIONS

The most important part of every situation within which action is taken is a set of personal relations: a *particular* relationship or a *set* of interlocking relationships, usually a mixture of both. All social acts either create, reinforce or otherwise modify such relationships. At the same time they are themselves influenced by the relationships already existing. Thus a reciprocal process takes place. On the one hand, existing relations – within the family, the work-place, the locality and the wider society – will be the main influence on all individual social acts that are taken. Conversely each social act will marginally modify (even if only by reinforcing) existing relationships. For this reason society – the overall set of relationships within which we live – is never stationary. It is continually being reconstructed by each new social action.

All this holds equally of international society. That society too is made up of a set of relationships: the relationships of individuals to their contacts abroad, of companies to economic partners in other countries, of states to neighbouring states and groups of states. There too these relationships are the central feature of the situation in which each international act occurs. And there too each act continually modifies relationships in such a way that international society is continually transformed.

The relationships of which society is created are of many kinds. Some are close, some are distant; some are friendly, some are hostile; some are threatening, some inviting. Other members of society may be seen as passive instruments or active opponents; as neutral bystanders or as dynamic forces for change. Whatever our image of others, our own acts, we quickly learn, must be adjusted to their known behaviour and beliefs. To secure our own aims effectively, we often need to know *their* aims, motives and habitual conduct; for this is an essential part of *our* situation. By securing greater knowledge of that situation, we are able to act more "rationally": that is, better able to adjust reality in our own favour.

In international society, likewise, relationships are of many kinds. Individuals may have many and close relations with other individuals in foreign states, or almost none; an economic organisation may be closely tied with similar organisations in other countries, or have no such links; states may have flourishing ties with neighbours or be self-sufficient, be on friendly terms with them or on terms of enmity. In international society too action is modified according to knowledge of the motives and actions of other international actors. And here too the *extent* of the knowledge we have of other actors may determine how far the action we take is "rational"; and how far, in the long term, it maximises our interests.

The effect of a relationship depends partly on how long it lasts. Some relationships are more permanent than others; and so become more powerful in influencing social action. The relationship that results from a short-term situation will affect that situation alone and almost nothing else: for example the relationship of a commercial transaction or a bureaucratic encounter. In many cases of this kind the relationship is *instrumental*; that is it is undertaken not for the sake of the relationship itself, but because of other ends that are to be secured. The relationship resulting from a more long-lasting situation, between pupil and teacher or, still more, between father and son (which, however its character may change over the years, will last as long as both are alive), will not only affect a much wider range of activity, and influence other relationships with other people; it may be valued in itself so that actions are taken, or goals modified, for the sake of the relationship, rather than the relationship being established for the sake of external goals.

So it is in international society. The relations of individuals or groups or states within that society can be fleeting or long lasting; influential or casual. A state may enter into an alliance with another state that lasts for many centuries (like that between Britain and Portugal, first established in the fifteenth century); or it may enter into a short-term trade agreement that is valid for a year only. The longer the relationship lasts the more it will be valued for its own sake rather than for the immediate practical advantages which it may bring, and the more effect it will have on other relationships. A long-lasting agreement will have a greater effect on foreign policy generally because it will affect the way in which *all* situations are perceived. Actions will be habitually adjusted so as to avoid offence to a state seen as a long-term friend. Conversely, a long-term *enmity* among states – such as that between Spain and France in the sixteenth and seventeenth centuries (resulting in nearly twenty wars between them during that period), between Russia and Turkey in the eighteenth and nineteenth centuries (resulting in eight wars during that period) or between the US and the Soviet Union today – will also influence other relationships (for example to their own and their opponent's allies) in a way that isolated conflicts, even of a very intense kind, will not do. In other words relationships, as they become more firmly established, increasingly influence the way society as a whole is perceived and the sort of action that is believed suitable for securing a state's objectives.

But relationships vary in their *intensity* as well as in their permanence. Even one that is not long-lasting may be important in its influence on action if it is intense (a close friendship that lasts for a few months, a marriage that breaks down after two years). Again the same is true in international society. A sudden and unexpected war, a brief union between two states, may have *temporary* consequences which are very significant, at least for the parties themselves; and those consequences may continue to be felt for years. Even a single individual, such as a Napoleon or a Hitler, can (like a Savanarola within a smaller society) for a brief period transform international society altogether and leave scars that last for a long time. Yet it will still remain generally the case that, in international and domestic society alike, it is the longer-term relationships which have the greater influence on actions, and so on the structure of society as a whole.

The way in which relationships influence social action is by affecting the *expectations* of the society's members. The established relationship of king to lord, lord to squire and squire to servant in the feudal system, the known and expected relations between long-term friends or long-term rivals, will determine the conduct not only of the parties themselves but that of others in society, who adjust their behaviour accordingly to these expectations. In the same way the known alliance between Britain and Portugal over centuries, the recognised enmity between France and Spain three hundred years ago, the close economic and political ties between members of the EEC today, influence not only the way those countries see each other, but the way other countries see them too, and in this way determines the conduct which is undertaken towards them. Expectations in other words, derived from repeated social experience, bring about particular types of social action which is adopted in the light of that experience. Eventually they establish a common, or at least a widely shared definition of the social situation and so of the social relationships required among all members of a society.

Expected relationships may be established by explicit agreement or by custom only. Within states the relationships of central government to local government, and of local government to citizens, are laid down in acts of parliament; the relationship of husband to wife, or son to father, or pupil to teacher, are established only by custom (which may change over the years). Some relationships – for example of employer to employee, or of banker to customer – are determined partly by written legislation, partly by custom. Others are determined by specialised codes of their own: for example the relationship of doctor to patient.

In international society likewise, the obligations demanded by some relationships are laid down in written form: for example in bilateral treaties or multilateral conventions, committing states to particular types of action towards other states. Other obligations result only from long-standing custom: for example the conventions surrounding the treatment to be accorded to a visiting head of state. Sometimes relationships that have traditionally depended on custom are eventually codified in multilateral conventions: as has occurred, for example, in the case of the diplomatic privileges to be accorded to ambassadors and their staffs, some aspects of maritime law and the law of state succession. In international society, as in smaller societies, there will always be some aspects of relationships which will not be readily codified in a written contract: for example the relations between great powers and small, between aid-donors and aid-receivers. But there will be others, such as the action to be taken by members of an alliance in time of war, or the organisation of telecommunication links, which are more likely to be laid down in formal undertakings.

In international society as in other societies, therefore, social action is taken within the framework of a set of expected relationships. But these expectations, even in domestic societies, differ marginally for every member of the society. In international society, with its looser framework and conflicting value-systems, differences in expectations will be much wider. There is thus greater scope for variety among the responses of each individual member and greater likelihood of a conflict of expectations and so of greater social disorder generally.

DECISIONS

The social act occurs, therefore, in international and other societies alike, within the context of a general situation which includes a set of relationships. The act itself results from a *decision*.

This does not mean that action necessarily results from a conscious examination of the situaiton to be confronted, the relationship it involves and a particular end to be achieved. Only a small proportion of action is as deliberate and rational as this model would imply.

In some cases action, including social action, is instinctive and unconsidered: as when a man, enraged by an insult, strikes another in the face. In international society actions are rarely totally instinctive in this way: the woman who suddenly decides, because of a personal crisis, to seek a job abroad may not have thought much but she has thought a little; the company that dismisses all its employers in a foreign subsidiary because of a strike may act hastily, but it is unlikely to be without any discussion at all; the state that declares war because of an insult from another state may take the decision in a few days or even in a few hours, but it will not be taken altogether without deliberation. Even so these represent the extremes of rapid and scarcely considered responses. In other cases a situation may be seriously debated for some time before a decision on a course of action is taken. A woman examines the pros and cons at length before deciding to emigrate; the company decides the alternatives exhaustively before deciding to invest in a foreign country; the cabinet undertakes intensive discussion before deciding on war against another state.

But there is a wide range of other actions that do not fit into either of these categories. Some action is routine and habitual. Often it depends on a decision taken long ago, which yet still governs behaviour. So a man may continue in a particular employment, even though he dislikes it, because of a decision taken in the past; a woman may continue to live in a particular house or with a particular person because of a past decision she may now regret. Some international "decisions" are of the same kind. Individuals may continue to take their holidays always in the same foreign country, a company may continue to sell the same products in the same markets, states may maintain an embassy within particular countries, buy arms from particular states, maintain alliances with particular states, because of a past decision leading to action that has become habitual. Decisions *not* to act, not to intervene in a particular situation, often fall within this category. Because a person has *habitually* not taken part in the quarrels of their family or voted in general elections, they continue not to do so; because a state has habitually not joined in alliances, nor become a member of an international organisation, it continues not to do so, without renewing consideration of the matter.

Other actions are more considered but are based on irrational rather than logical reasons. A woman may decide to emigrate because she dislikes her ex-husband or because she expects to find employment of a kind which is not in fact available in the country where she is going. A company may invest abroad because of political prejudice against the government at home or because of false information about the opportunities for investment elsewhere; a state may ally itself with another because of traditional sympathies rather than national self-interest, or because of false intelligence about the likely effects on its other interests.

Whether a decision is "rational" or "irrational", deliberate or unconsidered, positive or negative, concerns immediate action or long-term action, it is normally directed at particular ends. This does not mean that the end is always clearly conceived. Nor is it always a single end or one that can be secured by one means only. States, like individuals, have a wide range of ends which are only indirectly related to each other and rarely have a clear-cut hierarchy, ranking one end above another (see p. 125 below). In some situations one particular objective (say security) may be uppermost in the minds of decision-makers; in another situation another (say prosperity). In some cases these two objectives may be in conflict. But this does not mean that decision-makers (for example a cabinet) make a conscious decision concerning the relative value to be placed on each. They rather reach a decision in a particular case which *implies* a particular valuation, though this might be different from that which they would attribute to each alternative if asked to make a conscious choice: they may, for example, attach greater weight to defence needs because of an immediate security scare or powerful parliamentary pressure, rather than because of a dispassionate decision on the allocation of resources.

The choice that is made between goals in practice may depend on the relative *influence* of particular groups. In most decisions, in international society as in others, a large number of different groups will be involved. If, for example, the decision concerns whether or not arms should be sold to another state, officials concerned with trade questions, defence questions and foreign policy questions will all be involved. They in turn will be subject to influence from business groups, trade unions, human rights organisations, politicians, churches and many other unofficial bodies. Each of these groups (which may themselves sometimes be divided) will seek to exert influence on different government departments and often in different directions. Eventually a decision will be reached, perhaps by the cabinet or a cabinet committee, which will often reflect the balance of influence among all these various groups, official and unofficial.

All of those involved in the decisions, however, including those seeking to influence it, are in turn affected by a number of other factors: their personal knowledge and experiences, their perception of the international and national situation, their remembrances from the past, their expectations of the future, the norms of various kinds which influence their beliefs concerning desirable objectives. These may influence different decision-makers in different ways. Thus in considering the decision whether to sell arms to another state, the minister of defence may be more concerned about maximising the defence potential of the alliance; a trade official with maximising revenues from arms sales; a church leader with the effect on human rights in the receiving country.

All may believe themselves to be aiming at the same objectives; the long-term interest of the state. But because of the different focus of their primary concern, each of them may conceive the interests of the state in different ways. Some will be more concerned with immediate advantage, others with long-term reputation, some with the effect on close allies, others with the effect on the international community as a whole, some with material consequences, some with intangible ones. Because there is no single, universally accepted and clearly understood measure of "national interest" which would automatically determine the weighting to be given to each of the various considerations involved (even within the cabinet alone, still less within society generally), there can never be consensus about the relative weight to be given to each factor and therefore about which decision is the right one.

In all international actions one of the most important choices to be made is that between internal, or autonomous desires, and external pressures. A woman's instinct, and even her judgment, may tell her she should emigrate to another country; but her friends and her family may tell her she should not. A company's directors and work-force may wish to expand its operations abroad, but a report of market researchers may advise them against it. All the domestic pressures operating on a government – press, parliament, public opinion, as well as government departments themselves – may urge it that it should go to war with a particular state which has offended it; while all international pressures – from allies, friends, international organisations and international lawyers – tell it that it should not. Here again it is the balance of influences that will be finally decisive. And often it is the degree of *attention* which a government accords to the two sources of influence which will mainly affect the decision that is reached. The government which has greater knowledge (and therefore greater concern) about the international environment may reach wholly different decisions, even in identical circumstances, from the government which has its attention focused almost exclusively on domestic influences.

But decisions are affected, finally, by another factor, which is among the most important of all: the availability of *means*. The decision of the woman who contemplates emigration will not only be affected by the relative influence of family and friends, but by her ability to pay the fare; the decision of the company contemplating investment abroad will be influenced not only by its knowledge of the investment opportunities there, but by the availability of the necessary funds; the decision of the government contemplating war against a neighbouring state will depend not only on the affront which it has received, not only on the relative weight of domestic and external influences, but on the strength of the armed force it can command relative to that available to its rival. Thus in every social situation a vitally important aspect is relative access to means, resources, power (in the sense of capacity to exert influence on others).

Nowhere is this seen more conspicuously than in international society. For in that society the means available to different actors vary even more widely than in domestic societies. The ability to emigrate to the US is very much greater for the middle-class university teacher in England than for the uneducated peasant woman in India. The ability to find a market in a foreign country is considerably greater for the large trans-national corporation of an industrialised country than for the small handicraft co-operative in Bangladesh. The ability to declare war on a contumacious neighbour is much greater for a wealthy and well-armed superpower than it is for an impoverished mini-state. In other words the inequalities that are such important influences on social action, and so of social change, within states are even more glaring within international society; and are therefore in that case a still more important determinant of social action (and potentially a still more significant source of social change).

The social act, therefore, though it represents the smallest input in every society, is ultimately the source of its widest transformation. Each act, taken alone, may be minimal in its significance. Taken together a series of such actions can be decisive in effect. Ultimately they will affect social relationships, social consciousness and so the structure of society itself.

3 Society

SOCIETY AND SOCIETIES

If individuals and groups, therefore, each take action to promote their individual or group objectives, often in conflict with each other, in what sense do they do so within a "society"?

It is clear enough that there exist numerous individuals, having a variety of contacts with other individuals, all reacting to each other in different ways. But what is it that they have in common which justifies us in lumping them together as members of a single entity? Is this "society" to which they belong the family, the locality, the town, the region, the national state or the world beyond? If all of these together represent the overall social environment, is it one society or many? Does the individual belong to one of them more than to others? If the demands of each conflict, must she always choose to obey those that derive from a particular society, or can she pick and choose? In other words what is the meaning, if any, to be attached to the word "society", as so widely used by social theorists (when they speak, for example, of the relation of the individual to "society")?

Is such a concept necessary at all? If all social action takes place in response to a situation, including a set of personal relationships, does not that set of situations and relationships itself constitute the social environment? If there are many relationships, in what sense is there one "society"? Is not the latter a redundant concept, the artificial construct created by the observer to refer to a number of *individuals*, related to each other in complex and often quite unpredictable ways?

The same questions arise in relation to international society. Indeed such questions are still more relevant there. If, at the lower level, it is the individual relationships that matter, rather than the artificial construct we call "society", is that not perhaps even more true in the especially amorphous and incoherent international society? Here surely, even more than in smaller groups, it is the particular rather than the general which counts: the series of separate inter-state relationships, not the sum-total of all such relationships indiscriminately added together.

There are, at root, two separate questions involved here. Both

55

concern the definition of "society". First, in what sense is society one? If it consists of a "network of relations", as is sometimes suggested, why do we need to use the former term at all? Is it not more meaningful, concrete and specific to refer simply to the relationships themselves, rather than to bundle them together in a spurious unity.

There is much to be said for the latter view. It is the case that essentially social existence consists of a set of relationships. But the latter expression alone perhaps does not tell us enough. To say that individuals exist within a set of relationships is scarcely more informative than to say that they live within a society. It is the concrete substance of the relationships, not their abstract existence, which matters. The same relationship – of father to son, employer to employed, doctor to patient – can take many forms. What is important is not the formal, or legal definition but the *substance* of the relationship: the behaviour to which it gives rise. The way in which father in practice behaves to son, employer to employed, doctor to patient, depends on a number of factors, which include the personalities and past experience of each partner. But it also depends on factors which derive from the culture as a whole. It is here that the concept of "society" (if properly defined) may have some relevance: that is, as an indication of the source of external influences on behaviour. The individual, in international and domestic society alike, lives not only within a set of relationships, but within an *expected*, that is a socially derived, set of relationships. Those expectations derive from *outside* the relationships themselves, and outside those who participate in them.

This immediately leads to the second question: from *where* outside? The expectations within the family about the proper relationship between father and son may be quite different from those that prevail in the village, and different again from those of the national state, which in turn may be different from those of the wider international society. Which of these is "society's" view. Is it meaningful therefore to talk about "social" expectations without distinguishing between them? All participate in many societies, not only of different sizes but of different kinds; a set of varying cultures which belong not only to different geographical areas but to different environments (the culture of the school, the culture of the work-place, the culture of the peer-group and so on), each of them affecting the relationships in which they engage in different ways. Some of them may be in conflict with each other. They cannot therefore be simply lumped together to create an amalgam called "society". It is thus in the strictest sense meaningless to speak of the relationship of the individuals to "society" without specifying to which of the many societies we are referring.

How is knowledge of these different societies acquired? And how are the boundaries between them established?

Some of our knowledge about expected relationships is *direct*. The growing child experiences direct physical contact with mother, father, siblings, neighbours and some more distant friends and relations. He can see, hear and personally experience these social partners and their expectations concerning relationships. He will later acquire similar direct knowledge of a separate society at school. But some of his knowledge of relationships is indirect. Gradually, by hearsay, reading, education generally, he will become aware of a wider society outside, which he never sees or directly experiences. He will become conscious of a political structure constituting the state to which he belongs. He will learn of the economic relationships in which he and others are joined. And he will finally absorb (partly through use of the language which transmits it) knowledge of the ideas, traditions, expectations and accepted norms of conduct among a wide range of people with whom he may never have any direct contact: international society as a whole.

But he will quickly become aware that he is surrounded in each of these environments, not by a single set of ideas, traditions, expectations and norms. Even within his own family these will not be identical. Within his school they will vary more. Within national society they will be actively debated and disputed. And within the wider world society there are even larger differences. Not only does he belong to many societies. Each of them is itself complex, fissured and divided.

What is more, there are no exact dividing-lines between these "societies". There is often a regional tradition and culture as well as a local one; there is a European and African tradition and culture as well as an international one, and there are the many specialised societies and cultures to which he belongs – those of school, work-place, professional group – which also do not always have clear boundaries (there is the culture of the class-room as well as that of the school). Which then is his own society?

He cannot make a deliberate choice to which he belongs; which set of expectations he regards as more authoritative. He can *declare* a loyalty: he can say that he regards his father's moral judgement as more binding than his community's, his government's as more authoritative than the UN's. But he cannot in that way alter or nullify the social expectations themselves. It is not his own decision but his own social *situation* which creates the expectations; and those expectations, his social situation generally, will exist regardless of his own choice.

Whatever individuals may "decide", therefore, they will continue to belong, willy-nilly, to many different societies. They will be subject to a variety of expectations. Most influential usually, as we saw, are those that come from nearest at hand: from family and friends. Only as individuals become equally conscious of other groups who are further afield, do the expectations of a wider society begin to play a larger role. Even then it will be for most the expectations that prevail within a national state that have the largest influence. The expectations of the international society beyond, which impinge least on consciousness, will have the smallest authority of all.

The degree of authority each type of "society" exercises will depend partly on indoctrination: social and political education. But it depends ultimately on the nature of social *action* (of which these are a part). Attention will be focused on the authorities and societies which are most active in determining the individual's life. Only as action embraces ever larger geographical areas does attention also expand outwards. Only as international action increases does the consciousness of international society also grow. Only as knowledge of the international society, of the relationships that exist there, of the behaviour that is expected there, of the norms that have been evolved there and the institutions that have been established there, gradually increases does the image of international society gradually become more significant in influencing consciousness and conduct.

SOCIALISATION WITHIN INTERNATIONAL SOCIETY

Knowledge of international society, therefore, is acquired slowly and only indirectly. But once acquired, it will modify, at least to some extent, social expectations derived from elsewhere. And as international action increases as a proportion of all action, the influence of the wider society slowly grows.

If an image is slowly established of international society in this way, how does it influence behaviour? In other words, how does the individual become aware of the expectations that prevail within that wider society?[1]

There, as in other societies, a process of socialisation takes place. Individuals, groups and states alike are slowly made aware of the demands of others within international society. They become conscious of the practices and conventions governing international behaviour accepted among other actors. They absorb, from the comments of politicians, editorial writers, television commentators and others within their own states, ideas concerning the standards that should be applied in judgements of international behaviour. They learn of the pronouncements of international institutions – the International Court of Justice and United Nations bodies – concerning the principles that should govern relations among states. They read of the rules of conduct established over the years by international law. They may even, through rational thought, acquire some conception of the principles of conduct which are a condition of peaceful co-existence among states.

There are, however, a number of reasons why the socialisation which occurs in international society is much weaker than that which takes place within smaller societies.

First, the period of socialisation is much later. The socialisation that takes place in domestic societies begins at a very early age. From their earliest years children are taught, by parents, teachers and other elders, the kind of behaviour that is expected of them. Since they are still at an extremely impressionable age, such influences are likely to have a powerful effect in inducing co-operative behaviour. Socialisation within international society, such as it is, comes far later. Only slowly, as he grows up, does the child become aware, from the watching of television, the reading of newspapers and books and from other sources of information, of the existence of a world society outside the national state. And only much later than this will he begin to be aware of the expectations that are held, often diverse or even conflicting, concerning behaviour within that wider society.

Secondly, socialisation that relates to the small-scale society is the *first* type of indoctrination of which most human beings have experience. For this reason it normally has an especially strong and lasting impact. International socialisation, on the other hand, is

1. The argument of the following passage is set out in greater detail in the author's *Conflict and Peace in the Modern International System* (Boston, Mass., 1968; 2nd rev. edn, London, 1988).

superimposed considerably later, over beliefs and loyalties which are already deeply entrenched. This reduces the impact the former can have, especially where any conflict occurs between the two. The sense of international responsibility is nearly always far weaker than that of national loyalty.

Thirdly, socialisation within the smaller society occurs in the form of direct and clear-cut injunctions which are unmistakable in meaning and immediate in their impact. They are received from parents, teachers and other respected figures, the authority of whom at the time is unquestioned. Even the instruction which is received concerning civic duties and national loyalties (the kind which is most relevant in this connection) may be directly instilled, in the home or at the school, in the same personal and persuasive way. Against this, socialisation within the international society occurs, if at all, only in the most indirect manner. Nobody gives an explicit instruction: "do not commit aggression". The citizen learns slowly, if at all, from reading and discussion, from the views of publicists and politicians, from resolutions of the UN and other sources, that certain international actions, such as "acts of aggression", are widely regarded as inadmissible and generally condemned (though he may also become aware that *specific* uses of force – especially if undertaken by his own state – are as frequently defended and justified, even by respected political figures, in his own particular society).

There are, in other words, many reasons why the messages that are received about desirable behaviour and relationships in international society are far weaker and more uncertain than those that concern the smaller society within. There is no consistent process of initial *inculcation*, subsequent *reinforcement* and eventual *habituation*, such as so deeply instil the principles and rules concerning behaviour within states. There are no widely accepted principles governing the judgements to be made: for example on the relative value to be placed on peace or justice, or on national sovereignty and the protection of human rights, concerning the definition of "aggression", or on the rights and obligations of trans-national corporations) of the kind which facilitate judgements on such matters in smaller societies. Still less is there any generally accepted authority which can give an undisputed judgement about such questions. On the contrary, there are sharply conflicting schools of thought concerning most such matters: conflicts not only between states, but between whole groups of states and between groups and individuals in the same state.

Even more serious than the *weakness* of the socialisation process in international society is its *diversity*. The effectiveness of socialisation in all societies must depend partly on its occurring in similar forms among all members of society. Without this, though each member or group may still have strong opinions about the principles which should govern social acts, they may strongly disagree about what these are, so that society is disrupted by continual conflicts on such questions. In international society this is precisely the situation that exists. Since beliefs about international behaviour among different states vary so widely, and since there is no generally agreed authority capable of pronouncing on such matters, there can, by definition, be no consistent socialisation process. Individuals, groups and states in different parts of the world acquire widely varying conceptions of the principles that should govern international action, and share no widely accepted value-system which might resolve such disputes.

Only if a more consistent set of principles and beliefs could be developed within the wider world, therefore, would the socialisation which occurs there be capable of promoting mutually compatible types of conduct, as the socialisation which occurs in smaller societies is able to do.

NORMS IN INTERNATIONAL SOCIETY

In international society, therefore, as in any other kind, effective socialisation depends on the establishment of commonly accepted principles of interaction. Without these the lives of its members are likely to be ruled by conflict and competition, violence and vagary alone, providing insecurity for the weak and instability for all. Self-seeking instincts and aggressive drives may establish a mode of existence governed mainly by brute force or intimidation.

In small-scale societies the basis for a more stable interaction is normally provided by the creation of a common set of expectations governing relationships within them. The main source of these common expectations are the customary norms of interaction that are established there. Such customary rules are of a number of kinds, of varying degrees of precision, universality and comprehensiveness.

First, there exist *practices*, *ad hoc* procedures and habits of interaction, adopted among two or more parties, which set up firm expectations concerning behaviour in specific situations. Here the object is only mutual convenience; and the sanctions against violation are those of reciprocity, the disapproval and retaliation of other parties, together with the less immediate disadvantages resulting from the disruption of established procedures. Next there are *conventions*, forms of behaviour that are approved by a wider society, and which thus come to enjoy an authority independent of the immediate advantages derived by the parties. Here the expectations are those of society as a whole, and the sanctions are the disapproval of society as a whole. Third, there is *morality*, including custom among primitive societies and ethical codes among more advanced ones, where the expectations aroused are more powerful and surrounded by a more emotional, often religious, sentiment of awe, fervour and dread. Here the sanctions are usually conceived as religious in form, imposed by supernatural beings, though immediately imposed through the self-punishment of the conscience; and because exhortations to conformity, and warnings against violation, are more intense and deeply instilled, they create a more inescapable personal imperative than surrounds any of the other codes. Finally, there is *law*, a code more explicit and detailed than the others, covering more varied fields of existence and practices and conventions, but less deeply internalised, and less coloured by religious emotion or conscience than moral codes. Here the sanction is the coercive power wielded by enforcement agencies, together with the shame involved in proved and public violation of the code.

Each of these codes creates norms of conduct of varying degrees of precision and persuasiveness. The effect is to set up expectations that, in given types of situation, a particular type of behaviour should occur. They thus come to modify motives deriving from other sources, including innate drives, self-regarding ambitions, group objectives and other goals. They create *rules*, to *regulate* conduct, by setting up *regularities* of behaviour.

In all societies such rules provide the main instrument of order. By reducing insecurity and unpredictability, they provide the stability essential to a harmonious and well-balanced existence for each individual member. They contain the element of impartiality and objectivity which arbitrary personal rule may lack. And even apparently coercive authorities depend in practice largely on principles of this type to maintain their power. Everywhere it is rules, rather than rulers that exercise ultimate authority.

But the *type* of norms predominantly employed will crucially determine the character of each community. Each type of norm possesses its own typical form of sanction. The function of the various sanctions is to create a self-regulating mechanism, which provides the subject with a self-interest against violation: the interest in avoiding the sanctions creates an interest in conforming with the norm. But the sanction characteristic of each norm is not exclusive of others. Law may be sustained by moral conscience, social convention and mutual convenience as well as by policemen. Practices whose original sanction is the partner's non-compliance may come to be reinforced by social disapproval, moral sentiments and even the force of the law as well. The specific element of each code consists in the particular emotional aura that surrounds it, as much as in the sanction which is typical for each.

In international society there are obvious difficulties about the creation of customary rules of this kind. The establishment of a system of laws is prevented by the lack of the enforcement powers which are their typical sanction. The establishment of a system of morality is inhibited by the existence of a wide variety of varying moral systems. Even the creation of recognised conventions and practices is made more difficult by the tradition of independence and autonomy among states and the lack of a strongly felt sense of solidarity between them.

None the less customary rules do exist within international society, as in other societies. There exist recognised international *practices*: agreed forms of interaction between two or more states to serve their mutual interests, as similar practices serve those of individuals. In the relations of states, as in those of individuals, there is often a need merely for set procedures or standardised forms – such as recognised diplomatic practices for example – on which each party is able to rely. A common interest in maintaining these may be held where little else is held in common. For many centuries such recognised practices have been established in agreements on trade and navigation, customs procedures, and a wide range of other activities: at first often in bilateral form, more recently increasingly in multilateral arrangements governing all or most states.

There also exist in international society *conventions* among states, which establish more general and formal understandings concerning their conduct. These may create common expectations more depend-able, permanent and universal in application than *ad hoc* practices (which may be abandoned by any state which so chooses if it decides to interpret its national interests in new ways). Conventions thus enjoy the more effective sanctions exerted by common international opinion, instead of remaining dependent on that of individual aggrieved parties. Such conventions are to be seen in the form of customs which have come to have the force of international law and other provisions of that law which are generally recognised.

There is even, in at least an embryonic form, a type of international *morality*. For even though the codes that are applied *within* states vary widely from one to another, there exists none the less throughout international society some recognition of the principles which ought to govern relations *between* them. The sentiments that have been established within the international community concerning genocide, acts of blatant aggression, war crimes, threats and bullying by states, terrorism and some other forms of international actions, whether by states, groups or individuals, have something of the same quality that colours moral revulsion in other spheres. While states, groups and individuals may sometimes engage in such practices, they are recognised by most as undesirable and "wrong". Such a code may be at present only embryonic, both in the scope of its provisions and in the degree of respect accorded it. Yet it none the less begins to have, at least for some, something of the compulsiveness and emotional aura typical of morality of other kinds.

We shall consider in greater detail later (Chapter 10) the particular form these various codes have taken in different international societies. For many reasons their influence is at present far weaker than that of corresponding codes within smaller societies. The process of socialisation through which they are instilled is, as we saw, later and more uncertain in effect. The system of communication through which they are spread is far weaker than that which operates within states. There exists no recognised authority for establishing rules. The effectiveness of the codes is gravely weakened too, as we shall see, by ambiguities and uncertainties about their provisions. Finally, widespread divergencies of interest – between strong countries and weak, rich countries and poor – create equally wide differences about the content or applicability of the codes.

Yet, for all these difficulties, such customary rules, though they may not play such an important role as in smaller societies, do exercise a significant influence both on relations among states and, to a lesser extent, on those among groups and individuals in international society. The need for order and predictability creates, there too, a willingness, most of the time, to conform to the expectations of society as expressed in codes of this kind. The sanction of widespread social disapproval, which is incurred by defiance of the rules, is usually sufficient to cause states and individuals, even powerful ones, to behave according to the conventions. This conformity is not total. Some states do from time to time violate the rules concerning diplomatic procedure or maritime conventions. Some companies cheat their customers in foreign states. Some individuals break the acknowledged code: violate human rights, undertake terrorist acts, or engage in subversion, torture or killing in foreign states. Yet it remains the case that in much of their international behaviour, states, groups and individuals alike will normally seek to adjust their behaviour to the customary rules established within international society.

In other words the kind of norms which operate in international society, though at present still weak and widely contested, are not altogether different from those that influence the behaviour of individuals in smaller societies. It is indeed perhaps only because of the existence of such codes that there can be said to exist an international society at all.

INDIVIDUALS AND COLLECTIVITIES IN INTERNATIONAL SOCIETY

The international society to which individuals belong is thus only one among a number of societies of which they are members; within it they are subject to a process of socialisation which is weak and unsystematic; but through that process they are made aware of a variety of norms and standards, however weakly defined and widely disputed.

They participate in that society in two different ways: as individuals and as members of the collectivities to which they belong. The same person may travel abroad on holiday; invest abroad on behalf of his company; and fight in a foreign war on behalf of his country. In each capacity he is subjected to a different set of influences from the wider society.

For international society is itself not one clearly defined society, but subdivided into a number of smaller societies. So a company belongs not only to a world economy, but to a regional economy as well. A state belongs not only to a world society of states, but to alliances, regions, economic groupings, groups with which it has historical associations (such as the Commonwealth, or the group of former French colonies). Which of these is the "society" to which it belongs? And which are the customs and norms that should carry greatest weight for it?

No clear-cut choice of this kind is made, either by states or by other international actors. Just as the individual does not feel obliged to choose between his family, his community, his region or his state, so the state itself – that is a government or a population – does not feel obliged to choose between any of the groupings to which it belongs. It is equally a member of all of them. But while it may participate in some sense in several societies, it does for certain purposes make choices among them. For different ends – defence, economic links or functional co-operation of various kinds – it will choose to participate mainly in particular organisations; perhaps NATO for one, the EEC for another, UN agencies for others again. In other words it will choose the type of "society" which it believes most useful for the purpose in question; that is according to its functional value.

In a sense a "functional" appraisal of international society is here adopted in a practical way. A "functionalist" approach to society (pp. 15 ff. above) can take two quite distinct forms, which need to be distinguished. Attention may be focused on individual institutions of society with a view to analysing the functional role which each plays: for example a particular kinship system, religious practice or set of myths in a simple society, or a particular type of educational system, political constitution or class structure in a modern society. The concern is not with the satisfaction which each particular institution may provide for *individuals* in each society (except perhaps in the most indirect way), but with the functions they perform for the society as a whole, seen as an entity in its own right.

There is, however, an alternative analysis that can be made. This concentrates on the functional value of particular institutions, or of social arrangements generally, for *individuals*: do they, for example, function in such a way as will procure survival, security, stability, social satisfaction (such as a sense of "cohesion", or "solidarity"), economic sufficiency, the opportunity of social mobility or social justice for each member of the society?

Either of these analyses may be applied to international society. It is, as we saw earlier (p. 17), possible to consider what functions particular institutions of society – the balance of power, national sovereignty, diplomacy or international organisations – provide for the international society as a whole. But it is also possible to consider the same institutions, or entire international societies, to determine the functions they perform for the individual members: for example do they assure for the state's independence, security, stability, peace, the conditions for economic development or social justice? This is a question we shall look at in greater detail in the following chapters. But the ultimate member of international society is the individual. And judgments of different types of international society must depend finally on the satisfaction they create for individuals. In many cases the benefits which will be gained by individuals depend directly on benefits secured by the states to which they belong. Thus the type of international society that secures independence, security, prosperity or peace for states, will tend to increase these values for individuals too (though they could still be threatened by the actions taken *within* states). Economic deprivation or economic injustice for the state will tend to entail economic deprivation and economic injustice for the individual (though the effect may be lessened for particular individuals by the distribution of goods and services within states). It is in this sense that individuals have a direct *personal* interest, as well as a collective interest, in the character of the international society in which they live.

As we have seen in the last chapter, one of the main factors distinguishing international actors is their differential control over resources, over the *means* for effective social action. This not only affects their capacity for action. It determines the nature of their *interests* within international society. In international society, as in domestic society, the distribution of resources is highly unequal. And the distribution of resources among states determines their distribution among individuals too. While at one time the main inequalities which existed (and the only ones that were *visible*) were those between individuals in the same state, today the most important inequalities and the most visible, are those between entire states. The position of the individual in international society, therefore, depends crucially on the situation of their own states within that wider society. For the most part, within international society whether individuals are rich or poor, privileged or underprivileged, depends not on their own position or achievements but on that of their state.

This transforms many of the assumptions of traditional political theory. One of the main demands that individuals have always placed on the societies to which they belonged is that they should afford a distribution of goods and welfare which roughly corresponded with their own conception of deserts or needs. With the increase in the scale of visibility of inequalities at the international level, that demand can no longer be satisfied by the arrangements made within particular states. It can be satisfied only by the arrangements which are made within international society as a whole. It is this capacity of the international society, and of the international society alone, to procure "justice" through the distribution of goods and welfare, which becomes the principal function it can fulfil for its members: states, groups and individuals alike. And individuals, groups and states, in seeking justice as they have from time immemorial, will increasingly recognise that this cannot be realised by changes in the arrangements and institutions existing within states. It can be achieved only by adjustments between states: that is by the creation of a different kind of international society.

It is thus the nature of international society, rather than of national societies, which in such a world becomes the principal concern of social and political theory. The decline in distance, which the communications revolution has brought about, has the effect that groups and individuals scattered about different parts of the globe become more closely interrelated. The relationships established between them are complex, and often indirect, but they are none the less real. The "interdependence" which is so widely discussed is not simply interdependence among states, but among individual human beings. The actions of multinational companies based in New York, or international banks based in Tokyo, affect, directly or indirectly, the well-being of peasants in Peru, or jute-workers in Bangladesh. The decisions of a commodity organisation in London, or of exchange dealers in Frankfurt, can determine the livelihood of millions on the other side of the world. Fashions in pop music, or clothes, or sexual morality, established in one part of the world quickly spread to others. It is in this sense that a single international society is created; a society which increasingly becomes more significant in determining the destiny of ordinary human beings than the lesser societies – national, regional, local – which exist within it. It is this wider society which increasingly becomes the one on which most ordinary human beings are most dependent; and so becomes also the unit of the most relevance for social study.

4 Structure

SOCIAL STRUCTURE

So far we have been concerned with international society in an abstract sense: with the character of all international action, the relationships undertaken within *every* such society. In other words we have been concerned with the general rather than the particular.

In this and following chapters we shall be increasingly concerned with *particular* international societies and the *different* forms which various social institutions and practices have taken within them at different times. This will enable us to undertake the comparison between societies which is an essential element of all social analysis.

Whatever the general image of society that is held, every particular society needs to be subdivided in one way or another. Fellow-members of the society need to be classified: into those that are similar and those that are dissimilar, into friends or foes, powerful or weak, rich or poor.

The type of classification made by each individual will depend partly on reality: the actual characteristics, behaviour and attitudes of other members of the society. But it depends partly on the classification made by society as a whole: in other words on the categories which each individual is taught to see. These categories vary widely from one society to another.

Members of society can be divided on the basis of a number of criteria: birth, status, occupation, wealth, power and so on. Sometimes classifications are made on the basis of a number of criteria in combination. But often one or other will acquire greater *saliency* than the others: will be more significant in influencing the perceptions that are made. So in one society there may be greater awareness of differences of wealth, in another of differences of status or power. In a feudal society there may be greater consciousness of the categories created by birth; while in modern industrial society there may be greater awareness of differences created by education or individual attainment.

Societies also differ in the degree to which such categories are seen as rigid and unchanging: how far passage from one to another is regarded as simple and frequent or difficult and rare. Thus in ancient

India it may be seen as impossible for a member of an Indian caste to move from one to another; while, conversely, in ancient China it may be thought possible for *anybody* (at least in theory) to become a senior mandarin, on the basis of examination success alone. But as important as the ease of transition from one group to another is the *effect* of membership of one group upon status or way of life. Whether membership of a particular group can be acquired by birth, education, ability, or competitive drive, the difference in life-style that results may be very great or very small. Thus in modern India movement from one caste to another may remain impossible, but the effect on life chances, whether in social status or income, may be relatively small; in the US transition from one class to another may be (or seem) relatively easy, but the difference in life-style which results may be great.

Equally important are the *sizes* of each group and the social distance which divides them. The division of society between small groups having very high status, or rank, or wealth, or power, and a large majority who are very low in each or all of these respects, will create a very different kind of society from one divided between two, ten, or a hundred groups, only marginally different in these respects; and those will be different again from a society divided into four or five groups separated by function rather than by rank – say, priests, nobles, warriors, landlords and peasants. Whatever the size of each group the social distance between them may be great or small; and this too will have a major effect on the character of the society generally.

There are also differences in the subjective effect of high or low position under any of these criteria. Very low rank may be more easily supportable (especially if it is shared among enough others) than very low status or very low wealth. But even this will vary from one society to another according to prevailing valuations. In one society differences of wealth may, because of the value-system which prevails, be seen as a matter of indifference, while differences of rank or status are deeply resented (as is sometimes said to be true in the US today). In another (say in Britain forty years ago or in Cuba or Vietnam today) differences in status are accepted as facts of life, while even small differences in income are resented. In other words, subjective as much as objective factors influence the effect of different systems of classification.

In most modern societies differences based on wealth have come to play a larger social role over recent times, while those based on rank, status and power have declined in importance: that is, categories based on wealth have become more salient than the others. This is partly only because categories based on the others have, for various reasons, acquired a *lower* visibility. Differences in power are less significant (at least in theory) in democratic societies where political power is supposed to be diffused and responsible to the electorate; a classification based on status is less influential because there are many divergent views of status (for example the relative status accorded to a priest, a politician or a pop-star); and one based on rank (that is officially *recognised* status) is less important because less value generally is placed on that criterion (for example awards and titles). It is also because there is a greater *awareness* of differences in wealth. The income of all groups is for the first time roughly known; political parties, trade unions and other organisations make individuals more aware of their relative position on this scale. But it is perhaps above all because in modern society differences in power, status and even rank are largely *determined* by differences in income, so that life-chances are more than ever dependent on differences in the latter alone.[1]

There is, however, another factor which affects the social classifications made in recent times. It is increasingly recognised that in modern societies the position achieved by individuals on any of these scales is not dependent on their own efforts and situation alone. Increasingly it depends on the collectivity to which they belong: the enterprise within which they work, the region where they live, above all on the state to which they belong. For most people wealth, status and power depend not on how hard they work themselves, not on the family into which they are born, not on the titles bestowed on

1. This was expressed by Max Weber, writing more than sixty years ago: "the way in which the disposition over material property is distributed among a plurality of people, meeting competitively in the market for the purpose of exchange, itself creates specific life-chances. According to the law of marginal utility this mode of distribution excludes the non-owners from competing for highly valued goods; it favours the owners and in fact gives to them a monopoly to acquire such goods. Other things being equal, this mode of distribution monopolises the opportunities for profitable deals for all those, who, provided with goods, do not necessarily have to exchange them. It increases, at least generally, their power in price wars, with those who, being propertyless, have nothing to offer but their services in naked form and goods in a form constituted through their own labour, and who above all are compelled to get rid of these products in order barely to exist" (*Economy and Society*, Tübingen, 1956, pt III, chap. 4).

them, but on which state they belong to. The individual born in, say, Sweden or Switzerland, even if relatively unsuccessful, will be richer, and may feel himself of higher status, than the one, even if relatively successful, born in Bangladesh. Life-chances depend more than in any earlier time on the success (the "life-chances") of the state. Collective inequalities, in other words, increasingly become more important than individual inequalities.

The effect of this is that the social structure of international society begins to become as important, perhaps more so, for the welfare, of individuals than the social structure of each individual domestic society.

SOCIAL STRUCTURE IN HISTORICAL INTERNATIONAL SOCIETIES

For there exists a social structure in international society too.

The social structure we are concerned with here is primarily the structure among *states*. In so far as there exists any social structure among individuals and groups in international society it is derived, directly or indirectly, from this primary structure. It is therefore with the social structure among states, and especially the system of stratification among states, that we will here be mainly concerned.

In international society too a variety of criteria have been used for dividing and classifying the principal members: that is the states.

The first classification that has been made in every society concerns the qualifications for membership: what makes a state eligible to be a member of the society at all. Distinctions of a number of kinds have been made for this purpose. In most ages, for example, some states have been regarded as outsiders, like the "strangers" not accepted as members of a simple society: beyond the bounds of civilisation and so not eligible for admittance. Typically some states have been seen as "barbarian", "primitive", "underdeveloped" and so on. The ancient Chinese system of states, for example, distinguished between those states which were members of the system, originally the Chou states that shared a common culture, and external states not so regarded (Ch'in, the state that finally emerged as the conqueror of all the others, was originally an external state of this sort); and later the Chinese empire regarded almost all states with which it came into contact as "barbarian", refusing them diplomatic representation at the imperial court on these grounds. Among the Greek city-states, such powers as Persia, Egypt and later Macedonia (again the eventual conqueror of the system) were seen as external powers which did not and could not participate in the system or the relationships maintained among the city-states themselves. In the Middle-Ages in Europe a similar distinction was made between insiders and outsiders. Italian writers, such as the historian Guicciardini, referred to all states of North Europe, that is beyond the Alps, as "barbarian" states, even at a time when much of Italy was controlled by France and Spain.[2] For centuries the Turks, though diplomatic representatives were sent to their Sultan and though they were frequently confronted in war, were not accepted as full members of the European state system (until the Treaty of Paris in 1856 explicitly admitted the Porte to the Concert of Europe). In the nineteenth century European powers would happily sign treaties with any African chief who was willing to sell rights in his territories, but did not enter into diplomatic relations with even the most powerful of them and certainly never regarded them as equals, nor even as "states" at all. In general, therefore, it has until recently always been the case that every international society has excluded certain states on the grounds of strangeness or lack of "civilisation".[3]

A second condition of membership in international societies has been the *independence* of the state concerned. In most periods some states have been excluded from membership – certainly from full membership – of the international community on the grounds that they were not fully independent: usually because they were seen as being, to a greater or lesser extent, under the tutelage of another power. Among the Greek city-states, for example, it was well known that some were directly dependent on a larger city-state and were therefore not accepted as independent members in their own right: for example Potidea, a colony of Corinth, or Argolis controlled by Argos. In Italy during the fifteenth and sixteenth centuries the same thing was true: only fully independent states, for example, became signatories of the Treaty of Lodi, setting up a collective security system for the whole peninsula in 1454. Diplomatic relations were not established with even large German states in the sixteenth and early seventeenth centuries because, being within the empire, they were seen by many as not fully independent of the emperor. Later

2. See, for example, his *History of Italy* (New York, 1969) p. 234.
3. Occasionally there has been an intermediate category of "semi-civilised" states; such as Morocco, Egypt and Persia, during the nineteenth century.

full recognition was not granted to some states because, however independent in practice, they were seen as judicially under the sovereignty, or at least the suzerainty, of some other state: so most of the European powers refrained from granting full diplomatic recognition to Egypt, Serbia and Montenegro, long after they were effectively independent, because they were regarded as being still under the suzerainty of the Turkish sultan. In the same way Tibet, despite being accepted as "autonomous", and in practice totally independent from 1911 to 1950, was not recognised as a member of the international community, nor granted diplomatic status, on the grounds that she remained under a vestigial Chinese "suzerainty". In more recent times colonial territories, even if totally self-governing, were not recognised as members of the international community until they secured full independence (so India, for example, though she became a member of the League of Nations, and subsequently of the United Nations, for thirty years before her independence, was not able to undertake diplomatic relations with other states). In some cases a position of total dependence on a major power has meant that a state, even if formally independent, was denied recognition: on these grounds Outer Mongolia and Manchuria were not granted recognition by most states during the inter-war period, while Trans-Jordan (later Jordan) was not recognised by the Soviet Union until the mid-fifties, nor East Germany by the US until the early seventies, for the same reason. In other words, in all international societies only states seen as fully independent have been regarded as qualified for full membership.

Thirdly, apart from these conditions of principle there has been another, based on convenience. In many societies a minimum size or power has been seen as a condition for effective membership. Most of the mini-states of Germany, for example (nearly 900 until 1648 and 350 from then until Napoleon's time), and the similar mini-states of Italy were effectively excluded from the international community of their day on these grounds. In the nineteenth century there continued to be a number of very small states which were effectively disregarded in the affairs of the continent as a whole. In more recent times attempts have been made to exclude the smallest states from full membership of the international community. For a time an attempt was made to limit membership of the UN to states with a population of 100,000 or more.[4] Though that policy has not been

4. This criterion was used for a period in the 1960s by the Security Council (which needs to authorise any decisions on admittance).

sustained, and a number of states with smaller populations have been admitted, many very small states – Monaco, Leichtenstein and San Marino, for example – are not recognised as full members of international society: no other countries maintain embassies in their capitals, for example, and they are not accepted as members of the United Nations. In other words in most international societies there exist some entities which, even if independent, are regarded as being so insignificant in terms of size that they are not recognised as fully qualified members by most other states.

Even among states that are accepted as full members of international society, a clearly defined class structure is usually visible. Differences in size, and especially in military power, are usually clearly recognised, sometimes in explicit ways. As a result varying types of social structure have been established according to the number of dominant powers.

Occasionally there has existed a single state disposing of far greater power than any others: so Rome and China at the height of their empires were both of overwhelming power in relation to all of the other states with which they had relations (most of China's neighbours were on these grounds tributary states). Sometimes there has existed a form of *diarchy*, with two superpowers, each of them often having large alliances clustered about them: like Athens and Sparta in ancient Greece; Spain and France in sixteenth-century Europe; the US and the Soviet Union today. At other times there have been *oligarchies*, with a small number of states clearly superior in power to most of the rest and accorded a dominant role in shaping the affairs of the entire society: thus in nineteenth-century Europe there were five, and later six, powers explicitly recognised as "great powers", and so qualified to take part in the regular conferences among such powers which surveyed, and to some extent regulated, the affairs of the continent as a whole (see p. 233 below). Sometimes a larger number of significant powers have participated on a relatively equal basis, with a considerable number of much smaller states left almost entirely out of account: this was roughly the situation between 1648 and 1789 when there were about 10 states of comparable size and capability,[5] together with a considerable number of much weaker states.

5. France, Austria, England, Russia, Sweden, Prussia, United Provinces, Turkey, Spain and Poland (Saxony, Portugal, Piedmont and Bavaria were at only a slightly lower level of power).

Inevitably these different types of social structure have involved varying types and degress of inequality. Inequality is obviously greatest in the first two we have described: for example between Rome and her smaller neighbours on the periphery, or between the US and, say, Grenada today. In others the visible inequality has been less: for example most of the significant members of the European society between 1648 and 1789 were of comparable size and power, and this led to a wholly different type of interaction among them than has existed in societies where one or two states have attained overwhelming dominance. Where the international community is very large and contains many small states, the total variation in power is naturally likely to be great: as, for example, in the ancient Chinese society with its 1700 separate states, or among the Greek city-states, of which there were three or four hundred just before 400 BC, or in Europe before 1648 when, if every kind of state, including free cities and bishoprics are included, there were around a thousand separate units. But the degree of disparity depends on many other factors than the number and size of states. It often depends especially on variations in the economic strength of states, and on the levels of military technology which often directly result from this. On these grounds the degree of inequality in power that exists in the contemporary international system is probably as great as in any earlier international society: differences in national income, for example, on which so much else depends, have probably never been greater than they are now (in 1984 the national income of the US was $4000 billion as against $76 million for the Maldives, while the average income a head in the US was $18,500 against $100 in Chad).

But the social structure established is affected not only by the number of states and their relative power but by the way they are grouped: that is by the alignments they establish. This depends on the motivations of states and the way they see the social structure as a whole.

Traditionally states have aligned themselves according to three major principles, which have largely determined the resulting social structure. In certain ages, each state, whether powerful or weak, has sought to promote its own interests independently against all other states. Because the power of even powerful states has always been less than that of many others combined, the aim of most states has been to enter into combinations which would not only maximise their own strength, but would, above all, prevent any single power, however strong, from dominating the entire system. This has brought about *balance of power* policies, of the kind most clearly seen in the period between 1648 and 1789. Because such a system requires above all flexibility in the formation of new groupings and alliance, so that a balance can be maintained, it is necessary that alliances should (as during that period) be made and unmade extremely quickly, and regardless of any other consideration. This means that alliances cannot be based on traditional national friendships or ideological commitment, but only on immediate self-interest. The social structure required is thus extremely fluid, somewhat unstable; but should prevent any large degree of domination by any single state. An essential condition of the system's operation is that each member-state should retain its own freedom of action and therefore its own individual sovereignty so that it may always remain in a position to influence the balance.

A second possible structure is one in which the entire society is divided into two, or occasionally more alliances that are relatively stable and unchanging. This system too can succeed in establishing a kind of balance, and so can prevent any one power, or group of powers, from securing domination of the entire system. But it may do this only by allowing a substantial degree of domination of lesser states by the leader of each alliance. This kind of system is especially likely to be adopted at a time of strong ideological commitment, when states are motivated above all by pressing religious or political concerns: for example during the age of religions between 1559 and 1648, or in the contemporary society beginning in 1917 (see pp. 101–7 below). In such ages the spread of a particular belief creates an automatic association among all those adhering to that faith (for example Protestantism or communism). This in turn leads to the establishment of a rival association among those hostile to it, determined to prevent it spreading further. However the system starts, it is to some extent self-perpetuating. Any increase in the strength of one bloc leads to increased fear within the other, and so to an attempt to redress the balance (for example by recruiting new states or by subverting members of the other alliance). This means that a considerable degree of domination by each alliance leader is likely to be necessary, though excessive domination may become unacceptable to allies and cause attempts by them to assert their own independence of action. None the less the overall social structure which emerges is one that is characterised by a substantial degree of cohesion *within* each bloc, but by sharp divisions between. The institutions of international society – diplomacy, procedures for peaceful settlements and international organisation – are frequently made ineffective as a result of the natural hostility divisions of this kind create.[6]

A third social structure is one that emerges when a *collective security system* is established among states. Such was the system which the Italian states sought to introduce under the Treaty of Lodi of 1454, and among the major European powers under the Quadruple Alliance of 1718 and again under the Treaty of Paris of 1814–15. In all these cases the signatories committed themselves to act jointly to maintain the peace against any state which disturbed it. Since these commitments, however, were vague (and in some cases insincere), no genuine collective security system was implemented on any of those occasions. More recent attempts to create a similar system were made in the League of Nations (providing for collective action on a voluntary basis) and in the United Nations (providing for a mandatory response to Security Council decisions calling for such action). Any system of this sort implies, like the first which we considered, a complete lack of prior commitment to particular allies by every member of the society: all must be prepared to join in armed action against *any* other, even if closely linked by ties of traditional friendship or ideological sympathy. In practice this has proved a condition impossible to fulfil. As a result no true collective security system has yet been established. The system requires the existence of an international authority commanding considerable respect: since in any real-life situation there are likely to be ambiguities about the precise degree of responsibility for a particular breach of the peace, some central authority is required to pronounce on each such breach, to determine responsibility and to decide on the retaliation – military, economic or other – required by each member-state. Here is another condition that, given the demand of states for independence and their conflicting national interests, is not easily fulfilled. The system, if working effectively, creates a social structure affording a substantial degree of independence and security for each member, bought, however, at the expense of subordination to the central authority having responsibility for peace and security. It implies, though does not demand, that there shall be no alliances or groupings of any kind which would inhibit the free mobilisation of the forces required at a

6. See Evan Luard, *Types of International Society* (New York, 1977) pp. 324–6 and 335–9, and Evan Luard, *War in International Society* (London, 1986) pp. 315–19.

time of crisis.[7] And it assumes that states of many different political sympathies and levels of economic development will be able to co-operative effectively in taking action against the state, or group of states, found responsible for breaching the peace.

It will be seen that each of these systems implies a different orgnisation of states within society. The balance of power system implies that there should be no long-term groupings at all: only short-term alliances, usually created for the sake of particular wars only. Such a system is likely to be highly unstable, since even if states are consciously pursuing the required balance of power policy – that is, are seeking to prevent any other power securing excessive domination – there is likely to be competition for alliances in order to secure pre-emptive advantage (as frequently occurred between 1648 and 1789 in Europe).[8] A system of ideological confrontation implies the establishment of large-scale blocs, often grouped round rival super-powers: while this may establish a much more stable and easily predictable set of relationships between states, it can only do this by severely inhibiting the freedom of action of all states within the different blocs. A collective security system implies that there should be no alliances, short-term or long-term, but that there should exist considerable willingness among all states to conform with the demands of an international organisation, and with the requirements of the system as a whole.

The system established within each society for maintaining stability has a crucially important effect on its social structure since it determines the kind of alignments and alliances created. Because military relations among states have in most international societies been more important than any other and have conditioned most other relationships, the overall structure of each society has been largely dependent on this factor. But though it is the most significant, it is not the only factor determining the social structure. Especially over the last century or so, the social structure has been influenced by other factors: political and especially economic. This has established a social structure more complex, and more closely inter-related, than any that has existed in earlier ages.

---

7. It was generally assumed at the time the League of Nations and United Nations were established that their creation excluded the formation of alliances among states.
8. Luard, *War in International Society*, pp. 49–52, 294–5.

THE STRUCTURE OF CONTEMPORARY INTERNATIONAL SOCIETY

The contemporary international society differs in a number of ways from any established in earlier times.

For the first time ever an international society has been created that is reasonably comprehensive. There no longer exist outsiders, "strangers", "barbarians", who are not accepted as qualifying for membership. Virtually every territory in the world – except for the tiniest of all – is today represented within the established international community: for example in the main international organisations.[9] In so far as there remain any conflicts over membership of that community, it has resulted from conflicts *within* states: because they are divided or because there are different authorities demanding recognition. To a considerable extent the international society, for the first time, is a complete one: it is, that is, one that now comprehends states claiming authority over virtually the whole of mankind.

One immediate effect of this is that it comprehends a wider *diversity* of states than at any earlier time. There are, it is true, some assimilating factors which have the reverse effect: rapidly improving communications, close cultural contacts, economic integration, travel and tourism on an unprecedented scale, all of which spread similar perceptions and ways of thought throughout the society. Yet it remains the case that the gap in perceptions, assumptions and aspirations is wider between, say, a Western industrial country (such as the US) and a small African state (such as Mali), between a communist regime in Asia (such as Vietnam) and a conservative, Catholic regime in Latin America (such as Chile), than between any states that were members of earlier societies: for example between the states of Europe even at the height of the religious wars. Wide differences in way of life, cultural background, religious beliefs, political tradition and ideological creeds make this a society of highly disparate units.

They are not only disparate but highly unequal. In this society there are greater differences in power, income and way of life from one state to another than have existed in earlier times. In some ways

9. Of significant states, only Switzerland and the two halves of Korea remain outside the United Nations today (and even these belong to many of the UN's specialised agencies).

states continually become *more* unequal: for example in standards of living, education, scientific levels and military technology. For all of these depend on income a head, which increasingly diverges all the time. In other words it is a sharply stratified society.

The inequalities that are most visible and most resented are economic inequalities. Increasingly the social structure, at least the most apparent and visible social structure, becomes dependent principally on relative levels of economic development. States are classified, above all, as "developed" and "developing". This classification is increasingly recognised as a crude one, even in its own terms. The variations in income a head, or in levels of industrialisation *between* developing countries are considerably greater than those between industrialised countries as a whole and the better-off developing countries. Yet these categories, once established, dictate attitudes and so class-consciousness. For example many oil-producing states continue to name themselves, and to feel themselves, as "developing countries" even though they have incomes a head considerably higher than most developed countries. Developing countries as a whole, for all the wide differences which exist among them, feel that the common interest which they share in relation to industrialised states is more important than any differences which may exist between them. Just as within states traditional labels – propertied or propertyless, white collar or blue collar, salary-earner or wage-earner, middle class or working class – may continue to influence the way people see each other (and themselves), even when they have become less relevant than when they were established, so in international society likewise traditional labels continue to influence the way countries see other states (and themselves); and, in influencing their perceptions, influence equally their actions and so the entire structure of society.

A society of states, like any other society, is classified in different ways for different purposes. When emphasis is placed on power relationships, they are classified as "big powers" or "small powers". When emphasis is placed on religious beliefs or ideological preference, they are classifed as "Catholic" or "Protestant", "communist" or "democratic". When emphasis is placed on commitment to a cause they are classified as "with us" or "with them", "neutral" or "non-aligned". But in the modern world states see themselves (and others) in terms of the difference which is most visible and most resented: the inequality in wealth and welfare which so obviously divides one people from another.

States no longer compare each other in terms of the size of their armies or the number of their warships, as in the nineteenth century, but in terms of levels of investment, growth rates and standards of living. This economic class structure largely determines the military one, but it is not identical with it. Some powers that are economically strong have small military ambitions (Japan, Switzerland, Kuwait). Conversely some that are poor have high military aspirations (Vietnam, Nigeria, Ethiopia). If social situation was based on economic power alone, Japan would be ranked as a superpower. But for most states the level of military power – or at least apparent military power – is closely dependent on their level of economic strength. And this is a further reason for competition in the economic field.

The inequality in economic power is the source of inequality of many other kinds. Divergent resources create a wide gap in levels of technology and science, and so in innovation. Cultural opportunities and cultural achievements are equally disparate, ultimately for the same reason. Environmental standards, originally much higher in poor countries which had not experienced the pollution and overcrowding brought by industrialisation, in time become far lower, with the problems of urbanisation found at their worst in the vast slum of big cities in the developing world and the eroded and deforested countryside of such countries. Whatever measure of achievement is taken, the richer members of society are not only the best off now: they have every prospect of becoming still better off in the future.

This increasing consciousness of economic disparity is reflected in the groups which are established among states. In earlier international societies the groupings formed were primarily military alliances. No groups were established on the basis of economic circumstances. Now consciousness of common economic interests become a major factor in determining alignments. So developing countries establish among themselves the Group of 77, as a pressure-group to promote the interests of poor states in negotiations with richer countries. Developed countries establish various fora to discuss their common economic problems and adopt a strategy for negotiation with poor countries: for example, the Organisation for Economic Cooperation and Development (OECD), the International Energy Agency (IEA) and the economic summits. Similar pressure-groups are established *within* particular organisations: for example the Group of 24 poor countries and the Group of 7 rich countries within the IMF. Because negotiations of many kinds are continually being undertaken between the two groups of countries, all are encouraged to see themselves, and to label themselves, in terms of this division.

Regional organisations are also now primarily economic, UN regional economic commissions are established to plan and oversee economic activity over a continental or subcontinental area. "Common markets" and free trade areas are established to promote trade within particular regions: as in Western Europe, West Africa, Central America and other places. There are increasing efforts to co-ordinate and integrate economic activity throughout an entire sub-region, or occasionally an entire continent. More significantly, economic interests are seen as being shared within such regions. Thus individuals now identify for economic purposes not only with their own states, but with their own regions. Regions too therefore become associated with an international economic class. The world is divided not only into rich and poor states but rich and poor continents.

This is, in other words, a highly unequal international society. The inequalities are no longer simply inequalities of size as in the past but, increasingly, inequalities of economic condition and so of military capacity as well. The myth of "sovereign equality" among states, to which all pay lip-service, is totally belied by the reality of economic inequality. In practice, status, influence and decision-making power are confined to a very small number of economically developed states. It is these states that established the institutions of the post-1945 world and laid down the principles which should guide them. It is they which hold the levers of financial power, determine the level of interest rates affecting the entire world, the volume of financial transfers and even (directly or indirectly) of commodity prices. It is they which take part in regular economic "summits", designed to chart the course of world economic activity for the following year or two. The inequality of power is even institutionalised in the provision of a veto power for the five "permanent members" of the Security Council; in the provisions for permanent or semi-permanent membership of the richest states in all governing bodies of other agencies; and in the concentration of voting power in the world's financial institutions in the hands of the major donors.

In international society, in other words, as in domestic society, inequality in economic conditions leads to substantial inequalities of other kinds: a small number of states are dominant and the great majority dependent.

CONCLUSIONS

Thus in different international societies a wide variety of social structures have been established.

This has depended, in the most obvious sense, on the variations in size and power among the members: whether there is a single dominant power, a diarchy, an oligarchy and so on. Which of these is established depends on relative power rather than relative size: such states as China and India for example, large without being powerful, have not exercised a weight within international society sufficient to influence the social structure significantly. Because force has been the major factor in determining whose will was to prevail in any given situation in the societies known so far, it is the capacity to wield armed force that has mainly determined the relationships among states. For this reason there has never yet been a genuinely democratic international society, in which all states had an equal influence; that is, an influence proportionate to their population. At all times the more powerful states have ensured for themselves an influence outweighing that of the less powerful.

The type of social structure which emerges does not, however, depend in any crude or automatic fashion upon power relationships. The effect of those relationships depends crucially on other social factors: the motives which are held among states, and the underlying ideology – the set of beliefs – which influences those motives. We shall be considering each of these factors in greater detail below, but for the moment it is sufficient to note that a set of relationships, in other words a social structure, dependent on power alone can be maintained only so far as states do in *practice* determine their disagreements in the final resort on the basis of armed power. The relevance of power will depend on the degree to which it is actually mobilised and used for that purpose, whether explicitly (through the overt exercise of armed force) or implicitly (through threats and intimidation). If the motives of states are different, if their aim is not to win military domination over other states, but, for example, to win cultural influence or popular goodwill or a willingly accepted political influence, relative power will be a less important factor in determining the social structure. In that situation it will be cultural levels, or conciliatory policies, or the power of political ideas, which will become the major influences in determining relationships among states. Since in contemporary international society relationships *are* influenced to some extent by these or other factors, and not by power alone, the type of social structure established is already more complex than that which would emerge if all relationships depended on power balances alone.

In other words the importance of power in determining relationships is almost never total. It is qualified by other factors and its significance varies from one society to another and from one relationship to another. Relationships among west European states today, for example, are not significantly affected by power factors: there is no longer behind all their dealings (as there was until relatively recently) an implicit threat that if one does not accede to the wishes of another, it might find itself constrained by the coercive power of superior force. On the other hand, between a superpower and small states in immediately adjacent areas such an implicit threat does often exist and does remain an influence.

How far does there exist any social *mobility* in any of the societies that we have been examining? If the structure – the pecking order – depended on size alone there would clearly be no mobility (except in so far as the type of population policy pursued might affect relative size: it was precisely in order to increase the relative positions of their own states in this respect that Hitler and Mussolini sought to increase the birth-rate of their countries through appropriate policies, and it is for similar reasons that one or two developing countries today are said to be reluctant to introduce effective population-control programmes). If the structure was dependent solely on relative *power*, then some mobility would be possible. A state wishing to improve its position could increase the size of its armed forces or the power of its armaments: it was partly on these grounds that Germany's naval building programme was undertaken in the early years of this century – to secure Germany's recognition as a "world power"; and it was on similar grounds that Germany, Japan and Italy determined to build up their armed forces in the inter-war years, and that the Shah of Iran and other leaders of developing countries have been willing to invest large sums in modern military equipment. If social position is judged in terms of levels of culture and education, increased expenditure in those areas will be undertaken to raise the apparent levels achieved. Finally, if social position is judged in terms of levels of economic development (and we have seen that this has become the most widely used measure of esteem in recent years) intensive efforts will be made to improve performance in this respect. In other words none of the factors that are widely held to determine a country's position within the international social structure is altogether outside its control. Even so, the position which each holds cannot be quickly or easily influenced in any of these ways. While the individual, in modern industrial societies at least, can, if fortunate, move relatively quickly from a position near the bottom of the social scale to one near the top, a state can only with considerable difficulty and over time, move from one social class to another.

The structure of all societies results from differences in the situation and capacity of the individuals which compose them: differences in power, wealth, influence, authority and intelligence. These create variations in the ability of particular individuals, and sets of individuals, to secure their own ends and satisfactions. Those who are best able to secure their ends within the present system will use the power available to them to maintain the existing social structure; those who find they are unable to do so within that structure will struggle to alter it. The structure of international society too derives from differences in the situation and capacities of different states. These differences are in some ways greater than those which exist among members of a smaller society. They derive, for example, partly from differences in size (of population), which will exist regardless of the social structure established. So, because of its size, China will carry a greater weight in international affairs than Costa Rica, whatever the social system, however democratic the constitution of international organisations, however firmly the principle of "sovereign equality" is established. But against these inequalities in size must be set inequalities of other kinds which may counteract them: for example differences in economic and military capabilities. Thus, for all its size, China in the last century carried a minimum weight in international affairs; and even today, despite having a population far larger than any other country in the world, is a lesser power in economic and military terms than others with far smaller populations.

The international social structure, therefore, like that of smaller societies, is affected by differences in capability of many kinds. As in smaller societies, the poorer and weaker will often combine to reduce the power of the larger and more powerful. They will seek greater influence in international bodies, demand economic arrangements providing for a transfer of resources, resist the claims of great powers to have a dominant say in world affairs. They will seek (though may not attain) an irreversible shift of wealth and power from rich to poor, from large to small, from strong to weak. Increasing consciousness of economic inequalities, and increasing recognition that they lie at the heart of inequalities of many other kinds, have the effect that a class structure among states emerges which is clearly based on differences in economic circumstances, just as the class structure within states once was. For these reasons – because differences in life-chances bring about a continuing struggle to change society – the international social structure will never be static: in international society as in smaller societies a continuing struggle will take place, among individuals and groups as much as among states, to adjust it in their own favour.

5 Ideology

IDEOLOGY AND SOCIETY

The most important single feature determining the character of an international society is the ideology which governs it.

Every society consists partly of the ideas which influence its working. These ideas will affect the way its members see that society and their own place within it. They will determine the kinds of relationships believed to be desirable and the kinds to be avoided. And in this way they will effect, above all, the *behaviour* of members, both to each other and to the established social institutions.

In many societies, especially simple societies, these dominating ideas stem from religious beliefs. Anthropologists have therefore been interested in studying the role of such ideas in influencing the life of society as a whole. They have shown how particular kinds of cult – for example totem religion – affect the entire structure of relationships and social attitudes within a community. They have examined the importance of myths, magic and other types of belief in influencing social behaviour (even, in some views, in creating a "deep structure", often unperceived by its members, which none the less serves to hold society together and give it its essential character). The importance of this common "ideology" is partly the very fact that it is *shared*, common to all members, and so creates a sense of solidarity among them; but even more that it can determine the whole pattern of relationships within society.

In more developed societies the prevailing set of beliefs – religious, social and political – have a similar importance. In ancient China the "hundred schools of thought" which flourished a few centuries before Christ elaborated different sets of ideas, concerned not only with the nature of reality, but, much more, with the desirable social and political relationships stemming from those beliefs. Some of these sets of ideas were put into practice in particular states; and two of them (those of Han Fei-tzu and Confucius), though totally different from each other, each for a time became the officially established ideology of the empire as a whole (the first for a decade or two only, the second for over two thousand years). In the same way the differing social and political views of Greek philosophers were sometimes put into practice in different city-states; the contrasting polities of Sparta and Athens, for example, implemented two political and social philosophies that were in radical contrast. In the cities of medieval Europe, widely varying types of social and political system resulted from varying religious conceptions – for example in Franciscan Assisi, Hussite Prague, Capuchin Camarino, Anabaptist Munster, the Florence of Savanarola and the Geneva of Calvin, not to mention Orthodox Kiev or Muslim Istanbul, each reflecting a different set of beliefs about God, man and social relationships; just as in the seventeenth and eighteenth centuries in America a range of religious communities established societies of widely differing structure and practice, each reflecting the beliefs, religious and social, of their members.

But it is especially in modern times that the role of "ideology" has been most generally acknowledged and most widely discussed. So Comte believed that the ideologies that governed earlier societies, based successively on "theology" and on "metaphysics", were now outdated, and believed that positivist science could establish a new set of ideas, founded on systematic examination of social needs, that would be able to create the "consensus" that every society required. Marx, condemning the "bourgeois ideology" that sustained existing capitalist society, which he saw as a "false consciousness" that blinded its members to their real interests, held that the political and social order was partly sustained by a "superstructure" of ideas and beliefs – religious, political and social – deriving ultimately from the system of production and the relationships it established. Durkheim believed that religion was the creation of the group, and became the inspiration and binding force of society, so that, in worshipping a god, its members were in fact worshipping society itself.[1] Lenin accepted (as

1. "There is no doubt that a society has everything needed to arouse in men's minds, simply by the influence it exerts over them, the sensation of the divine, for it is to its members what a god is to its faithful. . . . In either case the believer feels that he is obliged to accept certain forms of behaviour imposed on him by the nature of the sacred principle with which he feels he is in communication. But society also maintains in us the sensation of a perpetual dependence, because it has a nature peculiar to itself, different from our individual nature, and pursues ends which are likewise peculiar to itself; but since it can attain them only through us, it imperiously demands our cooperation. It requires that we forget our personal interests and become its servants; it subjects us to all kinds of inconveniences and hardships and sacrifices without which social life would be impossible. So it is that at every moment we are obliged to

Marx had not) that even a socialist society required an ideology. And even those who believed in a democratic political system came to believe, in response, that they too required an "ideology" to justify and sustain that system.

The ideologies such thinkers have discussed have been of two distinct kinds. For the most part they have been concerned (as we are in this chapter) with a *social* ideology: a general set of ideas that guide and influence and justify the life of the society as a whole, a "set of closely related beliefs and ideas, or even attitudes, characteristic of a group or community".[2] This might be regarded as the original, and perhaps more authentic, use of the word. It is not unlike what Marx described as the "superstructure", the intellectual underpinning of society. It is to be contrasted with the alternative, and now perhaps more common, use of the word, to refer to a *political* ideology: that is a set of ideas that explains and identifies the beliefs and attitudes of a *particular* group or class. While the latter is usually concerned, directly or indirectly, to criticise the existing social order, and to show reasons why it is to be changed, or must inevitably change, the former will seek to justify and maintain the existing order. In other words, while the assumptions of a political ideology will be accepted only by a particular group, usually a group seeking radical change, the assumptions of the social ideology will be shared to some extent by most members of society, even if in varying degrees.

How does a social ideology act to influence behaviour and relationships within society? It does so, first, by the language which it uses; by establishing a set of concepts and categories which serve to explain and justify the existing social relationships (just as political, that is critical, ideology, will set up a rival set of concepts and categories, which explain and justify a *different* set of social relationships). This justification is not necessarily explicit; often it is only implicit in the choice of terms and the way they are used. Secondly, the concepts and categories will establish an *image of society* that influences action within it. And they will, finally, establish a set of *value-standards* which will imply approval for existing relationships (as the political ideology will imply approval for *change* in those relationships). In this way they will win legitimacy for the approved social or political

submit to the conduct and ideas which we have neither made nor willed, and sometimes even oppose through our most fundamental inclinations and instincts" (quoted in R. Aron, *Main Currents in Sociological Thought*, vol. II, London, 1958, p. 51).

2. J. Plamenatz, *Ideology* (London, 1970) p. 15.

system and surround it with an aura of respect and veneration which may deter attempts to overturn it.

These concepts and categories may be supported by a more explicit and clearly articulated "theory" which can be used to buttress its assumptions. Such theories (whether social or political, supportive or critical) are typically of two kinds. One type is based on assertions about the "nature" of man. It is suggested that, because humans are of a certain kind, have particular characteristics "by nature", particular types of social or political organisation will suit them best. For example because they are "by nature" good or sociable or co-operative (as was generally believed, for example, in differing degrees, by Mencius, by Aristotle and by Rousseau, among others), a type of social organisation which facilitates this co-operation will be most suitable; or because they are "by nature" bad, aggressive and prone to conflict (as asserted, for example, with different emphases, by Han Fei-tzu, Machiavelli and Hobbes), a different type of system will best meet their needs.

The second type of argument is based on a theory about the inevitable course of history (p. 27 above). In this case it is suggested that a proper understanding of these successive stages of history can show either that an existing type of society precisely corresponds with the requirements of these historical forces (as Hegel, for example, found the existing Prussian state to correspond with the most advanced manifestation of the Idea, and so to represent "God walking on earth"); or that, on the contrary, an existing form of society is destined to be eliminated and replaced by some other kind which the writer favours (as Marx held that bourgeois society and the capitalist state were destined, as a result of inevitable historical processes, to be replaced by the proletarian society and the socialist state).

Whatever the arguments deployed, the importance of ideology is its effect on *action*: on the aspirations and behaviour of the members of society generally. This effect can vary widely. Among simple societies, for example, one ideology will promote the acquisition, display, and even the conspicuous destruction, of wealth as the principal source of status and the objective towards which action in society is to be directed (as among the Kwakiutl of the North American Pacific coast). In another society the dominant idea will on the contrary deprecate all personal possessions and self-interested activity, encouraging on the contrary a commitment to group econ-omic activity and group possessions (as among the Zuni of New

Mexico). In another again it will demand the use of violence and treachery against groups outside the society, the use of supernatural powers and charms to outwit other members within it, together with close co-operation for common purposes within the small matrilineal family (as among the Dobu of Melanesia).[3]

The ideology may teach not only what is to be desired but how it is to be obtained. So, for example, though most modern societies set a high value on the production of wealth, different ideologies may encourage wholly different ways of securing this, each having quite different social consequences. Thus early Soviet society, the Israeli kibbutz, the Chinese commune and the modern Japanese state, while each stressing the importance of productivity, propose totally different ways of securing it. Each establishes wholly different life-styles and different social relationships as a means to that end.

The ideology of a society, in other words, teaches not only what is to be attained but how it is to be got. Thus the ideology teaches people how to see their own society, the relationships they should adopt, and the behaviour they should undertake. It can teach duties, interests, even wants. For these reasons it is this, more than any other factor, which will determine the differing characteristics of each society.

IDEOLOGY IN INTERNATIONAL SOCIETY

In international society too there will exist a "set of closely related beliefs and ideas or even attitudes, characteristic of a group or community": in this case characteristic of a particular *society of states*. Here too an ideology can teach how the society will be seen, what relationships should be adopted and what behaviour therefore should be undertaken. And here too the ideology promotes above all the aspirations which inspire the actions of the society's members.

Before considering particular international ideologies, there are three points that should be made clear.

Of the two types of ideology described earlier, social and political, our concern is with the former: the ideology of an entire society, having an influence to some extent on all its members, rather than with a political ideology, often hostile to existing social arrangements,

3. These three contrasting types of social organisation are described in Ruth Benedict, *Patterns of Culture* (Cambridge, Mass., 1934).

designed to justify the attitudes of particular groups. Ideas of the latter kind are not impossible within international society; and in the concluding section of this chapter we shall consider the forms which they might take. For the most part, however, we are concerned with the sort of ideas that have been widely held throughout a society and the way they have influenced social relationships: the "closely related beliefs and ideas, or even attitudes" characteristic of the entire society.

Second, we are concerned here only with ideas that relate to *international* society. Of course in many cases these have co-existed with other ideas relating to the domestic society: the assumptions held concerning social and political relationships *within* states. We shall consider later what is the relationship that exists between the two; how far domestic and political social ideas influence the international ideology or vice versa. For the moment, however, it is important to be clear that we are concerned in this chapter with ideas relating to relationships between states rather than to those within them.

Third, it should be made clear in addition that we are primarily concerned with the ideas relating to *political* relationships between states. Often these have co-existed with other ideas concerned with other areas: for example cultural relations and especially economic relations. These too can, of course, have significant effects on the operation of international society as a whole (just as economic beliefs and doctrines can be important factors in the operation of a smaller society). It is for this reason that, within the general study of international society, economic as well as political relationships, and the ideas that affect them, need to be considered and analysed.[4] But though they are certainly not without importance, this is not the kind of "ideology" we are concerned with in this chapter.

Having clarified these points, let us now try to make the concept of "international ideology" a little more real by describing, even if very briefly, the main features of the ideologies that have existed in different international societies over the last few centuries and the way these have influenced attitudes and behaviour in each.[5]

In the late Middle Ages the prevailing international ideology was

4. This author has attempted to do this in the case of economic ideas in *Economic Relationships among States* (London, 1984).
5. For a more adequate account of each of these societies and of the characteristic ideology in each, see E. Luard, *Types of International Society* (New York, 1977) especially chap. 5.

that of *dynasticism*: a belief that international action was concerned above all with the promotion of rival dynastic claims to particular territories. The conflict fought out in international society was seen as a struggle between ruling *families* rather than between states or between peoples. They fought for the right to a crown rather than to territory or resources for their own sake; for the right to rule, based on a claim to succession, rather than on mutual agreement, still less on the will of the people. Just as, within states, it was the desire for land and title, through marriage if possible, but by seizure if necessary, which mainly preoccupied the great magnates and even lesser mortals, so it was the desire to acquire land and titles *abroad*, again if possible through marriage, but if necessary through conquest, which was the prevailing ambition among the kings and lesser rulers in their foreign actions. A large proportion of the wars of the age were thus dynastic wars directed at enforcing such claims. A large proportion of the diplomacy of the age was devoted to securing the alliances required to win such wars, or marriages which could make them unnecessary. Though the aspirations were originally those of the dynasts themselves and their close adherents, they were shared by many other sections of society too. So the great magnates and their knights supported the claims of their royal masters in their struggles abroad. The ideology of dynasticism determined many of the prevailing attitudes to international society. Efforts to win power, whether by pretenders at home or by conquerors abroad, had to be put forward on the basis of claims to succession, never on an appeal to force alone.[6] The settlements reached at the end of wars had to take account of claims widely held to be legitimate; and a conqueror who had occupied a foreign land would still seek, long after the event, to legitimise it through an appropriate marriage.[7] Successful matrimony was often seen as a more effective means to territorial power than the use of armed force – as the huge empire accumulated by that means by the Hapsburg family vividly demonstrated. The institutions of the age reflected the assumptions of the dominant ideology. Diplomacy represented a form of communication between the princes themselves (rather than their governments). Treaties were personal undertakings between rulers, sealed by their hand, and they expired on the death of one of them. The most important diplomatic meetings were the meetings of the dynasts themselves, undertaken to conclude such agreements or pledges of marriage. And the principal institution for

6. See Evan Luard, *War in International Society* (London, 1986) pp. 87–8.
7. Ibid., pp. 138–9.

promoting peace was mediation by a foreign prince (unless the pope himself could be brought to perform the service). So the social institutions of the day, as well as the prevailing ambitions of each state, reflected the dominant ideology of the age.

From 1559 (when the longest and bitterest dynastic conflict – the sixty-five-year struggle between Valois and Hapsburg – came to an end) a new age began, governed by different assumptions and different concerns. Now the main preoccupation everywhere was *religion*: above all the battle between the established Catholic Church and the new reformed faiths which challenged it all over Europe. International society is now seen as the arena for a cosmic struggle between faiths: Christendom and Islam, Lutheran and Calvinist, Roman and Greek, but above all between Catholic and Protestant. That struggle was waged partly *within* states (for thirty-five years in France in the early part of the period and for thirty years in Germany in its latter half, among many other cases). But it dominated relations between states too. A substantial proportion of the wars of the age were fought over religion.[8] Governments and rulers of one state persistently intervened to secure the victory of the faith they supported in other states (or, more often, to prevent the victory of the rival faith there). This new concern overlay, and partly transformed, the dynastic principle of the previous age. Questions of succession became important for religious as much as for dynastic reasons (for example in Scotland, England, France, Sweden, Cleves-Julich, Bohemia, Denmark and other cases). For the most part Protestant rulers would not now take Catholic wives and vice versa (so the Protestant Elizabeth rejected the Catholic widower of her Catholic sister, while fifty years later James I's attempt to secure a Spanish princess for his son also ended in failure largely because of religious differences). Diplomacy was equally affected: to a large extent diplomatic ties, like royal marriages, were confined to others of the same faith.[9]

8. Ibid., pp. 93–4.
9. Cf. G. Mattingly, "International Diplomacy and International Law", in *The New Cambridge Modern History* (Cambridge, 1958) vol. III, p. 154: "As religious issues came to dominate political ones, any negotiations with the enemies of one state looked more and more like heresy and treason. The questions which divided catholics from protestants had ceased to be negotiable. Consequently . . . diplomatic contacts diminished. Special embassies continued to go back and forth from time to time between powers in opposing ideological camps, but they were less frequent, and, instead of expanding, the network of resident embassies actually contracted."

Alliances too were now established mainly on a religious basis. In other words, a wholly new type of international society emerged, in which international activity and international relationships were everywhere mainly governed by this new concern.

The Peace of Westphalia, concluding the thirty-year struggle which brought that era to an end, ushered in a new age and a new type of society, which lasted for 150 years. The concern of the sovereigns and their great ministers who now controlled each state was no longer with the winning of crowns elsewhere, as in the age of dynasties, nor with the type of faith that was practised in other countries; it was with building up the power of their own states. The settlement of 1648 sanctified above all the principle of *sovereignty*. Even in Germany the sovereignty of princes, however tiny their territories, was strengthened in relation to the suzerainty of the emperor. In France the sovereign equated himself, in fact as well as in words, with his state. In England and the United Provinces republics demanded and maintained a sovereignty equal to that of sovereigns (and fought each other for "sovereignty" in the North Sea). Everywhere the dominant aim was the building of powerful and self-sufficient states, each able to deal on a basis of at least theoretical equality ("sovereign equality") with other states. Each was concerned to protect its own power by limiting the power that could be attained by any other, that is to maintain the "balance of power". Religious questions now affected international relations hardly at all; dynastic questions only a little. And in each case they were now resolved on the basis of the new assumptions of sovereignty. It was for rulers to decide, as the peace of Westphalia laid down, the religion their people should follow; while dynastic questions too were settled now not on the basis of dynastic rights but on the basis of the balance of power.[10] It was thus overwhelmingly about this balance of power that the wars of the age were fought: the balance that was to prevail, for example, between Sweden and Russia in the Baltic, between France and England overseas, between Austria and Prussia in Germany. It was to undertake that struggle that alliances were regularly made and unmade with breathtaking speed. A new type of international

10. See Luard, *War in International Society*, pp. 50–1, 100–2. Though a number of "wars of succession" were fought, they were fought now to *prevent* a succession that might have excessively favoured a particular state rather than to *win* control of new areas elsewhere (and in every case succeeded in that aim): ibid., p. 102.

society emerged, in which individual states, unaffected by religious allegiances or political sympathies, now competed with each other, on the basis of all against all: a billiard-ball society, in which each state was self-sufficient, enclosed within the hard shell of sovereignty, and relationships were dominated by external forces – collisions and conflicts with other states – almost never by internal developments *within* each state. It was the belief in the primary importance of state interest – *raison d'etat* – that became the dominant idea governing international action.

From 1789 there was another change in the prevailing ideology. The French Revolution ushered in a new age in which internal forces once more became more powerful than external.[11] International relations were now governed by the ideology of *nationalism*: the power of nationalistic movements within states and of nationalist rivalries between them. This new principle challenged the whole basis of the traditional order, the entire concept of "legitimacy". A new consciousness of "national" identity created demands among many peoples of Europe, claiming ethnic, linguistic, cultural or historic ties, for the establishment of new states reflecting that unity. For the first time it was proposed that the boundaries of states should correspond to the will of their peoples. In effect the history of Europe from 1815 was the progressive rewriting of the map of the continent so that it conformed more closely with this national principle. So wars of national revolution brought national *independence* to Greece, Belgium, Romania, Serbia, Montenegro, Bulgaria, Albania and other states; other wars brought national *unification* for Germany and Italy. Another half dozen national states – Finland, Lithuania, Latvia, Estonia, Hungary and Czechoslovakia – were born at the end of the concluding struggle of the age on the widely acclaimed principle of "self-determination". This outburst of national revolution interacted with nationalistic rivalries between the major states. These frequently intervened to promote, or to impede, the success of each such revolution: Russia to prevent it in Hungary but to promote it in Greece and Bulgaria; Prussia to prevent it in Poland but to promote

11. Even at the time many recognised they were witnessing the birth of a new age. Goethe said (of the Battle of Valmy): "From today begins a new era, and you will be able to say you were present at its birth." G. P. Gooch made the same point: "While patriotism is as old as the instinct of human association, nationalism as an articulate creed issued from the volcanic fires of the French Revolution" (*Studies in Diplomacy and Statecraft*, London, 1942, p. 300).

it in Germany as a whole; France to prevent it in Spain but to promote it in Egypt, to promote it in one part of Italy and prevent it in another. As a result, a large proportion of the wars of the age were connected, directly or indirectly, with the search for national independence. Even countries which experienced no national revolutions themselves were affected by the surge of nationalistic sentiment. It intensified the rivalry for domination in Europe and encouraged the struggle to win colonial possessions elsewhere. Most of the wars of the age, including that which brought it to an end, were caused, directly or indirectly, by national movements of this kind.[12] So a new kind of society emerged. Many of the assumptions of sovereignty – especially the obligation of non-intervention in neighbouring states – were abandoned; the ambitions of the next age – to influence the political character of governments in other states – had not yet been acquired. A new type of international society emerged governed by a widespread belief in the legitimacy of national unity, national independence and national power.

Towards the end of the First World War a new type of society was born. The typical concern of the age was no longer nationalism and the creation of new states on a national basis (except among those territories held under colonial rule, where nationalistic sentiment remained strong); still less with the aspirations of sovereignty, religion and dynasticism that had ruled in earlier societies. The main preoccupation now was political: with what type of government should hold power in other states all over the world. It was in other words an age of *ideology*. The First World War was said by some to have been fought to "make the world safe for democracy". The Russian Revolution towards its end was directed at creating the first communist state. Soon afterwards, in several countries of Europe, especially in Italy and Germany, governments proclaiming new authoritarian creeds sprang up. For a time an ideological struggle took place between these three forces, reaching a climax in the Second World War. At its end the two forces which survived proceeded to turn on each other in a new ideological battle that dominated the succeeding decades. The struggle was now no longer between individual states, fighting for territory or other assets. It was between entire blocs and alliances, favouring the rival creeds; or between groups and individuals within particular states owing allegiance to one or the other. So each ideological alliance struggled

12. See Luard, *War in International Society*, pp. 87–8, 108–10.

to secure the establishment elsewhere of the type of political regime it favoured. As a result wars now took place within states rather than between them, often with massive intervention from outside. New weapons were employed appropriate to such struggles: propaganda, subversion, manipulation, aid to minorities and political factions, in the final resort substantial military intervention. The leaders of each alliance, were not only deeply committed to the ideological cause they favoured, but, because of their power, felt themselves to have a special responsibility for ensuring the victory of that cause. Yet wars never took place between the main protagonists themselves, only in the territory of third parties where each struggled to secure influence. So a new type of international ideology created a new kind of society, in which a world-wide struggle for political domination was fought out. The dominant concern now was above all with the political situation in other states, especially neighbouring states, rather than the acquisition of territory or other material assets.

These are highly simplified accounts of complex international systems. But they give some idea of the way in which the assumptions and ambitions that dominated in each, the prevailing *beliefs*, determined the nature of relationships and the character of the society as a whole. The temporal dividing line between one society and the next was naturally never sharp and abrupt. In each society there would often remain for a time *vestiges* from that which had preceded it, continuing to influence thinking at least among some in the age that followed. Conversely, towards the end of each period, there were sometimes *anticipations* of the age to come. But this does not alter the fact that there were real and important differences between the type of international society existing in each of these five periods. And the differences stem above all from differences between the barely conscious beliefs and assumptions that prevailed among the decision-makers in each period.

What is the source of these ideologies, and how do they emerge? There are rarely clear-cut origins, or "causes", of ways of thought current in particular periods. The climate of belief changes over time because of a whole variety of different factors and influences. But some reasons at least can be suggested for the changes we have traced.

First, the dominant ideas in each age have mainly been those of the élites which dominated at each time. The ideology of dynasticism reflects the preoccupations and concerns of the dynasts themselves and their immediate supporters, exercising power within each state;

preoccupations that came to influence the beliefs of all within that society (so that even humble English soldiers would cry for King Harry as much as for England). The ideas of sovereignty reflected the interest of sovereigns and their governments in the age when that ideology prevailed: above all their interest in the power of the state, abroad as well as at home. But they dominated the thinking of most others of the time, especially the powerful ministers who served them. The ideas of the current age reflect the concerns of political leaders in an age when most have secured power through a political struggle involving strong commitment to a political ideology. But the ideas of the leaders are reflected in the attitudes of most of their populations. Thus some part of the explanation for each change is perhaps to be found in the changing character of the leadership from age to age: the "rotation of élites" to which Pareto attached such importance.

But this is not a *sufficient* explanation. For example the ideology of nationalism was in many ways contrary to the interests of many of those in power at the time when it became dominant: indeed in some cases it threatened the existence of the states they ruled. In that case it emerged because of the sentiments existing within an *emerging* élite: because of the support and enthusiasm of middle-class political leaders, acting in opposition to the governments that prevailed in the majority of states.

Again a change in international ideology has sometimes reflected a change in *domestic* ideology. It was when concern with religion became an increasingly powerful factor within states that it became so abroad as well. It was when there developed an increasing concern with strengthening the power of sovereigns at home (as expressed in the writing of Bodin, Hobbes and others, as well as the actions of governments to assert their control over all sections of national life) that this came to be reflected in the doctrine of "sovereignty" applied to relations with other states. It was when ideological concern became a major issue in domestic policy (as shown in the age of McCarthyism in the US) that it became a particularly important factor in international relations too.[13]

However they are derived, international ideologies have an important impact on the kind of international society established. Of the

---

13. In this last case the reverse process is also at work: because "communism" was a major international concern, it became a concern of domestic politics too.

ideologies we have described two established a pattern of interaction that was largely *trans-national*, rather than international. In the age of religion and in the most recent period the concern of governments was to communicate direct with the people of other countries, rather than through their governments; and in both periods there was widespread intervention in the civil conflicts of other states. Conversely cross-border activities by individuals – for example Calvinist preachers and Jesuit priests, the Comintern and multinational companies – directly affected relationships among states. In other periods relations have been conducted mainly through inter-state activity: especially in the ages of dynasties and of sovereignty (the age of nationalism comes in an intermediate category). Equally the motives of states, especially the kinds of demands they have made upon other states – for thrones in one age, for religious rights in another, for trade and territory in a third, for national unification in another, and for acceptable political regimes in a fifth – have changed according to the dominant ideology. The kinds of institutions established, especially the methods for securing peace, have been equally affected by the character of the ideology.[14]

The entire nature of an international society in other words has been decisively influenced by the set of ideas which have prevailed among those exercising positions of power within it.

IDEOLOGY IN CONTEMPORARY INTERNATIONAL SOCIETY

Let us now examine, in slightly greater detail, the type of international ideology which prevails in the existing international society.

As always ideology affects, first, the *image* held of society as a whole. It will affect, in particular, the way the world is divided. Every ideology implies a division of a sort. So different domestic ideologies imply a division, for example, between heaven and earth, Christian and pagan, ruler and people, rival estates or competing classes, propertied and propertyless. In the same way, the international ideologies we have surveyed have implied a division of international society: among dynasts in the one, among religions in another, among states or among nations in others. The ideology of the current

14. For further details, see Luard, *Types of International Society*, pp. 312–41; *War in International Society*, pp. 273–328.

international society – an ideology of political competition – implies a world that is divided, and contested, between rival ideological forces: forces that are seen as historical, transcendental, often as moral forces. This inevitably encourages a Manichean division of the world: between supporters of good and of evil, between light and darkness (with very little twilight in between them). While, therefore, the ideologies of dynasticism or sovereignty or nationalism presupposed a world divided between (say) a dozen or twenty, or almost any number of contending states, the contemporary ideology of rival political forces (like the ideology of religion four hundred years ago) presupposes a contest between only two or a very small number of such creeds.

Logically these need not be confined to two. Between the world wars, as we saw, there was for a time a contest in which three rival ideologies were engaged, each radically different from the other: in the sixties again, ideas of Maoism, differing radically from Soviet communism especially in its international aspects, and having a substantial influence in many parts of the world, again created a world of three contending political ideas. Today the ideas of Islamic fundamentalism, which have a strong influence in many countries, might be held to represent a third force in the world ideological contest. There are always, however, strong pressures in favour of a dualistic division. For the belief that the contest represents a struggle between good and evil (which, even if it is not *consciously* maintained, still often affects the subconscious assumptions of those engaged in it) is much easier to sustain if the world is seen as divided in this way. A third force, if it is recognised at all, must be categorised as being on the side of evil or on the side of good; with them or with us. So Maoism, if it is recognised as a significant force at all, must be bracketed for a time with the evil forces; or, if it shows itself sufficiently hostile to those forces, relabelled and aligned with our side after all. By devices of this kind it is possible to maintain the image of a world divided between forces of light and forces of darkness.

Second, an ideology of political struggle will affect not only the way that society is conceived but the nature of *conflict*. In such a society the struggle is no longer between kings or other leaders and their followers; nor between geographical entities, whether "states" or "nations", as in most previous international societies. It is now, or at least is conceived as, a struggle between *ideas*. This form of conflict is encouraged by the character of the forces that rule within each state. In every state leaders have acquired their positions not, as before, because of birth or influence, but because of their commitment to a particular set of ideas, in other words because they are party politicians, especially concerned with political issues and especially expert in the handling of political arguments. Such people inevitably become committed to the primacy of the struggle between political ideas, in many cases attaching an importance to it far greater than do most of their peoples. And it is above all they who, in their international activities, attach the greatest weight to the ideological struggle in which they see themselves engaged. The battle of ideas takes place, for them, not only within states, in the political struggle which divides every nation, but between them too. It even takes place within each *ideology*. For those who are expert in political controversy are likely soon to find themselves engaged in political struggle against opponents among their colleagues: the accusation of ideological error which they cast at their opponents abroad is equally readily cast against opponents within their own camp (for example by Stalin against Trotsky and vice versa, by Mao against Li Li-san, Liu Hsao-chi and Deng Hsiao-ping and vice versa, by Taft against Roosevelt or Reagan against Carter; or at the international level by Russia against Yugoslavia, China against Russia, Albania against China; or by Syria against Iraq, Libya against Syria and Iran against Libya). So the primary ideological struggle, by sowing the suspicion that anything less than perfect doctrinal purity may endanger the ideology's survival, breeds many lesser struggles, each equally ideo-logical in character.

Third, because the struggle is now seen as one of ideas, there is no clear geographical basis for the confrontation. While in previous international societies, even in the age of religions, conflict has always been undertaken between fairly clearly defined geographical areas, this is no longer the case. The world as a whole is the arena of the struggle; and it takes place, at different intensities, in all parts simultaneously. Some adherents of each faction exist in almost every state. Thus the ideological conflict within states is almost as bitter as that between them. In previous international societies the political regime existing within states was regarded as a given, which changed only rarely and was not to be influenced by outside states. The struggle took place over the externals; the distribution of territories or trade *between* states for example. Now, on the contrary, it is the territorial disposition that remains stable – it rarely changes at all and is certainly not a major source of conflict – and it is the *internal* situation within states, increasingly unstable, which is the main object of concern among governments. Political stability and territorial instability have been replaced by territorial stability and political instability. In consequence the conflict takes place everywhere alike; and results not in changes to the externals (transfers of territory, colonies or trading posts) but in changes to the internal political structure of particular states. So the whole process of change in international society is differently conceived.

Fourth, such an ideology transforms the nature of *loyalties*. Here too the basis is no longer geographical. For some at least, even if it is only a minority, loyalty to the ideological faith transcends loyalty to the state. For the first time since the age of religions significant sections of a population may accord a higher importance to a cause supported and led by another state elsewhere than to that of their own state. So the adherents of one state will betray their own state for the sake of that faith. So volunteers will travel from one country to another to support a particular cause against its opponents (as in Spain, Korea, the Congo, Bolivia and Nicaragua). Fifth columns, defectors and dissidents become, as in the age of religions, a significant factor within international society. Traditional state loyalty is increasingly irrelevant to the type of struggle which is mainly undertaken within international society.

Fifth, the image of the "enemy", the opponent to be defeated, is also affected. Friends and enemies alike are chosen on the basis of ideas. So international action is undertaken not against Russia but against "Bolshevism"; not against Germany but against "Nazism"; not against the US but against "imperialism". Assurances are given that there is no hostility to the "American people" or the "Russian people": only to the creeds they have adopted and the leaders who have misled them. Though the world is still divided into friends and foes, it is now ideological friends and ideological enemies, rather than allies chosen on purely tactical grounds. The international ideology encourages the kind of activity previously undertaken only within states: a political battle, a competition for "hearts and minds".

Sixth, because objectives are now ideological, because it is internal rather than external change that is desired, the *means* by which change is to be secured are transformed. In a struggle of ideas the instruments used are now words as much as weapons; arguments as much as armaments, propaganda as much as planes. Typical strategies demand the use of powerful intelligence agencies, with many contacts in other states, which cannot only acquire information about the political situation there, but if necessary undertake covert action to overthrow a government or organise an armed coup. By such means like-minded groups can be helped to acquire power on behalf of a particular ideology or ideological alliance. So the more powerful states can secure their purposes, at little risk and no cost, without firing a shot, simply by giving support to favoured factions through concealed channels. A different type of objective brings about a totally different form of activity to secure change in international society.

Seventh, because the ideology is one of political struggle, the aspirations it creates are, as we saw, *trans-national* rather than international. As in the age of religion, they are directed to what happens *within* states, not what happens between them. The concern is, in other words, not so much with bilateral relationships between states, but with relations between groups and individuals in other states; not with the acquisition of territory or other state assets, but with the acquisition of political power and other intangibles in other states. The competition is therefore not a zero-sum game between states or even between alliances, but a general mêlée in which *trans-national* political forces and ideas are struggling for advantage in every state simultaneously. Because this is a world-wide struggle, no place is so distant as to be immune from the conflict. It is not thought possible to allow other continents (Africa or Asia) to go their own way; nor to allow individual countries (Nicaragua or Afghanistan) to choose their own political system free of external influence. Whatever their own populations may feel, they must not be allowed to fall into the hands of the enemy. The motive is often essentially defensive: to ensure that the enemy does not secure dominant influence in some state where it did not have it before (especially if that state is strategically important) rather than to win totally new areas. Fear of the insidious influence of rival creeds is often the main impetus to action. It is the balance of *ideological* power in the world as a whole that is at stake; and no part of the world can be left out of the reckoning.

Eighth, the nature of alliances is transformed in such a world. Unlike the short-term opportunistic arrangements of the age of sovereignty, or the rather more long-lived alliances of convenience of the age of nationalism (each of them unconcerned with the internal characteristics of the chosen ally), alliances depend now entirely on the political viewpoint of governments. Thus a state that changes its regime is virtually bound to alter its alliance too (which is one reason why such strenuous efforts are made to secure changes of regime in other countries). Conversely without such a change alliances are likely to be maintained unchanged over very many years. So eventually much of the world is organised into relatively stable rival blocs of this sort. Most states, even if not members of the alliances, at least stand in a recognised relationship to them. In every continent a few states are known as reliable friends and partners of the chief ideological blocs. Even the others are obliged to orientate themselves to that struggle rather than to any closer concern of their own particular region: even distant or indifferent states now label themselves as "non-aligned", that is state their position on the east–west rather than the north–south divide. Similarly, because of the dominance of the world-wide political struggle, the more ardent ideological leaders denounce any abstention from that contest, renaming neutrals as "neutralists"; or even claim that neutrality is "immoral".

Ninth, economic relationships too, in such a world, are determined by ideological alignments. Trade *between* the rival blocs is heavily circumscribed by strategic and other controls; trade *within* them on the contrary increases at record rates. Most-favoured-nation treatment is accorded readily to ideological partners; it is refused to ideological opponents. Aid is slanted in favour of ideological friends: the main bloc leaders give generously to those who share their views but not at all to those of the opposing camp. Within international organisations similar preferences are shown; so major donors in the World Bank and the IMF try to ensure that these bodies only give assistance to countries with which they are ideologically in sympathy. Economic relations between states are thus now largely determined by political relations.

Finally, in such a world there is a special role for the leaders of each ideological bloc (the "superpowers"). Each is required not only to be the main source of economic assistance and military equipment for members of their own bloc; they must also be the main source of ideological encouragement and political propaganda. They become therefore, spokesmen not for their own states, as governments have been in former ages, but for a system: for "democracy" and the "free world", "communism" and the "socialist commonwealth". So each must devote substantial resources to attacking the other, and the ideas that the other propounds; and to demonstrating the superiority of the ideas its own bloc is advocating. At the same time each must undertake the role of negotiator with the rival superpower and must seek to carry its partners, themselves often divided, with them in such negotiations. The role of chief propagandist and war-leader therefore has to be combined with that of chief negotiator and peace-maker: roles that are not always easy to reconcile (for example the concessions which superpowers might be willing to make in the latter role may be prevented by their need to maintain the cohesion of an ideological alliance as a whole). At the same time they must cope with attacks on their strategies or objectives from dissenters within their own state or alliance as well. These are roles and relationships quite different from any which have been performed in earlier international societies.

This is inevitably an over-simplified picture of a complex world scene. The society is itself, moreover, not static, but in a state of continual change (the picture here represented is perhaps closer to the state of international society as it existed twenty or so years ago than to how it is today). The picture none the less portrays at least some of the more prominent features of the society which now exists; and it perhaps serves to illustrate the way in which a particular international "ideology" affects many aspects of the way such societies operate. As in other ages, the beliefs and attitudes of the dominant élite within the society have brought into being a type of social interaction quite different from that which has existed in other ages. A new international ideology has created a new kind of international society.

CONCLUSIONS

Are there any general conclusions that can be drawn about the various kinds of international ideology and their role in each international society?

There are some parallels that can be made between international ideologies and those that influence domestic societies. We saw that a domestic ideology is often based on an assumption concerning the "nature of man" and the kind of society that this is held to make necessary. An international ideology, by contrast, is sometimes based on an assumption concerning the nature of *states*. For example, the ideology of sovereignty is based on the assumption that the essential nature of a state is its *independent* character; this means that recognition of this independence is more important than concern about the kind of religion practised, the system of government or the

protection of human rights in other states. By contrast the two trans-
national ideologies – those of religion and of ideology – deny that
independence is a natural prerogative of states and believe on the
contrary that concern over those latter issues can and should transcend
state boundaries. The ideology of dynasticism on the other hand
implies that the state is essentially the personal possession of its ruler,
that it has in other words a personal rather than a territorial basis
(so that its boundaries can suddenly be expanded if the ruler succeeds
to a crown elsewhere). This personal character of the dynastic state
again contrasts with the state in the age of sovereignty when it is held
that the interests of states are more fundamental than those of the
ruler: that the latter was, in Frederick the Great's words, the "first
servant of the state" and at all times bound to respect and promote
the state's interest. While the state belongs to the ruler in the age of
dynasties, in the age of sovereignty the ruler belongs to the state.
The ideology of nationalism sees the state as coterminous with the
"nation", the ethnic or cultural group: it is thus the political
embodiment of the national sentiments of a people (so states which
include several nations may legitimately be dismembered to create
separate states for each). The ideology of the current international
society sees the political foundations of the state as its most important
character (so that if that character is subverted – a democratic regime
replaced by a communist one or vice versa – intervention to reverse
the situation is permissible).

The other basis we found for domestic ideology was a theory of
history demonstrating that a particular type of society corresponded
with the demands of historical development. Here too there are some
parallels to be found, if less exact, within international society. Such
theories, let us recall, for the most part represent *political* ideologies,
justifying opposition to the existing social and political order within
states. We must therefore look for parallels not in the kind of
international ideology we have been examining – that is ideologies
that influence an entire society – but in theories that might be put
forward to justify the replacement of those societies. Thus a theory
of the kind held by Mazzini and some other nationalist leaders in the
nineteenth century – that there were deep-seated historical forces
which made the creation of states on the national principle inevitable
and war for that purpose justifiable – could be seen as an ideology of
this kind: one that challenged the basis of existing international
society. So too could a theory in the modern world which proclaimed
that the forces of history made it inevitable that all states would in

time become communist states (or democratic states): that is, that the existing pluralistic international society based on political competition would in time be replaced by one of political uniformity. Of this sort too would be a theory which suggested that the kinds of institutions demanded by the so-called "new international economic order" were certain to be established in due course, and that international action should be directed to that end. All of these would represent "ideologies" in the modern sense (that is, not the sense mainly used in this chapter): theoretical arguments designed to show that a *desired* state of affairs must inevitably come about, rather than the beliefs underlying an existing social order.

If these are the theoretical explanations that might be put forward to explain the transition from one kind of society to another, what are the real explanations? Is there a simple reason for the transitions we have described above? How is it that relatively distinct phases in the evolution of international society of the type we have described are to be discerned.

The reasons are naturally complex. They are related to many different types of change taking place in each period, both within individual states and in the relations between them. There is inevitably a relationship between the kind of ideology powerful *within* states and the type that governs relations *between* them. In both cases these reflect changes in the social structure of states and especially in the character of the élites which control them.

Thus the international ideology of dynasticism flourished in a period when dynasts dominated in national states; the age of religion occurred when religious forces became powerful at all levels of society within states (often gaining a strong influence over the rulers themselves); the ideology of sovereignty flourished when the dominant forces within states – the monarchs and their great ministers – became mainly concerned, at home as much as abroad, with the establishment of "sovereign" independent states which were militarily powerful and economically self-sufficient; the ideology of nationalism emerged when groups that were strongly imbued with nationalistic sentiment secured positions of power and influence among the populations of many states; the age of ideology when those who controlled each state were party politicians concerned above all else with political dogma. It is not perhaps surprising that changes of this magnitude in domestic societies should have an impact in the way each state undertook its foreign relations.

This was not necessarily, however, the only influence at work.

International society is influenced by other factors that do not derive quite so directly from the domestic systems. Changes in military technology and the level of communications between states certainly have an influence. It is even perhaps possible to trace the slow and hesitant development of a form of international morality, embryonic principles governing the way relations among states should be conducted: rules that are specifically international and unrelated to development within states. These too bring about changes in the prevailing ideology.[15]

Whatever explanation of the way international ideologies emerge may be favoured, what kinds of ideology – in other words what kinds of international society – are likely to emerge in the future?

There is an almost indefinite number of types of international society, and so of types of ideology, that are theoretically possible, reflecting an almost indefinite number of essential wants and aspirations, whether among states or individuals. It is proposed here to sketch only five possible sets of ideas which might become influential in the international society of the future.

These sets of ideas may be distinguished in two ways: between those which are mainly concerned with the *political* order among states, and those concerned with the *economic* order; and between those that are mainly concerned with the position of *states* in international society, and those that are concerned mainly with the position of individuals. The first three ideologies we are to describe are concerned mainly (though not exclusively) with political relationships, the last two with economic; the first, second and fourth relate mainly to relationships among states, the third and fifth mainly to relationships among individuals and groups.

The first possible ideology is one concerned with establishing a more harmonious and co-operative international society. In other words the ultimate objective would be to achieve the kind of *integration* of society we considered in Chapter 3. This integration would in the first place affect the relationships of states, though (because of the importance of state action in affecting the relationships of individuals) this would ultimately imply a greater integration for individuals as well. The prime objective of such an ideology would be internationalism: the strengthening of international authority in as many spheres as possible. The activity of states, therefore, and of

15. For a more detailed examination of these factors, see Luard, *Types of International Society*, chap. 12, and *War in International Society*, chap 8.

individuals supporting these ideologies, would be directed to ensuring that there was a transfer of power and authority to international organisations. This might occur first in the case of functional organisations (since in that case the sacrifice of sovereignty involved is often more acceptable): by an increase in the role played by the WHO, ILO and IMF, for example. Subsequently efforts could be made to increase the authority of political institutions such as the UN Security Council, to enable them to be more effective than today in maintaining world peace. Efforts would be directed at securing the progressive reduction of armed power in the hands of individual states, matched by an increase in that available to the UN, together with improved, mutually acceptable arrangements for the supervision and control of national armed power. The implication of such an ideology is that the sacrifice of power and independence which each state would have to undergo is a price worth paying for the creation of a more stable and peaceful world society. It is an ideology that might be expected to appeal above all to weak states, which find themselves at a disadvantage in a competitive world society dominated by armed power. But it might appeal also to individuals (within all states) more than to states themselves and their governing authorities (which will suffer some loss of independence and autonomy if the ideology triumphs).

A second, almost diametrically opposed, ideology would be one designed to maximise the independence and *autonomy* of each state. This would imply not only a reduction of the already weak power of international organisations but, more importantly, a reduction of the activities of private organisations, especially large corporations, originating in one state but operating in another. All trans-national influences, in other words, whether political or economic, would be reduced or cut off altogether. Trade might be deliberately inhibited, by import controls, tariff and other barriers, in order to promote economic self-sufficiency, even if this took place at the expense of optimal growth rates. But the primary effect would not be so much economic as political. Ideological blocs, regional groups and bilateral alliances would be abandoned. Each state would conduct its relationships on a strictly bilateral basis with all other states. The ultimate effect, and the main objective, would be to maximise *diversity* among states. The independence acquired in this way would be for the state rather than for the individual (who would probably be made more dependent on the government of his own state). Each state would act as it thought best to develop its own culture, its own political system and its own way of life, free of all interference from other states. Weak states might therefore be advantaged by being freed from unwelcome influence or domination; strong states would be disadvantaged by being prevented from undertaking such domination. There would be less intervention by outside states in the affairs of another to influence political developments there. But there would also be less intervention for the protection of human rights or for any other purpose, so that the efforts to promote international standards in such fields would be halted. This then is an ideology that might be expected to appeal to *governments*, especially in weaker and poorer states, and those who supported strong governmental power, but not to those concerned with the interests of individuals in such states, who would probably see their standard of living fall, still less to individuals elsewhere, who would be left at the mercy of their own governments.

A third possibility would be contrary to each of these. This would be an ideology favouring the maximum possible international *competition*, both political and economic (at the cost of both political integration and political independence). The ultimate objective would be to create greater efficiency in the way in which international society operates. Competition would be seen as the means of maximising wealth and promoting progress, by ensuring the survival of those states, and those enterprises, which were most efficient, and the elimination of the weakest. The kind of competition aimed at might be that of states or of individuals. If the objective was the former it would be left to governments to promote the success of their own enterprises. States would each need to build up their own economic power by protectionism, state support for industry, subsidies for exports or particular manufactures and every means available to each state to improve its competitive position in relation to other states. Inter-state political activity would be promoted by more intensive propaganda, information work and cultural imperialism, designed to influence opinion in other states. If military competition was also favoured, existing restraints on warfare too would be abandoned so that the states which were more efficient in the development and use of armed power would be in a position to impose their will on others. If, on the other hand, it was competition between individuals and groups which was seen as the best means of securing progress, a different type of international society would be implied. In this case restrictions on economic activity between states would be removed. Free access would be granted both to imports and to foreign investment in order that the most efficient economic *organisations* should be able to prevail. Under this system, in contrast to the former, poor states, with cheaper labour available, and coveted raw materials, might benefit from increased inward investment, but at the price of losing some of their economic independence to large trans-national corporations. Political competition too could be maximised, by the abandonment of all restrictions on free communication and political activity between states, in order that the type of political system having the widest possible support would eventually prevail everywhere. The objective would be the elimination of all barriers between states, including those restricting travel, employment and investment to create a single international economy.

A fourth alternative would be an ideology concerned with promoting *justice among states*. The objective would be a substantial shift of economic and other power from rich states to poor states; a redistribution of wealth and welfare comparable to that brought about within states by the welfare state. In world society this would be done through the actions of international organisations, such as the World Bank and the IMF, by actions to increase aid programmes, to provide better trading opportunities for poor countries, through new commodity agreements, through the transfer of technology, and by a variety of other means (the main objectives would be not unlike those that have been called for in recent years in demands for a "new international economic order"). It is an ideology which would appeal to particular *states* – that is poor states – rather than particular groups and individuals, and which reflects the interests of those states. It would appeal (unlike the ones previously described) to nobody in some states and to almost everybody in others: in other words it would divide state against state, rather than individuals and groups in all states. Finally, the changes which it calls for could often be brought about only through the decisions of states – in changing existing international arrangements – not those of groups and individuals (and often would require decisions by those states having a direct interest *against* the changes that are demanded).

A final type of international ideology would be concerned above all with promoting the interests and influence of particular economic *classes*. The objective would be to transform the economic system *within* states, but through activity undertaken jointly in many states: for example through the mobilisation of the proletariat or the peasantry, or other groups, to promote their interests by jointly co-ordinated action. Here the ultimate objective is the establishment of greater *justice among individuals* in international society. This would imply that loyalty to states would decline, being replaced by loyalty to international class interests (rather than to international political creeds as today). Political competition, it would demand, should no longer be undertaken by blocs and camps formed of governments, as in the current society, but by individuals and groups, acting independently of governments, and often against them. The opponents would not be other governments and states preaching a different ideology, as today, but other *classes*, also operating simultaneously in a number of states: employers, shareholders, ship-owners, motor corporations or trans-national corporations generally. The ultimate object would be an irreversible shift of wealth and power in favour of those at present most disadvantaged in all states. It would imply the use of revolutionary techniques, revolutionary slogans, revolutionary forms of political organisation within states. In this case international organisations would have little part to play, since they would remain under the control of existing governments, and their actions would be irrelevant to the kinds of change this ideology implies (and might even be used to prevent such changes coming about). This would therefore be an ideology concerned with trans-national rather than international action; with the interests of individuals rather than of states or governments; above all of disadvantaged individuals in all states, rather than the citizens of particular states.

Each of these possible ideologies corresponds to the interests of particular groups and organisations within international society (respectively the people of poor states; governments generally, especially in weaker states; powerful states and groups, including trans-national corporations; poor states; and the underprivileged everywhere). Each might for this reason become a *political* ideology: that is the basis for demands for change in international society, perhaps in rivalry with each other. Only when one had finally prevailed in that competition would it become the ideology of a society as a whole.

These are, of course, only examples of the types of ideology which might become influential over future years. The international society which comes about in fifty or a hundred years time will not necessarily be governed by any of these possible aspirations. But whatever kind of society does emerge, it will be supported by a set of ideas influencing motivations and behaviour among its members. That set of ideas will have an influence not only on the shape of society as a whole, but, as we shall see, on many individual features within it. The study and analysis of such general ideas is therefore an important aspect of the study of international society generally.

6 Motives

MOTIVES IN SOCIETY

One of the factors that distinguishes one society from another is the nature of the motives influencing their members.

Motives of course vary from individual to individual in the same society: according to innate character, teaching, and experience, and especially according to the differing *situations*, short- and long-term, in which individuals find themselves. But they vary at least equally widely from one society to another.

There exist wide variations in the motives that dominate in different societies. This is not only, and not mainly, because the situations, social and personal, in which individuals find themselves vary from one to another. It is much more because the way they respond to such situations are influenced by the society's teaching concerning appropriate responses: co-operative or competitive, by strength or by stealth, based on immediate impulse or careful thought.

But a society influences the responses made in a more fundamental way from this: it teaches what to want.

It is above all the ideology of each society which has this effect. The long-term importance of this ideology is not so much in the beliefs that it instils as in the *effects* of those beliefs on what people desire and what they should therefore do. The widely contrasting societies of the Kwakiutl of the Pacific Coast, the Zuni of New Mexico, and the Dobu of the Pacific (pp. 91–2) resulted partly from widely contrasting beliefs about the world. But they resulted especially from beliefs about what people should *desire* and therefore what they should do: in one case to accumulate wealth which could subsequently be consumed or destroyed in a way that would bring prestige to the owner; in another to join in co-operative economic activities for the benefit of the society as a whole; in another to seek to destroy, by magic or other means, enemies believed to exist everywhere outside the close matrilineal family.

Motives in different developed societies may be equally divergent. One may encourage its members to value success in this world, another salvation in the next; one to value individual achievement, another to value group solidarity; one to value martial glory, another

116

to value artistic attainment; one to value dedication and service to the state, another to value personal freedom and individuality. And so on. The variety of ends which society can instil in this way is almost infinite. And though, as we saw, each society often maintains that the motives it demands are those which closely correspond to "human nature" (p. 91 above), in fact there is no evidence to suggest this is more true in one case than another. Humans appear to be capable of a variety of natures, which can secure satisfaction in different types of social environments in response to different value-systems. And the motives they in fact acquire are determined far more by the nature of the social influences to which they are exposed than by the inexorable demands of innate desires.

Even in the same society motives are of course not identical for all individuals. However intensive socialisation may be, it is never so perfect that those factors which promote individuality – differences in genetic endowment, in parental and other early influences, in education and social situations – can be entirely overlaid. In modern societies especially, socialisation allows for a much wider variety among individual personalities and demands than in most simple societies where it is more uniform and more intense. In every society, therefore, there will be some individuals whose motives diverge from the norm (and may even be closer to those characteristic of some other society than those common in their own). But variations of this kind are usually much less than the differences between the kind of motives, or mix of motives, which predominate in different societies; and in particular between the motives which are given *primary* emphasis in each.

The motivations of individuals result partly from their conceptions of their interests. The way they see their interests, like the motives themselves, is partly influenced by the ideology of the society. As Max Weber put it: "Interests (material and ideal), not ideas, dominate directly the actions of men. Yet the 'images of the world' created by these ideas have very often served as switches determining the tracks on which the dynamism of interest kept the action moving."[1] Some of the interests of individuals are peculiar to themselves. But others are shared with others: those of the same locality, enterprise, class or sex. These latter interests can often only be promoted by joint action of the group as a whole. These common interests may sometimes come to be more important to individuals than their more

1. Marianne Weber, *Max Weber* (Tübingen, 1926) pp. 247–8.

personal interests. Because important changes in their situation can only be brought about by joint action with others, they become increasingly conscious of the common interest they share with these and of the need for common action. This consciousness of *collective* interests then becomes a primary source of motivation and an important influence on action.

But with other groups individuals find they have a different relationship. With some they have *mutual* interests: some of the things that benefit that group will benefit themselves too, or at least an exchange of benefits can be easily made between them. With other groups, on the other hand, they have a direct conflict of interests: what will benefit them will harm the other group, and vice versa. More frequently they will have with another group common interests (or mutual interests) in some respects and conflicting interests in others. As their knowledge of their social situation increases, each individual and group becomes more closely aware of the areas in which they have common or conflicting interests. These perceptions affect the way they perceive society and so their motivations. They encourage action that is favourable to some groups, and action that is unfavourable to others.

The motives of individuals, therefore, are modified by their conception of interests. This can induce them to look more favourably at particular groups, at least for certain purposes, and less favourably at others. They may be modified also by the norms established by society, suggesting which goals "ought" and which "ought not" to be secured, and by norms approving certain *means* of achieving goals more highly than others. They may be modified also by conditions, favourable or unfavourable, for securing goals. Thus the acquisition of military glory will be a more important goal in a society where the conditions for individuals to acquire it exist; the acquisition of wealth may be more significant in another society where there is more opportunity for individuals to acquire this than to win success through military exploits.

So motives derive partly from individual endowment and experience, but far more from social influences and social conditioning. And they derive in particular from the underlying ideology which teaches what kind of attainment, what kind of activity, are most to be valued in each society.

MOTIVES IN INTERNATIONAL SOCIETY

In international society the motives we are concerned with are those of individuals, groups and states. Among these too, motives will vary from one to another within the same society, according to their own character and endowments. But, here too, they are also strongly influenced by factors deriving from the society generally. And here too, therefore, there will be some similarity in motives in the same society, while motives may vary widely from one society to another.

The motives we are concerned with here – even those of groups and states – are ultimately those of individuals. Individuals have desires and aspirations that relate to the wider world beyond the borders of their own state. Some of these relate to individuals' personal situation, some to the situation of their group or enterprise, some to the situation of their state. Their desire to emigrate, the desire they have for their company to invest abroad, for their state to recover lost territory, all of these are examples of the international motives of individuals. But once again it is collective motives – those of the group, and above all of the state – which are most significant in their effect. The motives of individuals, and for the most part the motives of groups as well, have consequences that are limited. The desire of the individual to emigrate, or of the company to invest, will not have great consequences for international society generally. But the desire of the state as a whole – for territory elsewhere, for example – can have a major effect on the character of international society. What individuals and groups can achieve is constrained, moreover, by what states – their own and others – will allow. For both these reasons in the study of international society it is the motives of states which are of primary concern to us.

To speak of the motives of states is clearly to use a form of shorthand.[2] The state itself is an impersonal entity, incapable of feelings or desires. We are speaking ultimately of the "motives" of a large number of individuals related to each other in a particular way within a state. Each individual can influence in quite different ways and in different proportions the actions which are taken by the state. Whatever their influence, they may or may not support its policies, share its desires and aspirations. Only in so far as they do share its

2. The following paragraphs are based on a passage on the same theme in Luard, *Conflict and Peace in the Modern International System* (Boston, Mass.).

collective concerns – the determination to recover territory that is lost, the desire for revenge for a humiliation in the past, the concern to secure economic advantages at the expense of another state – can they be said to be impelled by the motives attributed to the "state" as a whole.

Thus though we can reasonably attribute purposes to a collective body, on the basis of the sum-total of its actions, those aims will not be shared equally among its population. Some citizens may be more or less aggressive, co-operative, concerned with the wealth or status of their nation, worried about world peace or the international environment. Individuals, interest-groups, departments of the government, ministers or politicians will often be more concerned about some of the state's goals than others. Defence departments will be more concerned with promoting its interests in the field of security, and less with winning goodwill and popularity abroad. For foreign offices the reverse will normally be true. For this reason the policies of states – that is their aims – vary according to the relative influence of particular statesmen, political parties, interest-groups, government departments and sections or individuals within a foreign office.

But despite variations of this kind individuals do to a considerable extent identify with their own states. They see success, glory, greatness for the state, as success, glory, greatness for themselves. The situation which the state confronts – the threat from a neighbour, the humiliation from a rival, the danger to an ally – is the same for all its members and most will react in similar ways to the shared situation; will be equally concerned to defy the threat, to avenge the humiliation, to assist the ally. Here is another case where the individual becomes aware of having a common interest with others sharing a common situation. Citizens of international society are conditioned to think in terms of the collective interest they share with others within the same state rather than in terms of the *individual* interests which are peculiar to themselves alone.

For these reasons the motives of individuals within states, though not identical, do not vary widely. Foreign policy decisions are made in a national framework and it is national aspirations and interests which dictate them, not those of individuals, groups or parties. Assessments of state interests may, of course, vary to some extent: for

3. Cf. H. J. Eysenck, *The Psychology of Politics* (London, 1954); G. W. Adorno *et al.*, *The Authoritarian Personality* (New York, 1950).

example along the progressive–conservative and liberal–authoritarian axes.[3] But the homogeneity of national mood and emotion within particular national situations, the consistency of foreign policies pursued by successive governments of different parties, the predictability of national policy in particular situations, suggests that differences of this kind are usually marginal. It is because of this consistency that it is reasonable to speak of the "motives" of states.

The motivations of different states in the same society, like those of individuals in a domestic society, are not identical. They too vary according to national temperament and political traditions; according to the institutional machinery within each state; and even according to the personalities of the leaders involved in making particular decisions. But they vary above all according to the situation, short term and long term, in which each is placed: the threats it may perceive, the opportunities it may enjoy, the enemies it faces and the allies it can depend on. On these grounds some states may be aggressive, some peace-loving; some expansive, some inward-turned; some with political influence, some with economic power. No two states, therefore, will be wholly alike in the principal concerns and aspirations of their foreign policies.

But these variations between states, and between types of states, are not usually decisive. The differences between the structure of governments in the modern world becomes less and less, even between governments of totally different ideologies and traditions. The basic pattern of diplomatic intercourse, bureaucratic techniques, foreign office and parliamentary procedures, the number of people involved in decisions, do not vary decisively between types of state. So many people today take part in most decisions that variations in individual temperament or aggressiveness are evened out. Above all, the traditions and norms of the international society as a whole are, at any one time, common to all states. For these reasons, though the objectives of states in different ages vary considerably, according to the prevailing ideology, there is often a remarkable similarity between the aims and aspirations of different states within the same international society.

The important difference, therefore, is between the international societies of different ages, rather than between different states within the same society. Some of the differences in the motivation which predominate in different societies are not unlike those that exist between different domestic societies. Just as some of the latter promote a kind of activity that is primarily co-operative and some activity which is primarily competitive, so in some international societies motives are primarily co-operative (for example among West European states today) and in some they are generally competitive (as in the state system of ancient China and in eighteenth century Europe). In general, because of the long history of rivalry and conflict among states, competitive motives have been more prevalent than co-operative ones in most international societies. And the kinds of activity which are inherently competitive (warfare, competition for status and trade rivalry) have been more prominent features of most of them than activities which are by nature co-operative (joint action to overcome common problems or to secure common objectives).

International societies vary not only in the degree of competitiveness among their members but in the *type* of competition that occurs, and so in the dominant motivation. In one kind of society competition may occur mainly for territory (as in the age of dynasties and the age of sovereignty); in another it may be primarily for control of governments (as in the age of religion and the age of ideology). Among some groups of states it will be primarily political and among others primarily economic. The type of competition will determine the type of relationships established. If the competition is for territory, the likelihood is – given the reluctance of most states to concede territory willingly – that it will be undertaken mainly through war. If competition is mainly economic it may be undertaken mainly by peaceful means. Where competition is a sufficiently powerful motivation, however, even in areas where co-operation appears the most suitable form of interaction, disputes may be ultimately resolved by armed force. For example, in the ultra-competitive age of sovereignty even economic aims were promoted sometimes through war; conversely, among West European states today, where a tradition of peaceful co-operation has been established, even motivations that are predominantly competitive, such as the contest for status, may be pursued only by peaceful means.

The character of the motivations that prevail, in international as in other societies, is determined above all by the character of the international ideology. Thus the ideology of dynasticism automatically promoted aspirations and activities directed at the acquisition of foreign crowns. Similarly the ideology of the age of religions inevitably meant that the primary concern of each state was to influence the kind of religion practised in other states. The ideology of sovereignty made it unavoidable that each state demanded above all to assert its own independence, abroad as at home, and conduct its foreign policy accordingly. The ideology of nationalism inevitably made the promotion of national power and the creation of national states the supreme end of policy. The ideology of the current international society dictates policies designed to promote, or combat, the aims of particular ideological alliances.

But it is not only the main direction of concern that is determined by the ideology. It will dictate not only which motives are dominant but the precise forms they will take. Thus, for example, the demand for territory, while it is an important motive in a number of societies, has taken different forms in different ages. In the age of dynasties what was desired was essentially a *title* to territory, which could add to the glory of the ruler and lend lustre to the royal house. There was little desire for direct control of territories so acquired: that is why in many cases what occurred was a "union of the crowns", which allowed the life of the territory, and even its political and other institutions, to continue untouched, while only a nominal allegiance to the foreign ruler was required. In the age of religions, territorial aspirations were quite different: then at least sufficient control of it was desired to ensure that the true faith should be practised there. In the age of sovereignty the goal was different again: territory was desired not for a ruler but for a state; and it was not therefore any territory to which a claim could be found that was coveted, but particular territories that were of special value to the state – corridors to link divided territories (such as those acquired by Prussia), border areas to protect frontiers (such as were acquired by France), territory providing access to the sea (like those acquired by Russia), or to promote trading opportunities (like the colonies and trading posts acquired by England and the United Provinces). In the age of nationalism territorial ambitions were different again: now it was above all territory that could complete the unification of divided peoples (like those acquired by the wars of Prussia and Italy), or to create new states based on the national principle (like the states established in Greece, Belgium, Serbia, Montenegro, Romania, Bulgaria, Albania and other places). In the age of ideology territorial motives changed once more: the transfer of territory now ceased to be desired at all and frontiers everywhere remained almost entirely unchanged. It was no longer the acquisition of land, even of particular lands, that was desired, but a change of government. The essential objective was, while allowing the existing territorial disposition to remain unaltered, to ensure that governments of the opposing ideology did not come to power, especially in strategically important states.

Economic goals too have varied from age to age according to the ideas which prevailed in each.[4] In the age of dynasties foreign economic policy was designed mainly to fill the coffers of the royal house: so both exports and imports were taxed, to the detriment of producers and consumers respectively, and a principal objective was to acquire bullion from abroad, and so to ensure that imports were less than exports. In the age of sovereignty economic policies were designed to increase the self-sufficiency and independence of each state: so high protection is afforded to local industries, bounties provided for home production and colonial trade reserved exclusively for home merchants. In the following age the desire is to increase the market available to the newly developed manufacturing capacities; and this leads to the search for colonies or semi-colonies abroad and even, for the most developed states most likely to benefit, to a freeing of trade generally; while in the latter half of the nineteenth century, the surplus of investible funds brings a competitive search for opportunities to lend at fixed interest to governments all over the world. In the modern age governments seek to restrict the development of trade and the sale of technology to ideological opponents, while elsewhere promoting opportunities for favourable trade and investment, through bank lending, aid and multilateral assistance.

Thus even when motives remain stable, the form they take and the means employed change from age to age. Changes in ideology are not the only factor at work. Developments in technology, communications, economic organisation, alliance structure and other factors have the effect that new ways need to be found of securing traditional goals. So the demands for security, for independence, for influence, for prestige, each take different forms in different ages according to conditions prevailing and available opportunities.

Sometimes policies which are originally adopted as the means to other ends are transformed into ends in their own right. Thus the desire for security, independence and prestige leads to an expansion of armed power; and in time the development of such power becomes an end in itself. It is increasingly seen as a measure of status or even

4. These ideas, and their effects on foreign policy, are described at greater length in Luard, *Economic Relationships among States* (London, 1984) esp. chap. 2.

essential to national self-respect. The importance attached to power then feeds on itself. The estimates made of the armed strength available to other states, whether out of fear or prudence, are continually increased. The possibility of combinations among them is often believed to make necessary the development of sufficient armed power to match two or three of them combined. In this way the priority to be accorded to armed power is progressively raised.

There is in any case little evidence that states, any more than people, ever establish a clear-cut hierarchy of goals, allotting a recognised priority to some over others. There does not usually appear to be any clear relationship established between different goals, short term or long term; still less are all subordinated to one overriding long-term objective. Action is governed by a range of motivations, some comparatively stable and unvarying, and others more short term. The goal that is predominant at one time will depend, as for individuals, on the type of situation then experienced. Goals that at one point are thought of as means may become ends in their own right. Wealth, demanded first as a means, may become an end in itself. Conversely goals that are sometimes ends can also be means to other ends. Armed power may be desired as a way of winning influence, or influence as a means to power. Thus goals will be pursued in different proportions at different moments, in different spheres of activity and in different actions.

Among the most important long-term goals in recent times have been: survival; security; independence; status; influence; peace; prosperity; good name; protecting the interests, commercial and personal, of citizens; promoting a particular ideology or political creed and opposing others; and establishing a stable, harmonious or otherwise desirable international community. That these might be accepted as long-term goals by decision-makers if specifically questioned on the subject is no indication how influential such motives are in individual decisions. Probably many governments rarely formulate ultimate goals of this type; and for this reason alone their influence on statesmen or officials is reduced. Even where there are attempts to formulate such goals, they will usually have little influence on the actions taken in concrete situations (though they may be strengthened as unconscious motives). And among individuals in specific situations many decisions are made without any conscious regard for long-term objectives. The decision on how to respond to a particular diplomatic note, how to vote on a particular resolution, whether to ratify a particular convention, still more the far larger number of smaller decisions that are arrived at within foreign offices every day, are mainly influenced by other, and *short-term* objectives. These might include the need to promote relations with a particular country or type of country; the desire not to exacerbate relations with another; the need to promote the interests and cohesion of a particular alliance and to frustrate the interests of another; the need to promote *particular* rather than general interests of the nation and its nationals: the need not to offend a particular interest group or governing party at home. Among the most important and common of all such aims is simply the need to respond to an existing situation, to find a way forward from, or a solution to, the particular conflict or problem immediately faced. Though some of these goals may originally have been related, more or less closely, to the attainment of the long-term objectives, they can increasingly become ends in their own right, pursued without regard to their original instrumental purpose. There is thus no clear-cut division between first-order and second-order objectives.

For these reasons the policies pursued by states in international society, like those of individuals in smaller societies, rarely represent a "rational" implementation of clearly defined objectives. States, like individuals, have motives that are often incoherent and uncoordinated. To revert to the formulation applied by Schutz to individuals (p. 21 above), the public statements made of a state's aims are likely to be of the "because of" rather than of the "in order to" type: rationalisations of desirable, or most easily justified, objectives rather than objective descriptions of the motives really at work. The motives in fact at work, like those of individuals, will be a combination of vague and scarcely apprehended urges and desires with clearly understood and explicit policy objectives. They only partly result from desires that are peculiar to each individual state. They will be derived, to some extent, like those of individuals, from the society which surrounds them, which inculcates the ambitions and aspirations that inspire its members.

MOTIVES IN CONTEMPORARY INTERNATIONAL SOCIETY

Let us now go on to consider, in slightly more detail, the motives which dominate state action in the contemporary international society.

Again some of the most powerful motives derive directly from the ideology of that society. In this case that ideology inculcates above all a desire to secure victory for one political creed and defeat for another. It is a motive that is, inevitably, felt more strongly by some states than by others. It is felt most strongly of all by the leaders of such ideological alliance: the superpowers. Such powers not only *feel* most strongly about such questions, being politically deeply committed. They have the greatest power to put these feelings into action and the greatest responsibility for promoting the cause of their own ideological camp. It is they therefore that will be most passionately concerned to protect its interests; will be most involved in lending assistance to ideological factions in other states; and will do most to extend their own power and influence across the world to further that cause.

Such powers are not only leaders of an ideological cause. They are great powers in their own right. Their sentiments as ideological leaders and proponents of a cause are bolstered by their interest, not always identical, as great powers. This latter interest will sometimes demand an extension of their own national power and influence, occasionally at the expense of the ideological bloc or close political allies. So, for example, the Soviet Union will from time to time have to do deals with political opponents – to establish close relationships with governments in Egypt, Iraq, or Indonesia, for example – at the expense of local communist parties in those countries; the US will need to recognise the realities of power in China, Yugoslavia and Mozambique, even at the cost of abandoning political allies and hopes of political change in those countries. Their interest as great powers may sometimes induce a prudence and caution which ideological zeal alone would despise. Each will often in practice recognise the supremacy of the other in its own sphere of influence, and be reluctant to intervene there even on behalf of ideological allies: so the US does nothing to support democratic revolution in Hungary, Czechoslovakia or Poland, just as the Soviet Union refrains from giving effective support to left-wing revolutions in Latin America and the Caribbean. And on the same grounds the superpowers continue to search for deals with the other – superpower politics – deals which are undertaken independently of, and even behind the backs of, their closest political allies.

Ideological fervour, though felt most strongly by the superpowers, is felt to some extent by most other states. They too, if less intensely, desire to see the opposing faith contained, their own if possible spread wider. The version of the ideology they seek to spread is not necessarily identical with that of the superpowers themselves. There are many variants which correspond with the beliefs and interests of different states and groups of states. So communist regimes in China, Albania, Romania and Cuba proclaim messages that are not the same as that of their original sponsors and supporters. The anti-communist doctrines of military dictatorships in Latin America and Asia, and the views of some European states, though all belonging to the "free world", are not necessarily the same as those of the US. Some states are committed to different ideologies altogether – to "guided democracy" of some form or other, to one-party states, to Islamic fundamentalism – though, except in the last case, there is usually less zeal in seeking to defend and spread such doctrines elsewhere than in the main ideological blocs.

Motives of this kind are not those of governments alone. They also inspire many individuals and groups within states. In almost every country, whatever government may be in power, there exist factions or parties supporting one cause or another. Often they look to external powers of the same political persuasion to assist them in that struggle. Communist parties in the West, and indeed all over the world, look to Moscow (or Havana or Managua) for leadership; dissidents in the Soviet Union and Poland look to supporters in the West for moral support. In civil war situations the links are far closer: political support, propaganda, the dispatch of arms and volunteers, even overt military intervention, take place on their behalf. In other words political motivations, once directed almost exclusively to seek change within a single state, are now trans-national and are expressed in actions across international society as a whole.

An important element in the motivation of each state and of each group within states, is fear. We saw earlier (p. 102) how in such a society the world is seen as divided between forces of light and darkness. For each group the forces of darkness are different; but in each case they are full of danger. There is a widespread fear of mysterious enemies who, by subversive means – the communist "conspiracy", capitalist "plots", the corrupting influence of Western imperialism (or Islamic fundamentalism) – perpetually extend their influence all over the world and may eventually undermine the state. Such security fears heighten the intensity of ideological fervour.

But they also have the effect that motives are primarily *defensive*. On each side there is a greater concern to prevent the rival ideology from spreading its influence further than there is to spread its own to new areas. It is true that offensive objectives are occasionally proclaimed: an intention to "bury" capitalism, or to "roll back" communism. But whether or not genuinely intended at the time, such threats are less and less believed. When an acquisition is offered on a plate – when Cuba and Nicaragua decide to join the socialist camp, or when Yugoslavia and China decide to leave it – the opportunity is gratefully accepted. But there is little genuinely offensive action designed to bring such changes about. There is not even any intense concern to secure revolution in uncommitted areas, such as Africa and Asia, where neither at present holds sway. When action is occasionally taken to change a government by armed force – as in Hungary, Czechoslovakia and Afghanistan by one side, in Guatemala, Cuba, the Dominican Republic and Nicaragua by the other – it is always to *recover* a territory formerly held, which has defected or may defect, never to extend control to new areas. To a substantial extent there is a willingness (though it would never be admitted) to live with the status quo: a greater willingness perhaps than has existed in almost any earlier society.

Not all motives, however, are related to ideological concerns. In this age, with increasingly close economic interdependence, economic motives have higher priority than ever before among foreign policy goals. Once again, as in small societies, it is the perceptions of *interests* which dictates the motives acquired. Just as in smaller societies perceptions of personal or group interests mainly determine the actions to be taken, so too among states. And just as, among individuals, this perception may bring about a desire to join in common action with others of similar interests, so equally among states. So oil-producing countries join together to maximise their influence in bargaining with consumer states. Poor states as a whole band together to negotiate with rich states on trade, aid and other questions. The perception of common interests influences not only the means that are employed but motives themselves: poor states become more concerned to promote solidarity with other poor states and to avoid actions which may threaten it. They come to acquire a class interest, which sometimes conflicts with and overrides other interests, such as their membership of a common ideological grouping.

These class interests dictate the particular economic objectives that are pursued. Poor countries, seeking to develop new industries, demand the right to provide these with the same protection from foreign competition which rich countries themselves demanded a hundred years earlier. Rich countries, on the other hand, now want liberalisation of trade and the freest possible access for their own products to other markets elsewhere. Conversely, poor countries look for markets in rich economies, such as they themselves had once, as colonies, provided for the manufactures of the rich; rich countries, on the other hand, fearing threats to traditional industries, now themselves impose import controls of many kinds against third-world products. Poor countries want measures to stabilise raw material prices at relatively high levels; rich countries want no such stabilisation, or only stabilisation at low prices. Poor countries want generous credit terms from aid donors, international organisations and private banks, for long periods and with few conditions; rich countries want restricted credit, for short periods and under harsher conditions. And so on. Increasingly the economic motives of states become group motives, shared among large numbers of similar states rather than those of each state acting independently.

Other traditional motives take new forms. The demand for security, one of the most basic and consistent motives in all ages, now takes new forms. Major powers, because of the decline in distance, now demand wide defensive zones around their borders in which they reserve the right to intervene to eliminate unfriendly governments: this is seen not only in actions undertaken by the superpowers in Eastern Europe and Central America, but in those of China in Korea and Vietnam, India within the Indian subcontinent, South Africa in states around her border, Israel in Lebanon and other cases. These aims are reflected in the successive "doctrines" of the age. The Brezhnev doctrine, like the Monroe doctrine of a century and a half earlier, was designed to keep subcontinental areas close to a superpower immune from hostile influences; the Truman, Eisenhower and Nixon doctrines sought in different ways to preserve more distant regions from the influence of the opposing ideology. Even areas on the other side of the world are sometimes seen as essential to defence: thus Singapore and the Suez Canal were thought vital to Britain's security interests in the early post-war period, as later Vietnam and the Middle East were seen as vital to those of the US. Inter-continental missiles expose hitherto invulnerable areas and states, including the heart of Russia and the US, to the threat of destruction (a situation which the attempt to develop a "strategic defence" does not seem likely to alter). The decline in distance has another effect: for the first time security is no longer seen as the responsibility of each state acting individually, but of entire alliances acting together to promote their joint interests. In a world so diminished in size, both friends and enemies are pushed into closer proximity to each other than ever before. As a result, here too collective interests and motives replace those of individual states.

Finally, the demand for peace also takes new forms in such an age. The reduction in distance and the increasing power of the available weapons means that the risks of war are greater than ever before: for leaders themselves and for a large part of their population, as well as to their armed forces, which alone bore most of the danger in the past. More than in earlier times, therefore, there is a desire, at least among developed countries, to avoid all-out warfare. But the desire for peace does not reduce, and perhaps increases, the desire for armaments. Fear and suspicion have the effect that an increase in arms often appears a better safeguard than a reduction. Interminable discussions on disarmament produce no significant measures for a mutual reduction of armaments and only marginal steps for restraining their deployment and development. The alternative road to peace, through building up the authority of international organisations, is blocked for the same reason. Neither side will agree to an increase in authority for such organisations for fear that they may come under the control of a majority sympathetic to the other; and one or other bloc is always in that situation. So international institutions become a forum for ideological warfare rather than for the resolution of conflicts; a means of scoring off opponents rather than for negotiating settlements. Even though no all-out war among major powers occurs, therefore, this remains a world beset by fear, distrust and mutual accusations.

So once again a new set of motives emerges, typical of a new international society. Some of the motives held derive directly from the prevailing ideology. Others take entirely new forms. More than at any other time motives are now trans-national, they relate to situations *within* other states rather than to relationships between them. And this transforms the character of the actions and relationships to which they give rise. It creates a new type of international society.

CONCLUSIONS

Motives are important, therefore, in international society as in other societies, because they determine social action and the nature of social relationships.

The motives that matter are in the first place the motives of individuals; their concerns and desires in relation to the world outside their own states. But many of these concerns and desires can only be implemented through collective actions. It is thus often through the actions of their own states that they seek to achieve their ends. And, in so far as they are in a position to influence the actions of states, their motives are in turn converted into collective motives: the motives of the state.

In the course of a brief chapter it has clearly not been possible to undertake more than a superficial survey of the kind of motives which have influenced the actions of states over recent centuries.[5] But enough has perhaps been said to show why, in any study of international society, an examination of state motivations is of considerable importance. What motivates the members of a society will determine what kind of society it is. It is thus necessary to attempt to examine the kinds of motives states have displayed.

Such an examination is not easy. The stated foreign policy aims of a government do not necessarily correspond to their real aims. A study may be made of the speeches of prominent ministers at a particular time – for example when a war is declared. But this may not necessarily give a reliable indication of the real motives underlying their actions at that time. A study can be made of the memoirs of ministers and officials who have been closely involved in the formulation of policy. But this too may give an indication of the aims which a government would *like* to have had at a particular time, rather than of those which actually influenced them. Examination can be made, after an interval, of the discussions undertaken at the time an action was taken, in cabinet rooms, in foreign offices and defence departments. But even this may not be conclusive: often it will only show how different were the objectives of different elements within the government machine at any one moment in time. It may be, therefore, that the most reliable indication of the motives of an entire state is a record of its *actions*, which can reasonably be interpreted as the implementation of a consistent set of intentions.

It is not difficult to show, on the basis of such examination, that some motives have been widely held by states in all ages (p. 125 above). But it would also show that there has been a substantial

---

5. The author has attempted more detailed treatments in *Types of International Society* (London, 1977) esp. chap. 7; *Economic Relationships among States*, esp. chap. 3; and *War in International Society* (London, 1986) chap. 5. All of these are concerned with the motives of states, in particular fields or in general.

variation among the motives which have mainly influenced state actions in different ages. Aims which seemed of great importance to the governments of one age – the assertion of a claim to a throne elsewhere, promoting or preventing the spread of a particular religious faith, the conquest and acquisition of territory or trade, assistance to national revolutions in a neighbouring state (all of which were important goals, probably the most important goals, at different periods in the past) – have been of little significance in a later age (for example over the last fifty years). Nor are these changes which affect particular states only. To some extent at least they affect all alike. Thus it can reasonably be said that there is no state today for which any of the objectives just named, so prominent among the goals of states in earlier times, remain important foreign policy aims.

Does this mean that motives are identical for all states within the same "society": that is, at any one time? Clearly this is not the case. There will always be some which are more concerned over particular aims – to win a foreign crown, to turn back the Protestant advance, to win colonies, to succour (or prevent) national revolution elsewhere, to defeat communism (or imperialism). Often it is the strongest states in each age which are most concerned, or at least most active, in pursuing such objectives. And this is evidenced by the fact that in every age it is nearly always the strongest states which are often engaged in warfare.[6] It is true that this could simply reflect a superior capacity to *achieve* aims which are felt equally by all states. But it may also reflect the fact that those states which are most likely to succeed in particular aims are also those which feel most strongly impelled by them (p. 54 above).

Even apart from this difference, however, there will be variations among states in the strength of different aspirations: that is, in the *mix* of motives which influence their actions. Some of these reflect differences in their situation. Thus small states (which may be less likely to be militarily successful) may be more concerned about peace than large states; poor states may be more concerned about economic development than are rich states; the state that has recently experienced a revolution may be more concerned with ideological issues than the old and stable state. And so on.

Thus the motives of states, like those of individuals, are influenced partly by their situations. But they are influenced also by their histories. For example, a state which has only recently entered into

6. See Luard, *War in International Society*, pp. 14, 35, 45, 53, 63, 70, 78.

the international community may remain for some time unsocialised and unassimilated, showing some of the characteristics of the aggressive psychopath within states. So Japan in the eighty years of her first opening to the outside world in 1862, Germany and Italy in the seventy years after their unification in 1870, exhibited some of the aggressive, anti-social characteristics of states in that situation. Somewhat similar is the behaviour of states with revolutionary governments, which in the same way often remain for a time unassimilated within international society. China after 1949, Cuba after 1959, Libya after 1969, Iran and Nicaragua after 1979, were all in this situation and for a time sought to challenge the traditions of the international society and the legitimacy of the authorities already established there. Other states are marked by an acute sense of insecurity, which induces in them periodic bursts of pugnacity, especially towards those believed to represent a threat to their own security. Austria in the century before 1914 (in her actions against Sardinia in 1848 and 1859 and towards Serbia in 1881, 1908–9 and 1914) could be said to belong to this category, as could South Africa and Israel, each engaging in successive forays against neighbouring states today. States that believe they have suffered a recent humiliation and are sometimes more self-assertive and status-conscious than other states: France after 1815, 1870 and 1945, Germany after 1918, the US after setbacks in Vietnam, Iran and Lebanon, might be said to have shown some of these characteristics.

The motives of states even within the same society, therefore, vary according to the situation and life-experience of each. But these variations among members of the same society are far less significant than those that exist between the motives characteristic of entire international societies. Again an analogy may be made between smaller-scale societies. In that case too there may be substantial differences between the motives of individuals in the same society: between the aggressive and the mild, the ambitious and the contented, the sociable and the unsociable. These differences will be of considerable interest to the psychologist, seeking the reasons for such variations. To the sociologist, however, they may be of less significance than the variations in motives among entire societies; rural village and industrial city, pastoral tribe and agricultural community, developing country in Africa and developed state in North America. In the same way, while the student of international relations may be concerned with differences in motives between states in the *same* international society, to the international sociologist there may be still greater interest in the variations that exist between the characteristic motives of entire international societies.

The student of international society is concerned to know the reasons for such variations: why dominant motivations change from one society to another. It seems likely that the main reason is similar to the reason why the motives of individuals in small societies vary from one to another: differing traditions, differing social structures, differing systems of economic organisation, differing patterns of socialisation, produce a different range of aspirations. Objectives that seem important in one age may come to seem trivial in the next. Technical, economic, military and other developments cause changes in the kind of desires that are widely held. But changes in perceptions and motives result above all from the changes in ideology which we considered in the last chapter: changes which, as we saw, derive ultimately from the changing character of the ruling groups which dominate in each society. It is because of the changing ideology that in one age the dominant concern of states is with securing a throne in a foreign state; in another the spreading of a particular religious faith; in another the building of powerful and prestigious states; in another the promotion of national revolutions and national unity; in another the promotion of a particular ideological cause.

Here, as for other institutions of international society, it is the influence of the prevailing ideology which is ultimately decisive.

7 Roles

SOCIAL ROLES

Another feature distinguishing one society from another is the nature of the roles individuals are expected to perform in them.

Even the simplest human existence implies the performance of some social roles: those of mother and daughter, leader and followers, neighbour and neighbour, for example. As society becomes more organised, and the division of labour more complex, the roles each individual is expected to play become more numerous and more various. The members of the society are increasingly distinguished by their diffeent roles: medicine man, war leader, village elder and so on.

Roles are essentially parts to play, expected patterns of behaviour, corresponding to each position held within society. Because they are social roles, they are independent of the particular individuals who hold them: the expectations of society remain the same irrespective of the particular people that hold each position at any one moment in time.

Some of the roles are reciprocal. The part played by one person demands the playing of a corresponding part by another. These may result from a one-to-one relationship (doctor to patient); others from one-to-several relationships (mother to children); others again from one-to-many (teacher to pupils, king to subjects).

In some cases reciprocal roles are equal, or approximately equal – for example the roles of brothers, neighbours or partners in business. In others the roles are unequal: one is more dominant or authoritative than another – the roles of employer to employed, teacher to pupil, parents to children.

Some roles are permanent: those of son or brother last as long as either partner lives. Others are relatively short term: those of student or lodger last a few years or a few months. Roles also vary in the area of life which they affect: some belong to the family or kinship group, some to the work-place, some to the neighbourhood, some to recreation, some to the wider society or state as a whole.

Roles vary according to how far they are unique or shared. There are some roles which everybody performs: for example that of citizen.

There are others that very many perform: the role of parent, householder, pupil or employee. There are others that very few perform: the role of priest, doctor or elder statesman. And there are a few that only one person in each national society performs: those of king or prime minister, for example.

Some roles are deliberately chosen, while others are imposed or demanded by society or some part of society. The person who decides to become a priest, or a doctor, chooses to play that role within society. But the person who becomes a son (by being born), who becomes king (where kingship is inherited), who becomes lord of the manor (by succession), who becomes a brahmin (by being born into the appropriate caste), who is elected the leader of a jury, who is unexpectedly appointed advertising manager, or is suddenly promoted to general, has not chosen those positions: they have been thrust upon them largely irrespective of their own wills. This again reflects the fact that roles exist independently of individuals. In many cases, therefore, if one person dies or falls ill or resigns a post, somebody else must be found to take his or her place. The role is a require-ment of society rather than of the individual who decides to perform it.

A role will always imply certain types of behaviour but not, as is sometimes suggested, particular rights and duties. The person who performs the role of father is in most societies expected to perform certain duties and can expect to acquire particular rights. So does the person who performs the role of teacher. But there are not always such clear-cut rights and duties. Neighbours or tennis partners adopt certain roles towards each other, but there are no clearly laid down rights or obligations (other than negative obligations) which either can demand of the other. All that can be said of any role is that it creates expectations of a certain type of behaviour. That behaviour is not necessarily socially approved behaviour: the criminal or outlaw performs a role of a kind, may even be said to conform to social expectations, but they do not perform a socially sanctioned role.

Because a role is that expected by society, it may not be precisely the same as the role actually performed by any particular individual who holds the position. Role *performance*, in other words, may differ from the demanded role. The behaviour expected may be narrowly defined or may cover a broad range of alternative conduct. There may also be varying degrees of social consensus about the precise nature of the behaviour expected: variations not only between the expectations of society as a whole and of particular groups and individuals within it, but between both of these and those of the individuals who undertake the role.

But there are also differences between the expectations of entire societies. Societies vary in the precise way in which they expect particular roles to be performed: for example those of priest, war-leader, mother, son or wife. But they differ, even more significantly, in the kinds of roles which they demand. Some may provide an important role for the village elder, some none at all; some an important role for grandmother, some only an insignificant one; some an important role for husband's brother, another for mother's brother; and so on. It is the total *mix* of roles which are demanded, as well as the way in which each individual role is to be performed, which will, as much as anything, distinguish one society from another.

ROLES IN INTERNATIONAL SOCIETY

In international society too social life brings about the adoption of expected social roles: the pattern of behaviour believed appropriate to particular positions in society. And here too different societies are distinguished by the different types of role which they demand.

Some roles in international society are those assigned to, or adopted by, individuals. The prime minister and foreign minister of each state have important roles to play there; diplomats have a role of a kind; and every individual can play a minimal part within international society. A few individuals play far more important positions. They popes in medieval times, the Secretary-General of the UN today, have performed important roles within their own international societies. Occasional unusual individuals, a Napoleon or a Hitler, leave a personal stamp on the society of their own times. Groups equally may exercise an international role. So, for example, religious organisations and churches – the Calvinist preachers of the late sixteenth century, the Jesuit preachers of the century that followed – secret societies – such as the Carbonari and the Nihilists in the nineteenth century – international political organisations – such as the Comintern or the Socialist International – international labour organisations – such as the ICFTU or the International Metal Workers Union – all these have played significant roles in particular ages. For the most part, however, the roles that are important in international society, and those with which we will be especially concerned here, are the roles of states. Most individuals – military leaders, prime ministers and foreign ministers – and even many groups, have an international role only as the representative of their own state; and it is the national roles, rather than individual roles, which are of greatest importance in determining the character of the society as a whole.

In international society, as in domestic society, some roles are widely shared, others unique to a few individuals. Just as every individual plays the role of tribesman or citizen, so every state plays the role of member of international society. Other international roles, however, are confined to particular states. So, just as most individuals are friends and neighbours, so most states are allies or reliable partners; just as only a few individuals are teachers or doctors, only a few states are aid-donors or bloc-leaders; and just as only a single individual is king or pope, only a single state can be President of the Security Council, or leader of the Non-Aligned Movement.

Again, as in domestic society, many roles in international society are reciprocal. In this society too these may be either equal or unequal. The role of ally or trading partner is, in normal circumstances, a relatively equal role, freely entered into by both parties. But there are a number of international reciprocal roles that are highly unequal: for example, those of superpower and satellite, colonial power and colony, lender and borrower.

In international society as in domestic society, some roles are individually chosen, some imposed or inherited. In most cases the role of ally is freely chosen by a state. But that of satellite to a superpower may be imposed against its will. Some roles are inherently voluntary or compulsory. The role of coloniser is invariably freely adopted, while that of colonised is invariably imposed. But there are some roles that can be either freely chosen or imposed. The role of neutral, for example, may be voluntarily adopted by a state: as it has been by Sweden or Switzerland today. But it may also be imposed on states whether they like it or not, to suit the interest of external powers; like the neutrality imposed on Belgium in 1839–40 and on Austria in 1954. Similarly some international roles, like some personal ones, are inherited. All might be said to be inherited in the sense that they are inherited from the past: thus Britain and Portugal remain as allies because such an alliance was concluded by their rulers several centuries ago, and neither country has wished to do away with it, rather than because of any conscious enthusiasm for the partnership on either side today. Switzerland remains neutral because she has inherited that role as much as because she has chosen it. Because states do not change identity from one generation to the next as individuals do, there is no precise analogy to be made here with the roles inherited by individuals. All that can be said is that inherited roles can be abandoned by states, as by individuals. So Belgium was able to abandon the neutrality that brought her so little benefit in 1914, just as the US could abandon the role of isolationist in 1940–1, and Britain that of colonial power after 1945.

So far we have looked at the ways in which the roles of states *resemble* those of individuals in smaller societies. But clearly the particular roles that have been played by states within their own societies have been in many cases quite different from those which are performed by individuals in theirs. Let us now look at some of the roles that have been widely performed in different international societies of the past, before going on to examine those which are most characteristic of contemporary international society.

In international as in domestic society there are some roles which are peculiar to particular societies, and some that are played in all or virtually all societies. The role of "hegemon", as played by particular states in the multi-state system in China, was peculiar to that society and has not been exactly reproduced in any other. The roles played by Rome at the time of the Roman Empire, and of the Holy Roman Emperor in late medieval Europe, are almost equally unique. Against this the roles of ally, neutral and superpower (in one form or another) exist in virtually every international society and can be seen as archetypical social positions. One of the things about which we need to be concerned is the reason for differences of this kind; and in particular the reason why the *same* role – superpower or satellite for example – has been played in different ways in different international societies.

Superpowers of one kind or another have existed in almost every international society. But the precise role performed by superpowers has been different in each, reflecting the different relationships and the different prevailing ideologies within each society. In the ancient Chinese system, there often existed one or two dominant powers, one of which usually took the position of "hegemon" which meant that they could perform some of the functions of the ancient Chou dynasty, and could exercise considerable power over members of the society. For example the hegemon "directed punitive expeditions, acted as arbiter of differences between feudal rulers, punished those who disobeyed the orders and received the revenues which had formerly gone to the [Chou] king".[1] It could call meetings of the other rulers and could intervene in the territory of its allies. But there were nearly always one or two other states of almost equal power, sometimes themselves seeking to secure the position of hegemon, sometimes organising a rival alliance against the hegemon of the day.[2] In ancient Greece Athens and Sparta, later joined by Thebes, acted as superpowers. As in China they could call meetings of members of their own league and recommend action of a particular kind to its allies. They could expect to exercise command in the field, and sometimes domination of other kinds: Athens, for example, held the treasury of her alliance in her own hands, placed military garrisons among her allies and often used force to compel them to join a particular operation. During the sixteenth and early seventeenth century Spain was the acknowledged European superpower. She too frequently intervened by force, for example in north Italian cities, to secure her strategic position and promote her dynastic interests. A century later, the France of Louis XIV was almost equally dominant, intervening against the United Provinces (1672), Luxembourg (1683–4), Genoa (1684) and the Palatinate (1688) as well as in Alsace (1680–1) and Lorraine (1662 and 1670) to promote French interests. Each of these was seen, by others as much as by themselves, as superpowers, and each finally succeeded in uniting much of the rest of the continent against them. In the eighteenth century no state was sufficiently dominant to be rated a superpower, though Napoleon at its end might have succeeded in restoring France to that position, had he not finally once more united the rest of the continent against him. In the nineteenth century too there were no true superpowers, but the five "powers" were quite as willing as their predecessors to intervene in areas of concern to them to promote their interests: Austria in Italy, France in Spain, Russia in Greece and other parts of the Balkans, Prussia in Schleswig-Holstein and other parts of Germany, Britain in Egypt, among other cases. Only Germany might, among the European powers, have made herself a superpower; but she too, like those before her, eventually succeeded, in two successive wars, in uniting much of the continent against her. In the contemporary age two superpowers have once more re-emerged, each flanked by its own alliance. They, like their predecessors, have been willing to intervene by force in neighbouring areas (p. 129) where they have

1. W. G. Creel, *The Birth of China* (London, 1936) p. 244.
2. R. L. Walker, *The Multi-State System in Ancient China* (Hamden, Conn., 1953) pp. 67–8.

felt it necessary to promote their own strategic interests and expect a dominant voice within their own alliance. In every age, therefore, a few powerful states have enjoyed a privileged position. While they have usually seen themselves as having responsibilities as well as rights, they have often been more conscious of the latter than of the former, and have in particular reserved the right to intervene, among allies or in strategically sensitive places, whenever they believed their interests demanded this.

Reciprocal to the role of superpower is that of its dependencies: client-states, camp-followers or satellites. In the ancient Chinese system the converse of the dominance of the hegemon was the subordination of its allies. They were expected to show continual marks of deference, for example by sending regular visiting missions to the leader of the alliance, missions which were usually not returned.[3] They could be bullied into joining a war, or have their quarrels with one another settled, with or without their consent. Among the Greek city-states, similarly, the smaller cities were in a position of constant dependence on the larger. While middle-sized cities (such as Corinth, Argos and Thebes) could switch their support to Athens or Sparta according to which represented the greater threat, the smaller had little choice but to remain in close obedience to the immediate protector: as the Euboean cities did to Athens, Mantinea to Sparta, Tegaea to Thebes, Nautila to Argos and so on. In late medieval Europe the small cities of Italy were in the same way usually subject to the dominant influence of their powerful neighbours: as Pisa was to Florence (except when she revolted), and later many were made subject to the domination of external powers, such as Spain and France: so Naples was swallowed by Spain, Milan by France and Spain in turn, Florence made dependent on the emperor, while even the pope saw his city ravaged by imperial troops. In the age of sovereignty after 1648 the small states sometimes had to play a role of abject dependence: so Louis XIV compelled the Doge of Genoa, having mercilessly bombarded his city, to travel personally to Versailles to make a humiliating submission to him there; and sought to compel the United Provinces to send a delegation to him once a year to present him with a gold medal thanking him for his benevolence. In the nineteenth century small states had to play an almost equally humiliating role: for example the newly created Balkan states were compelled to offer deference to their larger rivals –

3. See Walker, *Multi-State System*, pp. 57, 80–1.

Prince Milan of Serbia was forced to declare to Austria that he would enter into no foreign treaty without her consent (and even agreed to make a declaration of submission "in whatever terms you care to notify me") while Russia in the same period (1880–1910) demanded an equal submission from Bulgaria. Finally, in the modern world, though the "sovereign equality" of small states is in theory generally recognised, in practice dependence is equally brutally imposed: so East European states suffer invasion from the Soviet Union if they dare to change their political regime, while those of Central America and the Caribbean may suffer invasion or substantial intervention from the US if they show similar independence of mind.[4] In each of these ages, therefore, though the forms of dependence have varied according to the motives of the most powerful states, small states have often found themselves obliged to adopt a role of considerable subordination to the wishes of powerful neighbours.

Another role to be found, in one form or another, in almost every age is that of *neutral*. In theory this is an honourable role which may allow the state concerned to play the part of mediator and impartial observer. But in many societies the more powerful states have been reluctant to acknowledge such a role. In the ancient Chinese multi-state system, for example, it was not in practice possible for any small state to withdraw from the struggle for power that dominated their larger neighbours: "within such a system neutrality was an impossible and futile hope. Those states which attempted to remain neutral usually suffered extinction at the hands of one of the power-blocs seeking to swing the balance in its favour."[5] Among the Greek city-states, though the role of neutral was acknowledged, it was not accepted as a part which could be freely chosen by each state. Sometimes a city was *prevented* by its more powerful neighbours from adopting that position: for example Melos was ferociously punished by Athens in 426 BC for daring to declare herself neutral at

4. Only six left-wing regimes have been established in Latin America. The first, that of Arbenz in Guatemala, was overthrown by an invasion organised and assisted by the CIA in 1954; the second, Castro's Cuba, was invaded by US-supported rebels in 1961; the third, that of Caamano in the Dominican Republic, was overthrown as a result of a US invasion in 1965; the fourth, that of Allende in Chile, was overthrown by a revolution believed to have been encouraged by the US; the fifth, in Grenada, was overthrown by a US invasion; and the sixth, in Nicaragua, has been consistently under attack by US-supplied forces.
5. Walker, *Multi-State System*, p. 101.

the beginning of the Peleponnesian war.[6] In other cases neutrality was *imposed*, by agreement among the great powers. Plataea was compelled to undertake neutral status by Sparta after the Persian war (and was therefore condemned when she forsook it fifty years later by aligning herself with Athens); Argos was made neutral by a treaty between Athens and Sparta in 446 BC; while under another treaty between those two countries in 421 BC six cities were, regardless of their own wishes, prevented from aligning themselves with Sparta.[7] In the later Middle Ages in Europe the role of neutral was only marginally acknowledged. No state could make itself immune from the dynastic claims which were the principal cause of war, and few rulers wished to do so. The Swiss Federation adopted "eternal" neutrality in 1516, but this was virtually forced on it as a result of defeat at the hands of France. In the age of religion which followed, the role of neutral was seen as scarcely a respectable option. On such issues every state, it was generally felt, should be willing to stand up and be counted. As Gustavus Adolphus declared "I will not listen to talk about neutrality. . . . If he [the elector of Brandenburg] wishes to hold with God, good, he is on my side. If, however, he wishes to hold with the Devil, then in truth he must fight against me." For this reason it was not easy to find mediators when peace was negotiated: at the Peace of Westphalia there were practically no powers which were not seen as committed on one side or the other – and almost all had taken part in the conflict at one time or other – and the pope, so often a mediator before, was now by no means accepted as neutral by Protestant (nor by all Catholic) states. In the age of sovereignty, neutrality was more often imposed by outside states than voluntarily chosen. Just as the major powers distributed territories among each other, regardless of their inhabitants' views, to suit state interests,[8] they also decided on which places should be neutral for the same reason. So several of them were able to agree to the imposed neutrality of north Germany during the Great Northern War; and so

6. Even when it was voluntarily chosen, neutrality did not always provide security; as the representative of Corcyra told the Athenian assembly at the beginning of the Peleponnesian war, "We used to think that our neutrality was a wise thing, if it prevented us being dragged into danger by other people's policies; now we see it clearly as a lack of foresight and as a source of weakness" (Thucydides, *Peleponnesian War*, vol. I, p. 32).

7. N. G. L. Hammond, *A History of Greece to 233BC* (London, 1967) p. 388.

8. For details see Evan Luard, *Types of International Society* (London, 1977) p. 93.

Prussia and Britain were able to agree together in 1756 on the neutrality of German states which had not themselves been consulted on the matter. The role of neutral was in any case not too clearly defined at this time:

> The notion of neutral status remained somewhat nebulous . . . because the practice of the time had blurred the line separating war and peace. A neutral abstained from direct acts of hostility; but he could send auxiliary troops to a belligerent . . . without compromising his neutrality, and could allow the troops of a belligerent "innocent transit" through his territory to attack the enemy.[9]

In the nineteenth century the role continued to be more often imposed by outside powers than voluntarily chosen: for example in the multilateral agreements providing for the neutrality of Switzerland in 1815, of Belgium in 1840 and of Luxemburg in 1867. Such treaties were designed to serve the purposes of outside powers, by insulating a particular region or state from their own competitive struggle, rather than that of the countries most directly concerned. Even in the modern period this remained a common motive. Though some states, such as Sweden, have made a deliberate decision to choose the position of neutral, in other cases neutrality continues to be determined by outside powers to suit their own interests: as for Austria in 1954 and Laos in 1962. While therefore the role of neutral has served different functions in different international societies, it has normally been one determined by the needs of society as a whole rather than by the autonomous choice of a particular state.

In most international societies there has existed, as in smaller societies, the role of *rival*. Often a traditional rivalry that exists between two states largely determines their attitudes towards international society as a whole and conditions most other relationships. In the ancient Chinese system, for example, Sung and Lu, Chin and Cheng, were pairs of rivals of this kind; and the attitude they took up towards the contests of the superpowers and the larger leagues was mainly influenced by the usefulness it was thought they would

9. See *Cambridge Modern History*, vol. vi (1970) p. 174. The Catholic forces of the emperor in the Thirty Years War occupied parts of Brandenburg for several years while that state was still neutral. France and Britain were engaged in war against each other for four years as auxiliaries to other combatants between 1740 and 1744 before finally declaring war against each other in the latter year.

have in prosecuting their local contests. In ancient Greece, the wider contest between Athens and Sparta was mirrored in many such local rivalries; between Plataea and Thebes, Mantinea and Tegaea, Corinth and Corcyra and so on. To each individual city these tended to be of more importance than the struggle between the main leagues to which they belonged. In medieval Europe the rivalry was often between two families (Luxemburg and Wittelsbach, Hapsburg and Valois); or between two individual rulers (René of Anjou and Alfonso of Aragon, Matthias Corvinus and George Podiebrad, Francis I and Charles V). Increasingly these personal contests developed into the rivalries of states (Venice and Genoa, Naples and Milan, Sweden and Denmark, Spain and France). Though these were complicated for a time, between 1559 and 1648, by the rivalries of religions (between Calvinist and Lutheran, Orthodox and Roman, as much as between Catholic and Protestant), state rivalries re-emerged more powerfully than ever in the age of sovereignty. Often particular pairs of rivals struggled for power in particular regions: Russia and Sweden in the Baltic; Spain and Austria in Italy; France and Britain in Canada, the Caribbean and India; Prussia and Austria in Germany. This competition between states became in the following age a rivalry between *nations*, mobilising popular passions and loyalties and inspiring strong patriotic feelings: for example between the newly emerged states of Serbia and Bulgaria, between Austria and Russia in the Balkans, between France and Germany on the Rhine, between Britain and France in North Africa, and between Britain and Russia in Asia. This national rivalry sometimes now had a racial foundation: Germans and Russians alike preached an inevitable struggle for existence between Teutons and Slavs; while English statesmen spoke seriously of the benefits of a "natural alliance" between Britain and Germany because of their common racial stock. In the most recent age this rivalry between states has become closely entangled in the rivalry of ideological beliefs. Though in some cases national rivalries are able to survive despite ideological alignment – for example between communist Hungary and communist Romania, pro-Western Turkey and pro-Western Greece – in other cases ideological differences *reinforce* existing rivalries for power: for example between the US and the Soviet Union, communist China and democratic India, Shia Iran and Sunni Iraq. In such cases an ideological superstructure can give the justification which an ideological age requires for rivalries and resentments which have far deeper historical roots.

The role of *ally* is another that is found in almost all international societies. But here too the form which the role takes depends on the character of the society as a whole. In some cases the ally is a genuine partner, sharing common attitudes and concerns, and making common cause as a result of shared beliefs. This is the role most often found in times of competing ideology, such as the ages of religion and of ideology. So between 1559 and 1648 a large proportion of alliances reflected common attitudes towards religion: for example, combinations between the provinces of the Netherlands and the states of Germany (the League of Utrecht and the Evangelical Union among Protestants, the League of Arras and the Catholic League among Catholics), and, with one or two exceptions, the combinations of the Thirty Years War. In the age of ideology likewise, members of NATO and the Warsaw Pact, as well as most regional groupings, are sustained by common attitudes on ideological questions. Since religious and political viewpoints do not quickly change, alliances on that basis are likely to be relatively enduring. But in a different kind of society the role of ally can be altogether different. It may then represent a purely opportunistic arrangement, designed to promote mutual interests at a particular point in time. In this case alliances may be short lived and continually changing: such as those that were made among the states of the ancient Chinese system and the continually changing combinations of the age of sovereignty in Europe. Sometimes the role of ally is that of an *accomplice*, a partner in crime – that is, in an act of aggression or spoliation – like the secret arrangement made between Russia, Saxony and Denmark against Sweden in 1699–1700, the agreements among Russia, Prussia and Austria for the partition of Poland, or the agreement of France and Savoy to attack Austria in 1859. Sometimes an alliance is based on kinship, the family ties of rulers, and in this case again will be relatively enduring: of this kind were the links between Lu and Chou in the ancient Chinese system, some of the arrangements between tyrants in the Greek city-states, and the links between Hapsburg Spain and Hapsburg Austria, Bourbon France and Bourbon Spain (almost the only pairs of European states which never fought each other at that time). So different kinds of alliance have been established for different purposes in different ages; and the role of ally is accordingly transformed according to the nature of the social structure in each period.

Another role that has been played in different societies is that of *balancer*. This is a role that needs to be distinguished from that of *opportunist*, or *tertius gaudens*, the state which remains deliberately uncommitted in order to maximise its own bargaining position and state interest. The latter role is an understandably attractive one that has been tempting to states in every age. The key distinction is that the true balancer will always side eventually *against* the stronger power or powers, while the opportunist will tend to side *with* it. Thus among the Italian states of the fifteenth century, Florence, siding at first always against Milan, the most powerful state and the main threat to the peace, and in the second half of the century against Venice, by then the most powerful, played a genuine balancing role. So did the popes of the following century, acting in turn against Spain, Venice, France and the emperor, when each in turn became the main threat to Italy's independence. So did Britain, in a somewhat half-hearted way, in the early years of this century when she finally decided to throw in her lot with her former enemies France and Russia against Germany, the most powerful state of the continent, and the main threat to the status quo. In many other cases, however, states that have appeared to play a balancing role have in fact been opportunists pursuing their own private state interests without any conscious desire for balance: so during the wars between Charles V and Francis I, Henry VIII more often joined the stronger party (Charles V) against the weaker,[10] while in the nineteenth century equally Britain pursued no consistent policy of supporting weak states against strong ones (for example Austria in 1866 or France in 1870), and at the turn of the century seriously contemplated allying herself with the most powerful state of the continent. Savoy, selling her favours to the highest bidder in the seventeenth and eighteenth centuries, and Italy doing the same at the end of the nineteenth equally pursued the role of opportunists rather than balancers. Here too the way the role is played – and the extent to which it can be played at all – depends on the character of the society as a whole. In an ideological society, such as that of ancient Greece and the present day, when most are committed by their own convictions to one side or the other, only wholly uncommitted or external powers, having no part in the conflict, are in a position to play the balancing role: thus in ancient Greece it was Persia, constantly switching support from Athens to Sparta and back again, which played that part, while in the modern age China, with her special and unorthodox political

10. Even when he joined the alliance against Charles in 1527 (for reasons partly connected with his desire for a marriage annulment) he believed himself to be joining the stronger side.

viewpoint, is most able to play the role. Conversely, in the non-ideological age of sovereignty, when there existed no long-term commitments of this kind and each state pursued its own interests independently, balance resulted often only from the chance result of opportunistic policies: from the self-interested combination of all states against Louis XIV, or from the unscrupulous abandonment by Frederick the Great of his ally in 1742 and 1744, and by Russia of hers in 1762.

Another role to be seen in most international societies, which again takes a rather different form in each, is that of the *challenger*. In nearly every society there exist rising powers which are seeking to challenge the existing order and carve out for themselves a larger place than had previously been accorded to them. In ancient China this role was played in the earlier part of the period by Ch'u, later by Wu, and finally by Ch'in, another barbarian power, which finally conquered the entire system. In the Greek city-state system, Thebes, which increasingly challenged the pre-eminence of Sparta and Athens from early in the fourth century, and later Macedonia, were the main challengers to the traditional order. In sixteenth-century Europe, in which Spain was predominant, France became the principal challenger, and the eventual humbler of Spanish power before herself being challenged at the end of the following century). In the seventeenth century it was Sweden and United Provinces which were the rapidly rising powers, enjoying a few decades of greatness quite out of proportion to their size and long-term capabilities. In the eighteenth century, Russia, Prussia and Britain were the challengers, each threatening in their own areas the traditional power of Sweden, Austria and France. In the following century the main threats to the status quo came from Savoy–Sardinia in Italy, from Serbia in the Balkans, from Japan in the Far East and from Germany in Europe as a whole. Finally in the most recent period a similar role has been played within their own regions by Indonesia (under Sukarno), Vietnam and Iran (both under the Shah and his successors). As these examples show, the chief challengers are not necessarily among the most powerful states of their age. Their essential characteristic is that their power is rising and that they seek for themselves a position in society greater than has traditionally been accorded to them.

Most of the roles we have described so far appear, in one form or another, in almost every age. But there are others that appear in some societies and not others. Thus for example in ideological ages (such as the ages of religion and of ideology) there exists the role of *champion* of a particular faith: leader and evangelist. This was a role played by Sweden in the former period, and by China and Cuba in the latter. Sometimes there exists the role of *revisionist*, the aggrieved state, which believes it has suffered some wrong and demands that it be put right: this was the role played by Spain after 1714, by Austria after 1740, by France after 1815, by Russia after 1856 and by Germany after 1918, each challenging the status quo and eventually undertaking bilateral action to subvert it. In some ages there exists the role of *extortioner*, or blackmailer, the ally which demands an increasingly high price of its protector: such as Piedmont, committing France in 1859, and Austria, implicating Germany ever more heavily in the Balkans, especially from 1908 onwards. In the more unscrupulous ages, there exists the role of *victim*, the weak or disorganised state which is constantly at the mercy of aggressive neighbours, and sometimes gradually dismembered; as Poland was in the late eighteenth century, Turkey during much of the nineteenth and Lebanon in recent times.

So a variety of different roles are performed in different societies. And just as in smaller societies, the roles that are performed reflect characteristics of the society, as well as of the individuals within it, so in international society too, the roles that are undertaken reflect the nature and needs of each international society as much as those of particular states.

ROLES IN CONTEMPORARY INTERNATIONAL SOCIETY

If these are some of the roles that have traditionally been played in international society, let us now look, in rather greater detail, at the chief roles played by states in the contemporary world.

Here too the roles played reflect the character of the society as a whole.

The most visible and well-recognised role over recent years is that of the *superpower*. This is not exactly the same as any part that has been played in earlier societies. In an age of ideology such as this, superpowers are not merely states with greater power than any other (though they are this too[11]). They are also the political leaders of

11. At present at least; but it is not inconceivable that Japan, or China, could eventually become more powerful than the Soviet Union without adopting the role of "superpower".

their alliance, the source of ideological inspiration and fervour, even sometimes the fount of authoritative doctrine. Within their own alliance it is their task to co-ordinate strategy; to be a source of technical progress, economic aid and other assistance; if necessary to supply arms and political support. Further afield they are expected to give assistance to factions of similar beliefs in any part of the world, especially in any state where civil conflict is taking place (just as their predecessors, Athens and Sparta, had to do in another ideological age). They come, therefore, to represent a powerful centre of gravity, leading many others to cluster around them. On the one hand, groupings that are linked by genuine ideological sympathies require a leader to give guidance and support. On the other, the increased vulnerability produced by new weapons creates the need among smaller powers for protection and patronage, and so places larger demands on the superpowers.

Complementary to this is the role of ideological *ally*. This usually creates a relationship more or less dependent on the superpower. The degree of dependence can vary, not only according to how far an ally is externally threatened, but on how far it is internally vulnerable. Countries that are seriously threatened in either way are willing to abandon some of their independence for the sake of the reliable support of a superpower: thus allies in one part of the world – for example smallish states in Indo-China or Latin America – are far more dependent on American aid and succour than those of Western Europe, since they often cannot survive without it. The role demanded of such allies is one of general support, verbal as much as military, in confrontations with the opposing alliance. Thus East European states are expected to vote with their Soviet ally within the UN and other international organisations, whatever the subject being discussed. Though a greater independence of action is allowed and taken in the Western world, there is a limit here too to the degree which can be shown, set ultimately by the need for the retention of US forces in Europe. Even where the role does not demand direct military dependence on the superpower it may be replaced by a form of economic dependence that is equally inhibiting.

The role of *neutral* also changes. Because those who are ideologically committed demand an equal degree of commitment from all other states, in such a society "neutralism" acquires a pejorative flavour: as when it is condemned by John Foster Dulles as immoral. Neutrals now term themselves as "non-aligned" (implying that alignment is seen as the normal state). None the less those that are non-committed, at first relatively few (since they forfeit the economic and military benefits of alignment), acquire a recognised position within society. Such countries as Sweden, India, Ireland, Austria provide the forces for UN peace-keeping operations; provide mediators (such as Count Bernadotte and Ambassador Jarring), in disputes; provide the first four Secretaries-General of the UN (Norway was still regarded as neutral at the UN's foundation). And they have had a more general role in breaking the log-jam in relations between the two main blocs. Thus individual non-aligned countries, such as Yugoslavia, India or Sweden, often have an important role as middlemen and compromisers in the overall struggle between the ideological alliances. And the non-committed groups in the Geneva disarmament talks and in the Helsinki review discussions succeed sometimes in launching new initiatives which prevent deadlock there.

The role of *balancer* also re-emerges in a new form. In a political sense the third world as a whole, as its name implies, represents such a balancing force between the blocs. Such countries as India and Egypt exploit this key position to some advantage, able to extort aid and other concessions from both sides. Most of the rest, instead of engaging in a self-conscious act of balancing, are willing to remain passive until wooed for their political support. In a military sense such powers are insignificant and do little to affect the military balance. Only China, as she emerges as a significant military power and detaches herself from the Soviet Union, begins to become a counterweight to the main superpowers, able to throw her weight from one side or the other as circumstances dictate. This maximises the power she can exert, though her reasons for changing are political and it is doubtful if she consistently supports the weaker side, as the role of balancer demands. All three of the great powers have an interest in showing themselves capable of friendship with either of the other two, and in this way increasing their bargaining power: for if any shows itself irrevocably committed to hostility to any other, the third can increase its own power by balancing between the two. Each must thus show itself as flexible and ideologically uncommitted as possible. For a time when the antagonism between Russia and China appeared the deepest of all, the US was able to perform the balancing role more effectively than either of the other two. Later, as China lost her own political inflexibility, she became the balancer and the US and Russia wooed her in turn. In general, however, ideological commitment prevents any state from consciously switching support from one side to the other, as the true balancer is required to do. For this reason Western Europe, which might otherwise have been in a position to perform a balancing role comparable to that of China, is in practice inhibited from doing so.

Fifth, the role of *rival* remains as significant as ever. There are a few states, in this as in earlier societies, whose attitude to the outside world is determined almost entirely by their relationship with a principal enemy, usually a close neighbour. Just as, in smaller societies, relationships with those who are close have far more influence than those with more distant acquaintances (p. 58), in international society too enmity with a neighbour will usually outweigh all more distant loyalties. On these grounds, because of the power of her fear of India, pro-Western Pakistan is willing to ally with communist China (even when China was at her most communist) against that threat. Conversely a deep-rooted antagonism will even burst the bonds of ideological alliances: so Hungary and Romania continue their long-standing confrontation, even within the confines of the apparently monolithic Warsaw Pact; Greece and Turkey maintain their own equally long-lived conflict within the constraints of common NATO membership. Traditional enmities of this kind are so intense and deep-rooted that they often survive even the most shattering political changes. So the deep-seated enmity existing between Cambodia and Thailand, Somalia and Ethiopia, Argentina and Chile survives even the most radical changes in political and ideological allegiance in one or both. Hostility between Honduras and El Salvador, Guatemala and Belize outlast all the traumatic political changes of Central America; that between Kenya and Uganda survives the successive revolutions in the latter country. Like neighbours in a domestic dispute, states become obsessed to the exclusion of almost any other concern by these most immediate preoccupations. Thus each will judge other states almost entirely by their willingness to take its own part in such disputes. Finally, even the most dominant political conflict of the age, that between the superpowers themselves, becomes in part a rivalry for pre-eminence – military, political and economic – between the two.

Sixth, there exists, perhaps more clearly than in most earlier societies, the role of *guru*, wise man, moralist or saint. A role of this kind – judge of the failings of other countries – was, as we saw, played for a time by the US in the days of Woodrow Wilson, and again later, to a lesser extent, in the days of Roosevelt, and of Dulles and Truman.[12] In the post-1945 world it was a role played above all by India, especially under Pandit Nehru, preaching to the rest of the world, above all to the great powers, about the way they should conduct their policies towards each other. More recently it is a part that has been adopted, in a more cautious form, by such states as Tanzania under President Nyerere and Zambia under President Kaunda, each judging the policies of the developed countries from the standpoint of the poor of Africa. Another variant of this role has been played by the Scandinavian states, seeking to persuade those more powerful than themselves to pursue more enlightened policies on disarmament and environmental questions, and themselves setting an example in their performance as peace-keepers and aid-givers. Finally, on a personal level, it might be said that the Secretary-General of the UN at any one time plays the part of the professional guru, put in his post precisely in order to be able to preach to all states of the world about their duties and responsibilities.

Seventh, there is the role of the *introvert*: the state that is absorbed in its own affairs and has little time or inclination to play a major part in the concerns of the outside world as a whole. Typical examples of states that have adopted such a role in the modern world are Burma, buried in her own problems in Asia, Paraguay, almost equally inward-turned in Latin America, Malawi and Cameroon in Africa. While motivated partly by a desire to devote themselves to the problems of development at home, this is by no means the whole explanation, since many countries at a similar level of development play a far more active international role. Nor is it a role confined to poor or weak states. Among developed countries, Switzerland, New Zealand, Austria and Finland have, for geographical and historical reasons, adopted a somewhat similar position. Even a very large and powerful state can sometimes, temporarily at least, take a similar stance of non-involvement; as did the US during the period of isolationism. Finally, there exists a variant of the role, which consists not so much in self-absorbed introversion as in self-conscious and deliberate abstention from participation in the affairs of a region, above all resistance to the demands of a neighbouring superpower – in other words independence, rather than isolation: the positions taken by France in de Gaulle's years, by Romania in Eastern Europe

12. It was against this tendency in US policy that Hans Morgenthau wrote his famous, but much-criticised, book, *Politics among Nations* (New York, 1948).

and by Mexico in the affairs of the western hemisphere, could be taken as examples of a social role of this sort.

Eighth, some states in the modern world are placed in the role of *pariah*, or whipping boy. This is of course not a role, like most of the others we have described, which is deliberately chosen, though it is one that the policies pursued by a state may make almost inevitable. The social importance of the role is that these are states against which any other state can with impunity vent its anger and moral indignation, and so demonstrate its own purity of intention and devotion to principle. The states chosen for the position are not necessarily those which, in terms of their crimes against humanity, might objectively be regarded as the most suitable incumbent: as for example Pol Pot's Cambodia or Nguema's Equatorial Guinea could reasonably have been. The states which have in fact mainly played the role in the modern world are South Africa and Israel. However well founded the grounds for indignation and denunciation against them may be, the vigour with which these are expressed may, like the scorn vented on the thief in the stocks in many European countries two or three centuries ago, serve other purposes as well. It may create a category of *universal* scapegoat for which many of the evils from which others suffer can be blamed; it may divert attention from the motes which the accusers have in their own eyes; it may pay dividends in the domestic political system of the accuser; and international credit and goodwill may be won by the accusing states even though they are in no way directly affected by the evils they denounce. In an ideological society, each bloc has an interest in placing its enemies in this role. So the Soviet Union will seek to win sympathy by denouncing the "neo-colonialism" or "cultural imperialism" of the US; the US and her allies will seek to place the Soviet Union in the dock for violations of human rights and other delinquencies; and each alike can freely blame the other for the tensions and instabilities of the world as a whole.

Ninth, there is the role of *fat cat*, Dutch uncle or sugar-daddy: the wealthy provider, the source not only of financial aid but of avuncular admonition and advice. So the major industrial powers, above all the US, the main source of aid funds in the world, are in a position (especially in controlling, as they do, the policies of the IMF and similar institutions) to deliver regular lectures about the economic policies pursued by receiving countries, and even to exercise substantial leverage to ensure that policy prescriptions they advocate are followed. The Soviet Union, as the main provider and only source of support for Cuba, Ethiopia, Vietnam and the countries of Eastern Europe, acquires an influence that is difficult for those countries to resist. OPEC countries, by raising oil prices in the early 1970s, not only increased their own wealth, but also could become the purveyors of substantial aid funds, enabling them too to acquire substantial influence on the policies pursued by the recipients. International financial institutions, such as the IMF and the World Bank, are in a sense *legitimised* sugar-daddies, which are able to give guidance and advice of an officially accepted kind (though this does not necessarily make it less resented by the recipients). Even international private banks can perform the role to a limited extent. So, in this society as in most others, money talks. Wealth itself provides an influence that is highly valued and gratefully exploited by those who wield it.

In contrast to these established roles, there are a number of anti-establishment postures which can be adopted. For example, there is the role of *revisionist*: the committed opponent of the existing social order, especially of the territorial status quo. This was the part adopted by Germany, Italy and Hungary after the First World War, each for different reasons demanding a revision of the Versailles settlement; and each eventually willing to threaten the use of force to secure change (a similar role had earlier been played by France, seeking to challenge the Vienna settlement, after 1815, and by Russia seeking, and eventually securing, revision of the provisions on demilitarisation of the Black Sea after 1856). After 1950 China was the main challenger of the established status quo: seeking and obtaining the recovery of Tibet, re-establishing Chinese control of territory disputed with India, threatening the offshore islands occupied by the Nationalists, demanding the recovery of Taiwan, and securing eventually the promised return of Hong Kong and Macao. Indonesia played a similar role in demanding and acquiring, largely by force, West Irian and East Timor, and seeking to win eastern Malaysia by the same means; as did Argentina in seeking to secure the return of the Falkland Islands from Britain, equally by force, and winning a settlement with Chile excluding the latter from rights in the Atlantic. Revisionists will be a disruptive force in any international society, usually the most important disruptive force. But the effect of their demands depends crucially on whether they seek to pursue them by force: thus Spain's claim to Gibraltar and West Germany's for reunification with East Germany have had little impact on the society as a whole because each state was willing to pursue them by peaceful means only.

The role of revisionist is one that is, in the terms we described earlier, essentially relational: it is directed at a *particular* state, that which at present controls the territory demanded. More disturbing to international society is the role of *revolutionary*: the state that demands radical change in international society as a whole. This is a position which has especially been adopted by a state which has recently undergone a revolution: an experience which often produces a revolutionary approach towards international society as a whole. So the Soviet Union, immediately after her own revolution in 1917, took up such a role: by establishing the Comintern, by repudiating all the previous undertakings of the Tsarist government and by her apparent support and encouragement of revolution in other countries, she issued, and was seen to issue, a challenge to the entire international order; though with time, and the consolidation of her own regime, she became, especially after 1950, increasingly a conservative, status quo power, concerned above all to hold what she already had rather than to stimulate dramatic change in other parts of the world (where she normally gave little support to revolutionary movements until they had already won power). For a time, in the 1950s and 1960s, her place as a revolutionary power was taken by China, actively preaching revolution in Africa and elsewhere. Later, after their own revolutions, a similar role was played by Cuba, Libya, Iran and Nicaragua. Each of these in their own parts of the world represented (or at least were seen to represent) the main focus for dissent, for radical social change and sometimes for revolution. As such they were resented and resisted by most other powers in those areas, which preferred the comfort of the status quo to the dangerous and unforseeable effects of revolutionary change, especially externally imposed revolutionary change. As in domestic societies, however, the revolutionary often becomes in time an accepted member of society, increasingly satisfied with its own position in the world; and its role as revolutionary is taken up, after the next domestic upheaval, by some new revolutionary power.

Finally, there is another form of anti-establishment role, more general in effect than that of the revisionist (concerned only with a particular, very specific change) but less clearly focused than that of the revolutionary state (which has a clear programme for change in all countries). This is the role of *maverick*: the unstable and unpredictable state, which may at any moment disrupt known relationships and established alliances by its unexpected conduct. Between the wars such a role was played by Italy, switching unpredictably from flirtation with the Western powers to alliance with Germany in order to engage in foreign adventures in Africa,

Albania and Greece in turn; by Japan, seeking first the slow dismemberment of China, then the establishment of a co-prosperity sphere, finally an assault on the Western presence throughout the area; and by Hungary, in turn adopting a communist, a parliamentary and then a violently right-wing regime, throwing in its lot with Hitler for a time in pursuit of the recovery of Transylvania, after the war attempting a brave but forlorn break-away from Soviet tutelage in 1956, and later still challenging her protector with experimental economic policies. More recently a fairly consistent maverick has been Iran, seeking to play off all the major powers before 1941, occupied by Western and Soviet forces during the war, engaging in brief and unsuccessful revolution against Britain and the West in 1953, later posturing as a substantial and strongly pro-Western military power, finally, after the revolution of 1979, rejecting the friendship of West and East alike, and seeking to export Islamic revolution to much of the Middle East. Others that could be placed in this category are Syria, the scene of countless military coups after her independence in 1946, subsequently in permanent conflict with her two powerful neighbours, Israel and Iraq, later still extending her dominance over Lebanon and defying most of her Arab benefactors in the process (supporting far-right Christians, socialist Druzes and dissident Palestinians in turn); North Korea, with a megalomaniac ruler, swinging unpredictably between Russian and Chinese tutelage and making occasional frantic forays against her southern neighbour (by land, sea, *under* the land or assassination); and Argentina, swinging from union-backed dictatorship to democracy, military junta and democratic regime once more, engaging in military adventure against Britain and military confrontation with Chile. By defying traditional categories and sudden switches of policy, such states lend a touch of the unpredictable and bizarre to the routine relationships which otherwise characterise modern international society.

All of the roles we have described represent distinct and relatively well-defined parts which have been played within the contemporary international society. Some of the roles are mutually exclusive; it is not possible for a state to be both an introvert and a revolutionary, a neutral and an ally. But others can be and often are combined, so that a state is not necessarily confined to a single role. The same states can (and do) play the roles of superpower and fat cat; of revisionist and rival; of guru and neutral. Partly for this reason no role will be played in exactly the same way by every power: there are always special factors in each state's situation (including the other roles which it is playing) which influence the way it performs a particular part. None the less each of the roles we have described is reasonably recognisable and easy to identify.[13]

The complete set of roles characterises the society as a whole. There is usually less difference between the way each role is played in the same society than there is in the way comparable roles have been played in different societies. The types of role adopted, therefore, and especially the way each role is played, has reflected the character of the society as a whole. Once again it is the structure of each society, especially its dominant ideology, which has had the greatest influence on the behaviour of each individual member-state.

CONCLUSIONS

Thus in different international societies a wide variety of national roles have been played. Some of these have been played by a single state only; some by some or many states; one or two by all. Some

13. K. J. Holsti, in his article "National Role Conceptions in the Study of Foreign Policy" (*International Studies Quarterly*, 14 (1970) 233–309), based on a study of speeches by high-level policy-makers in seventy-one countries in 1965–7, identified a somewhat different set of roles. These were the roles of "bastion of the revolution", regional leader, regional protector, active independent (such as Yugoslavia, India and Romania), liberation supporter, anti-imperialist agent (Soviet Union, Vietnam, Libya), defender of an ideological faith (US and East Germany), mediator and integrator (Canada, France, Yugoslavia), regional subsystem collaborator (members of the EEC and Comecon), "developer" (the role of aid-giver and helper of poor countries), "bridge" (a state that sees itself as the link between geographical regions (Pakistan, Cyprus), "faithful ally", "independent", "example", "internal development" (comparable to "introvert" in our classification). Not all of these are very clearly distinguished from each other (for example "active independent" and "independent", "liberation supporter" and "anti-imperialist agent"). A more important distinction from the categories suggested here results from the fact that Holsti was concerned with "role conceptions", as seen by leaders within each of the states concerned, rather than with the roles actually played, as is our concern here. In addition we have been concerned only with roles undertaken within international society generally, and have not therefore mentioned regional roles. Holsti contrasted the specific roles he identified with more general "orientations" such as isolationism, non-alignment, coalition formation, though again the distinction between role and "orientation" (a concept probably drawn from Parsons) is not always clearly defined.

have appeared in every society, even if they have taken different forms in each; others only in one or two.

It need not surprise us that some of the roles have appeared in every society so far known. This is because they have reflected basic attitudes and tendencies among states which must be expected to be found at all times: the desire to dominate other states, the desire to band together against common dangers, the desire to withdraw from the dangers of the hurly-burly, and so on.

Even so, each role, however basic, is played in a somewhat different way in different social environments. So the role of superpower is different in ancient China from what it is in ancient Greece; that of ally different in the age of ideology from what it is in the age of sovereignty; and so on. These changes in part reflect changes in the available means. Modern weaponry, and the means of delivering it, new systems of communication between states, the availability of radio and television propaganda, the closer economic ties that now exist between states, all of these bring about substantial changes in the way roles are played. The kind of diplomatic or commercial links that exist inevitably affect the way each state seeks to influence others. Above all, the differing roles reflect changes in the underlying motives of states: so the superpower, the ally, has different basic objectives in the age of ideology from those they had in the age of nationalism, for example. It is these changing motives, derived from the underlying ideology, which more than any other factor determine what roles are adopted in each age, and the different forms which the same roles may take in different societies.

As we saw at the beginning of this chapter, some roles imply an equal relationship, some an unequal one. The complementary roles of superpower and client state, fat cat and aid recipient, are inherently unequal: in each case some degree of domination by one state over another is implied. Other roles involve a more equal relationship: for example those of alliance member, trading partner or simply neighbour. Some roles represent a reaction *against* inequality: those of neutral or introvert are usually adopted by smaller and weaker states to reduce the dependence which a fuller participation in international life may involve. Others are designed to *protest* against inequality: those of rebel and (sometimes) maverick are adopted to agitate against the unacceptable inequalities which are found to exist in international society. The insecurity of international existence may bring into existence other roles: for example those of balancer, ally, alliance leader or (again) neutral. Others derive from economic relationships and differences in levels of development: those of fat cat and aid recipient, for example. In these ways the roles reflect basic features of international life.

As in domestic society, some roles are deliberately *chosen* by the state concerned: for example those of ally, revisionist or balancer. Others are chosen only half-consciously, as a response to a state's situation: for example those of introvert or rebel or even superpower. Others again are chosen not by the state most concerned but by other states or by society generally: that of pariah for example, which no state deliberately chooses but which may be none the less imposed on it.

Roles therefore, as in smaller societies, come about for different reasons, some relating to individual desires and some to social needs. They cover a spectrum, ranging from those which are in the fullest sense social roles, determined by society, to those which are individually chosen to satisfy individual purposes. At the first extreme, clearly filling a social function, are official roles: for example those of king, prime minister or policeman within states. Because of the disorganised state of international society it prescribes few official roles of this kind, but within this category would come that of the current President of the UN Security Council and General Assembly, and that of peacekeeper or mediator. Next, there are roles played within and for society, though they have no official status. Those of the elder, or the priest within states, and in international society the roles of balancer, guru and rebel are of this sort. Then there are private but bilateral roles, undertaken between different members of society but having no public function. The parts of neighbour, tennis partner (or opponent) and doctor/patient within states are within this category; corresponding roles in international society are those of ally, rival, aid donor or aid recipient. Finally, there are wholly personal roles, individually chosen: such as those of hermit or busybody or outlaw within states, or of neutral, maverick and revisionist in world society.

Sometimes the way a role is played is more important in determining its social significance than the fact that a role exists at all. This too may be either socially or individually determined. The character of the society as a whole may make it inevitable that a role is played in a particular way. Thus the unstable and conflict-ridden character of the ancient Chinese international society made it almost inevitable that the role of ally would be played in an opportunistic and unscrupulous way.[14] On the other hand in an ideological society, where alternative alliances are not normally available (since no state will ally with states of opposing ideology), the role of ally is a far more stable one. Even in the same society a role may be played quite differently by different states. Thus the role of neutral in the contemporary international society has been played quite differently by Sweden, an active participant in world affairs, a frequent peace-keeper and sponsor of initiatives on disarmament and the environment, from the way it has been played by Switzerland, which has avoided virtually all involvement in international politics (and has not even been willing to become a member of the UN). Similarly the role of ally has been played quite differently by East Germany and Romania; West Germany and France. The role of rebel has been played differently by Cuba, preaching loud-mouthed defiance but cautious in action, by Vietnam, undertaking armed intervention in neighbouring states, by Iran, providing the ideological inspiration to fanatical followers in other countries, and by Libya, arming rebels and plotting assassinations in other states. The role of fat cat and aid donor has been interpreted differently by Saudi Arabia and the Scandinavian countries, by the Soviet Union and the United States.

What causes a state to play a particular role in different societies? Sometimes this results simply from changes in power relationships. The US and Russia were not in a position to play the roles of superpower in the fifteenth century, any more than Spain and France could do so today. Sometimes it results not so much from a change in power bur from a change in government: a state comes to play the role of rebel as the result of a successful revolution, or decides to become a revisionist, or a neutral, or a maverick (or to seek to be one), because a different political party has taken control of the government. Or there may be a change of policy even without a change in government: a government may at a certain moment reach a decision to enter an alliance or to become an aid donor. Finally, the role adopted may change (or the way it is played, the "role performance", may change) because of changes in society as a whole and the prevailing ideology: so the coming of an age of ideological conflict caused states to adopt the role of ideological ally, or to play the role of superpower in a different way from the way they had been played before.

As in smaller societies, there may exist a conflict between the

14. Walker, *Multi-State System*, pp. 24–9.

different roles a state is called on to play. So a state may find it hard to play the role of rebel and supporter of revolutions elsewhere, at the same time as that of acknowledged great power (like the Soviet Union after 1945). Or it may find it hard to play the role of guru, wise preacher to the world, at the same time as having to protect national interests in neighbouring areas (like India in the early 1960s). It may find it hard to play the role of fat cat at the same time as retaining the role of champion of the poor (like OPEC countries in the 1970s). It may find it hard to play the role of balancer at the same time as that of rival to a particular power or powers (like Britain in the years before 1914)[15] Some degree of role-conflict is likely to be experienced by almost every state. In general the greater its participation in international affairs, the wider the range of different roles it is likely to play,[16] and the greater the consequent danger of role-conflict. Thus it is that the US today, more actively engaged in international affairs than any other power, may find it especially hard to reconcile the different roles which she plays (for example as ally of particular states, often non-democratic, such as Marcos' Philippines and Pakistan, and as protector of democracy generally; as defender of human rights, and as defender of the Western hemisphere, including such states as El Salvador, Honduras and Chile, against perceived threats from a hostile ideology).

But not only may a state experience conflict between the different roles it is expected or seeks to play. There may also be conflict between its own conception of its role and that of society generally. The clearest conflict of this kind arises in the case of the pariah or of any other equally unpopular role: no state is likely to see itself in that role whether or not other members of society do. But a conflict may also occur in other cases. The guru may see itself as the wise observer and helpful mediator, while other states may see it as the sanctimonious hypocrite or meddling busybody. The superpower may see itself as the brave leader and defender of truth and justice, while others see it as a dangerous fanatic or ambitious seeker for world power. These differences in role conceptions reflect deep-rooted

15. In the last thirty years of the nineteenth century, Britain, faced by this choice, preferred the role of rival, seeking any possible ally against France and Russia, to safeguard her position in Egypt and India; only as her fear of Germany increased from 1900 did she begin to attach more importance to the role of balancer, and sought therefore to settle her differences with France and Russia.
16. See Holsti, "National Role Conceptions", pp. 305–9.

conflicts within a society concerning appropriate social relationships. Only the general adoption of a common ideology implying clearly delineated social relationships, could (as in smaller societies) reduce conflicts of that kind.

The roles we have been concerned with in this chapter have mainly been the *characteristic* roles of each society. They are thus in the nature of the archetypes Weber was concerned with in discussing "ideal types". What this means is that a role may never exist in its purest and simplest form. The actual behaviour of particular states will always represent a version, a particular form, of each role. Because states play several roles, and because they interpret each in an individual way, there will be no state which will be simply "the balancer", "the rival", "the guru" (any more than there exists in smaller societies an individual who is simply "the priest", "the elder", "the criminal" and nothing else). The part which a state in fact performs is highly complex and highly specific. In distinguishing some of the more striking features of their behaviour – that is in identifying their principal roles – we may help to understand particular features of the relationships in which they engage. But we also may learn something about the kind of society within which those roles are played. Whether the roles are individually chosen or socially imposed, they dictate, or at least encourage, particular forms of behaviour. And it is the type of behaviour adopted which gives the specific character to each international society.

8 Status

STATUS IN DOMESTIC SOCIETY

The roles which individuals perform, therefore, establish a place for them within society. Each comes to be seen more clearly by other members: as father, insurance salesman, secretary of the local choral society and city councillor. But these roles alone do not go far enough in classifying them. Other members come to learn not only *what* roles their fellow members perform but what *kind* of role: good or bad, one to be imitated or avoided, to be respected or condemned.

They are therefore made aware not only of the *positions* which other members of society (including they themselves) occupy, but of their status; how that position is rated by society generally. That rating is essentially a social measurement: it may or may not correspond to that which would be made by any particular individual. The fact that one person has a high regard for Mr X, or that another despises him, is irrelevant. Neither fact can alter (or only in the most marginal way) the "status" that Mr X, or the position he occupies, enjoys. The status of an individual, or of a group, or of an occupation, is the status that they are accorded by society as a whole: their *social* status.

Status, in other words, measures the differential regard in which particular individuals, groups or positions are held generally within society. A ranking system of this kind exists in some form in every society.

Such a system may perform a number of social functions. It serves, for example, to indicate which types of behaviour or achievement are valued, and which therefore are to be stimulated and encouraged. It serves to secure respect and regard for those who already occupy particular positions in society, or who follow prescribed patterns of behaviour, and so to stabilise society and legitimise an existing social structure. It makes it more likely that those who fill inferior positions in society will willingly perform, for low reward, the tasks that are assigned to them and obey the injunctions of those who feel superior to them: because they have been taught that the positions they fill are ranked as inferior (and that they themselves are thus ranked as inferior), they may subject themselves to the demands of those who fill the positions ranked as superior (and who are thus themselves ranked as superior).

All of these represent *effects* of the establishment of a status system. It does not necessarily follow that they are the *causes* of such a system being established. Under a "functionalist" interpretation, measures of status will be established in order to secure the performance of necessary social functions: thus if leadership and creativity are required by "society", then these will be highly rewarded; if economic prosperity is required, economic success will be rewarded by high status; if administrative ability is most socially valuable, the highest status will go to the best administrators, and so on. This may imply a greater rationality in the way measures of status emerge than they in fact possess. They may, more simply, merely reflect the valuations which are widely held within each society. So a society which values war may accord a high status to soldiers, one which values art may afford a high status to artists and so on. Or, more simply still, the distribution of status may result directly from the self-interest of those involved: those who already possess positions of authority have an interest in being accorded a high social status and use their influence to secure it. However derived, the conceptions of status which are held will reflect the ideology of society as a whole: indeed they are a part of that ideology.

The measurement that is made of status may be based on a number of criteria. In some societies status is measured largely by *possessions*. So in some African societies high respect is accorded to those who own many head of cattle; in some Asian societies to those who possess many wives; in some North American Indian societies to those who own many blankets, coppers, or spoons; in traditional European and South American society to those who own large amounts of land; in modern industrial societies to those who own many cars, houses or swimming pools (or *large* cars, houses and swimming pools). The possessions may result from abilities and skills in other fields. But often it is the possessions which are admired, and become in themselves the source of status, rather than the activities which made them possible.

Another way status is measured is by *positions* held. So in traditional Indian society a priest may occupy a status above a warrior, a warrior above a lawyer, and a lawyer above a trader, for example. So in modern industrial societies a company director may be regarded as of a higher status than a dustman; a judge than a doctor; a doctor than a teacher; a white-collar worker than a blue-collar worker (irrespective of the incomes they earn and so of the wealth which they may possess).

Sometimes differences in status of this sort are marked by *titles*, seen as badges of rank. So aristocratic titles, professional qualifications, military ranks, positions in a government, may be used as ranking systems (for example as a measure of marriageability, or of precedence in seating at table, or of eligibility for receiving an invitation). Titles of this kind may only *reflect* a status that would be accorded anyway on other grounds: the university graduate is respected as a graduate not because he places the initials B.A. after his name. But sometimes titles can *create* a status that is independent of the position held. So the trade union leader or the business tycoon who is made a peer may acquire a higher social regard than they possessed before (and be regarded, at least by some, as more eligible as a son-in-law, or a dinner guest, even though their substantive achievements are in no way greater than before).

Status, in other words, can either be *ascribed* to particular positions, often inherited, regardless of individual merit; or it can be *achieved*, earned through attainment of a particular kind. Thus under the Indian caste system members of a particular caste could inherit, regardless of their own individual merits or actions, both an occupation and the status that went with it: that of a Brahmin, or of an untouchable, for example. In most modern industrial societies, on the other hand, high status normally results from individual achievement of some kind. But even there, the status enjoyed, for example, by a pop-star or a social worker, though achieved, does not necessarily correspond to the real contribution each makes to society under most valuations. In other words, status sometimes measures immediate public success rather than long-term public achievement.

But while measurement of status reflects the values which prevail in society generally, they also help to preserve and ossify those values. They do this by making *explicit* valuations which might otherwise only remain implicit. The Indian peasant who perhaps knows little of traditional Indian ethical teaching may none the less be deeply influenced by the reverence paid to the guru or saintly person. The medieval European who was little concerned about the abstract duty to go to war on behalf of his royal master might none the less be strongly impressed by the honour everywhere done to the successful soldier. In this sense the status system reinforces the effect of motives and roles in instilling the pervading ideology among the members of a society.

Status can be attached both to individuals themselves and to the roles that they play. Individuals may acquire high status because of what they are or because of what they do. Put differently, they may be admired not only because of the position they hold but because of their performance within that position. But an individual plays many roles, and may enjoy different types of status in each one. Mr X therefore may be seen as a good father but as a bad insurance salesman; may be respected for his activities as secretary of the music society, but despised for his activities as a city councillor.

Nor are judgments, either of the role or of the performance within it, necessarily uniform. Though, as we have seen, status is a social measurement, it is not necessarily a consistent one. There may be a majority judgement by society of the status of, say, policemen, politicians or pop stars; but there may be a minority judgement which is totally different. So each of these may enjoy high status in the eyes of a part of the community but a low status in the eyes of others. Even in speaking of the status of a particular occupation, therefore, we are speaking only of an approximate judgement, based on an average opinion of a job. In speaking of the status of an *individual*, we are speaking in still more imprecise terms. Not only do individuals enjoy many different kinds of status in the different roles they perform. The status they enjoy in each will vary in the judgement of different individuals and sections of society.

Different types of society, therefore, establish different systems for distributing status, corresponding to the ideology and valuations of society as a whole. The distribution which is established will influence conceptions of desirable behaviour and achievement, and so the motives of all its members.

STATUS IN INTERNATIONAL SOCIETY

The members of an international society too are classified and ranked in terms of status.

Once again the status we are concerned with here is primarily that of states. Individuals and groups have a particular status (or, more accurately, a set of status positions) within their own society. But their status in international society is to a considerable extent that of their own state. The political leader, the businessman, the trade union official are seen in their international dealings not just as leaders, businessmen and officials, but as *American* (or Australian or Albanian) leaders, businessmen and officials; and the adjective is nearly almost more important than the noun. To a considerable extent those in each category that come from a wealthy or otherwise successful state will feel themselves, and be widely felt, to have a superior status to their opposite numbers coming from a poorer or less successful state. In their international dealings their national origin will affect the regard in which they are held much more than their personal abilities (for example as political leaders, businessmen or trade union officials).

In international society, therefore, importance has always been attached to the relative respect and honour accorded to each state. In the ancient Chinese multi-state system there existed a clear competition for status and regard: There was a widely accepted hierarchy of states in order of their power: with the "hegemon" at the top, a few large states, especially the league-leaders immediately below, and smaller and dependent states, some of them in effect colonies, held in least regard of all. The number and scale of the meals served at banquets for visiting statesmen or diplomats were taken as measures of the status of the giver as well as the honour being accorded to the receiver.[1] This division of status was formalised in the fact that increasingly it was only the smaller states that were expected to make diplomatic visits to pay their respects, while the larger ones made no such visits in return.[2] Among the Greek city-states the league leaders – Athens, Sparta and later Thebes – were, being larger and more powerful, of higher status than their followers and far more so than their colonies. The status of the cities was not measured by power alone, however, but by the respect secured by each for their political institutions, artistic accomplishments, success in the Olympic games and in other ways. In sixteenth-century Europe there was a competition for prestige among rulers, exhibited in the competitive display of ambassadors to foreign courts, or in the sumptuous receptions given to a visiting monarch. In the seventeenth and eighteenth centuries, sovereigns competed in the precedence to be accorded to their ambassadors in a foreign court, the titles to be

---

1. Cf. R. L. Walker, *The Multi-State System in Ancient China* (Hamden, Conn., 1959) p. 77: "The states strove to outdo each other in their ceremonies to such an extent that their ability to put on a rich ceremonial feast frequently determined their position among their associates".
2. Ibid., pp. 80–1.

accorded to themselves as rulers, the number of guns fired in royal salutes,[3] in the splendour of their court and in other ways. In the nineteenth century there was concern to secure recognition as a "great power", as well as to win success in the more general struggle for prestige, a struggle that was sometimes particularly fierce among the smaller states of the era (between Serbia and Bulgaria, Romania and Greece, for example). And in the modern world there is a similar concern to win the status believed to be associated with the possession of nuclear weapons or of a permanent seat in the Security Council.

In international as in domestic society, the competition for status has sometimes taken the form of rivalry in *display*. Just as the ostentatious display of wealth – in conspicuous consumption, or even the conspicuous destruction of wealth – is used as a method of demonstrating high status in domestic society, so it has been in many international societies. This was seen, for example, in the competition of Francis I and Henry VIII at the Field of the Cloth of Gold, where each vied with the other to demonstrate the magnificence and finery of their court. It was shown in the concern at the same period that ambassadors abroad should demonstrate, by the richness of their apparel, equipage and retinue, the opulence of their masters, and in the desire of the monarchs who received them to reciprocate in style.[4] It was shown a little later in the competitive building of royal palaces, such as Versailles, Sans Souci and Schönbrunn, which equally were believed to enhance the glory and reputation of the ruler who built them, and so of his state. It was shown in the ostentatious display of hospitality provided for a visiting foreign monarch: for example the

3. In its treaty with Algiers of 1681, the French government secured an undertaking that a vessel of the "emperor" of France would be greeted by a salute of more guns than would be accorded to any other ruler. At a later date the rulers of the princely states of India engaged in fierce competition among each other concerning the number of guns by which they would be saluted by the British authorities on official occasions – whether they were "three-gun" or "five-gun" rulers.
4. See G. Mattingly, *Renaissance Diplomacy* (London, 1955) p. 35: "Throughout the Renaissance the ceremony increased in splendour. The welcoming committee would often be headed by a great magnate – a peer or a grandee, perhaps even by a prince of the blood. The streets might be hung with banners and garlands, and the ambassadorial procession in its most splendid apparel would advance to the sound of music (really solemn embassies carried their own trumpeters), of clanging bells and booming cannon. The citizens might oblige with a pageant in appropriate allegory, fountains might run wine, and certainly the whole affair would wind up in a stately public banquet."

month-long entertainment provided by Catherine the Great for Joseph of Austria, or the sumptuous celebration of the visit of Peter the Great to Paris in 1717. And in more recent times it has been shown in the organisation of lavish royal weddings, funerals, coronations and other state occasions, sometimes used as the opportunity to impress foreign visitors and the watching world as a whole.

In many international societies an important form of this display, and an important symbol of status generally, has been the creation of large, well-equipped, efficient and above all spectacular armed forces. Though military expenditure has had an obvious functional purpose – to secure success in war – it has often been intended equally, and sometimes even more, to *impress* rather than to fight or deter. From the time when royal armies began to be established from the fifteenth century onwards, their purpose was always to proclaim the glory and authority of the monarch as much as to fight wars (for which mercenary contingents might have been more efficient). The concern of Henry VIII to build a powerful navy, and of Charles V to establish his famous *tercios*, though it had a military purpose too, was in part to create forces that would do honour to themselves and their royal houses. One reason that Louis XIV took such a personal interest in the size and equipment of France's armed forces (which became over half a million strong during his reign) was because he saw them as adding to the 'glory' which he valued above all other things. The military parades and tattoos, naval displays and manoeuvres, and in more recent times the air-shows and fly-pasts, which governments over the centuries have organised have been intended to demonstrate the might and prestige of their nations, as much as their efficiency as fighting forces. In many cases states would increase expenditure on a particular type of armament above that of another power as an overt demonstration of its superiority. So Lopez of Paraguay built up the strongest army in South America partly because he was planning for the possibility of war, but at least equally to demonstrate that Paraguay was a power that was to be considered the equal of her larger neighbours. Germany launched her naval building programme at the beginning of this century partly to promote her strategic interests, but above all to support her claims to be regarded as a "world power". Japan built herself a powerful navy after the First World War not because she anticipated the need to use it in the forseeable future, but as a means of demonstrating her emergence as a world power; and sought to negotiate under the Washington Agreement, a naval tonnage which recognised that fact.

Another measure of status in international society has been the *titles* accorded to rulers (just as titles and ranks have so often been the prized badges of status within states). In the age of dynasties rulers prided themself on their ranks and "styles", and were often insistent that they were used by the representatives of other rulers, for example in formal agreements or on state occasions. Thus the ministers of Charles V were able to describe him by an interminable list including several kingships, innumerable dukedoms and lesser titles, culminating in the appelations "lord of Asia and Africa" and "king of Jerusalem". Conflicts over such titles were almost as intense as those over territories themselves. Henry VIII intensified his conflict with France by styling himself "king" of France long after England had ceased to hold a square foot of French territory outside Calais (a claim that was maintained on British coins until the early nineteenth century); just as the Hapsburg rulers continued to style themselves dukes of Burgundy, and the French kings dukes of Naples and Milan, long after they had been expelled from those territories. The opening of the negotiations for the peace of Westphalia were held up for two years as a result of conflicts concerning titles and the precedence which they carried with them.

This concern was demonstrated in other ways. In the eighteenth century there was considerable eagerness for the more prominent monarchs to acquire the suffix "the Great"; that honour being appropriated in turn by Louis of France, Peter of Russia, Frederick of Prussia and Catherine of Russia. There was equal concern with the ranks which rulers could claim for themselves. So in Germany margraves, who were the rulers in many states, wished to become dukes; dukes to become electors; and electors to become kings. Thus the dukes of Bavaria and of Hanover struggled for years to win from the emperor the title of "Elector". The Elector of Prussia struggled almost as long to win for himself the right to style himself "King".[5] Even in the nineteenth century such questions remained matters of passionate concern. After the Congress of Berlin of 1878, under which Serbia had been granted *de jure* independence, its ruler Prince Milan negotiated with great assiduity before being graciously permitted by Austria to style himself "King" in 1882 (causing

5. The Duke of Savoy, by securing for himself the island of Sardinia and the right to declare himself its king in 1720, considered this a promotion, even though he was henceforth known as the ruler of a wild and insignificant Mediterranean island, rather than of the ancient and cultured Duchy of Savoy.

considerable jealousy in Montenegro, the ruler of which remained a mere duke even though his country also was an independent state). Those particularly concerned to assert their prestigious status claimed the title of "emperor". So Louis XIV, in his dealings with the Barbary states, used the title "emperor" (in rivalry with the German emperor); Catherine of Russia claimed the title; while Victoria, at Disraeli's urging, named herself "Empress of India" (an example to be imitated in a later age by the ruler of the minuscule Central African Republic, who had himself crowned "Emperor" and his state renamed "Central African Empire").

Corresponding with these measures of a high status were the various graduations indicating low or subservient rank. In ancient China there existed a class of dependent or "attached" states which were virtually colonies.[6] In Ancient Greece, apart from colonies there were very small states which became tributary to the more powerful and virtually under their control (as a number of neighbouring states were to Thebes, as Plataea was to Athens and Thebes by turn, and as Potidea was sometimes to Corinth and sometimes to Athens). In Europe, from the time the state system emerged in the late Middle Ages, there existed a wide variety of mini-states – principalities, duchies, margravates, free cities, associations of knights (such as the Teutonic Knights and the Knights of Malta) – which took no part in the normal diplomatic relations of the continent and were scarcely regarded as sovereign states in the full sense (some were theoretically under the "suzerainty" of other rulers). During the age of colonialism some territories which were not claimed as colonies were held to be "protectorates" or "protected states", under the protection or "paramountcy", of a major power, and deprived of the freedom to conduct their own foreign relations. In the same way during the dissolution of the Ottoman Empire a succession of states – Serbia, (after 1830), Romania (after 1856), Bulgaria (after 1878), East Rumelia (from 1878 to 1885) and Crete (after 1897) – were recognised as "autonomous" rather than independent, as was Tibet after 1904 in the Far East. Other states were deprived of a part of the normal attributes of sovereignty through the imposition of "extra-territorial jurisidiction": external powers asserted the right to try their own nationals in their own courts within their territories, a disability only gradually thrown off (by Japan during the 1890s, by Turkey in 1923, by Egypt in 1936, by China in 1943 and by the Gulf States only in

6. See Walker, *Multi-State System*, p. 25.

1971). The lowest status of all was that of colonies, without any claim to be independent states; though even among these a distinction was made in some places between "crown colonies", falling directly under the administration of the colonial power, and others which enjoyed limited rights of self-government from the beginning.

The competition for status was often expressed in the struggle for diplomatic precedence. Before the Congress of Vienna there were few rules governing this question and it was for the ruler receiving the ambassadors to determine their relative status. There was thus intense competition among all the powers to persuade the host government to accord superior precedence to their own representatives. Louis XIV was determined that his ambassadors be accorded a precedence above that of all other states at every court in Europe; and above all that they should be granted a precedence over that of the Spanish ambassadors. On his instructions the attendants of the French ambassador in London fought a pitched battle with those of the Spanish ambassador to establish their master's prior rights. Somewhat similar struggles took place at other courts. There was a similar and simultaneous struggle over the dipping of flags by ships at sea. A major cause of the first Dutch war between England and the United Provinces was the demand of each power that ships of the other should dip their flags when they met in the North Sea and the Channel. Once again Louis XIV was especially insistent on the superior rights of France in this respect, and French ships fought armed engagements against both the Spanish (1685) and the Dutch (1687) to demand the deference which they held was appropriate to the French sovereign.

A somewhat similar concern was shown in the competition during the nineteenth century for the status "great power". This was not a vague courtesy title with little meaning, which any ambitious state might arrogate to itself, but a definite position within society, carrying clearly defined rights and responsibilities exercised only by particular, named, states. The term came to be applied after the Napoleonic wars to states which were members of the "Concert of Europe" or, more accurately, which took part in the conferences of such powers which occurred regularly from 1814 onwards. These consisted at first of Russia, Austria, Britain, Prussia and after 1818, when she was readmitted, France. In 1856 Turkey was formally accepted as a member of the European Concert (but was not admitted by most to the status of a "great power"). Later in the century Italy was, with some hesitation, accepted as such a power; as was the US, in effect, from 1906 onwards. All such powers jealously defended that status. A humiliation at the hands of another power might be felt to put that status in peril, so that a failure to respond to a challenge would be seen as a weakness that was incompatible with the honour of a "great power". One of Austria's main reasons for seeking to crush Serbia in 1914 was that she believed that her status as a great power would be prejudiced if she failed to respond with sufficient vigour to her archduke's assassination: as Conrad, the Austrian Chief-of-Staff, put it, "it was not a question of a knightly duel with poor little Serbia. . . . nor of punishment for the assassination; it was much more the highly practical importance of the prestige of a Great Power."[7] An Austrian foreign office official told the British Ambassador in Vienna that Austria-Hungary was determined to take action against Serbia, whatever action Russia might take, because she "would lose the position of a Great Power if she stood any more nonsense from Serbia".[8] For Russia at the same moment the same consideration was almost equally important: at the meeting of the Russian Council of Ministers immediately after the assassination, Sazonov, the Russian foreign minister, after priding himself on the moderation which Russia had shown over the previous decade (Russia had, despite impassioned pleas from the Balkan states, totally failed to respond to the Austrian annexation of Bosnia-Herzegovina six years earlier), declared that "Germany had looked upon our concessions as so many proofs of weakness: if Russia now abandoned under threat her historic mission [to protect the interests of the Slav peoples] she would be considered a decadant state and would have had to take second place among the Powers."[9] Nor was Britain any less touchy about the matter. In his famous Mansion House speech of 21 July 1911, Lloyd George declared that it was "essential in the highest interests, nor merely of this country but of the world, that Britain should at all hazards maintain her prestige among the great powers": if she had allowed herself to be treated "as if she were of no account in the cabinet of nations", the peace so obtained, "would be a humiliation intolerable for a great country like ours to endure".

In some societies the demand for status has been expressed in territorial ambitions. In the age of dynasties the ruler who prided himself on his many titles was priding himself on his widespread

7. S. B. Fay, *The Origins of the World War* (New York, 1940) vol. II, p. 158.
8. Ibid., p. 247.
9. D. C. B. Lieven, *Russia and the Origins of the First World War* (London, 1983) pp. 142–2.

territorial possessions. Similarly in the age of sovereignty the extent of a ruler's possessions was often seen as a source of pride. In the nineteenth century the struggles between France and Prussia over Alsace-Lorraine, between Bulgaria and Greece over Macedonia, between Turkey and Russia over Kars and Batum, were seen by both parties as contests over status as much as over territory. And at the end of the century the demand for colonies (though it sometimes also had an economic strategic motivation) eventually came to be mainly another manifestation of the demand for great power status. The British people took pride in possessing an empire on which the sun never set. Bismarck, though he had once called himself "never a man for colonies", had by the mid-1880s succumbed to the ambitions of many of his people for such visible trappings of national power. And the eagerness which both Germany and Italy showed for new colonies (having arrived late in the race by reason of their late access to nationhood) in the years before the First World War demonstrated how strong was the belief that colonial possessions were the prized symbol of great power status.

That belief was an example of the fact that in international societies, as in other societies, there are often particular *status symbols* which become the object of competition among the members. In one age these may be royal titles and kingly munificence: in another royal palaces and triumphal arches: in another well-drilled regiments, strategic railways and ever larger dreadnoughts; in another space exploits, inter-continental missiles and ever more powerful nuclear weapons. Which are the symbols that are seen as significant in each age will vary according to prevailing beliefs. In one age to have been crowned by the pope was a supreme symbol of the emperor's status, a privilege accorded to few; while to Napoleon it was a symbol of status *not* to have been crowned by the pope but by himself alone. In one age lavish expenditure on royal pleasures and sumptuous display is seen as a source of pride: in another as a source of contempt. For Maximilian I in the early 1500s to be without an army was a source of shame; for Costa Rica today it is a source of pride. What does not vary is the desire among states in every age for prestige; not merely for respect but for marks of respect from other states. And the kind of prestige which is aspired to will in each case be a reflection of the values that prevail within international society as a whole.

STATUS IN CONTEMPORARY INTERNATIONAL SOCIETY

Competition for status remains a major factor in contemporary international society. Some of the forms which that competition takes are similar to those seen in earlier times.

Competitive display, for example, still occurs in various forms. Governments vie with each other in the splendour of the receptions they offer to visiting statesmen; in the lavishness of the parties they throw on national days; in the magnificence of the airports and highways by which visitors from abroad are to be impressed. Ambassadors of even the poorest states drive around in expensive limousines to demonstrate that they deserve equal respect with those of the richest. States compete to host the Olympic games and other major sporting events, so that they can show off to the world the quality of the facilities they can provide and their efficiency in organising such functions. They lay on impressive demonstrations of their armed forces on national days and other occasions, organise lavish presidential inaugurations, coronation ceremonies and other state occasions (so the Shah of Iran is said to have spent hundreds of millions of dollars in the celebration he organised of his state's alleged 2500th birthday).

There continues to be competition concerning diplomatic representation. In a sense there are (as in smaller societies) two contrary tendencies at work. On the one hand there is the concern of the small and weak to enjoy equal regard with the large and the powerful: a process of levelling down. This is seen in the demand for "sovereign equality" among states. Every country now, however small it may be, claims the right to send "ambassadors" (rather than the "ministers" previously sent by smaller states) and demands they should receive them from other states as well. Each demands to be accorded equivalent respect on ceremonial occasions: there thus continues to be controversy concerning such matters as the relative degree of courtesy accorded to a visiting dignitary, or the level of greetings offered at airports (so that the foreign minister of the Congo calls off an official visit to London because he feels that the rank of the official who greets him at the airport is not sufficiently elevated). There is competition in the effort to establish impressive diplomatic premises abroad. There is even competition in the number of representatives sent abroad, so that even very small states feel they must have at least a dozen or so posts and send ambassadors to distant foreign capitals where they may have little business to do. There is intense competition to be represented within UN bodies and committees: because of this competition it becomes almost impossible to set up a UN committee with less than forty-five members, and occasionally the only way to satisfy the competing claims is to create a "Committee of the Whole" in which all 160 member states are represented.[10]

This demand for equality among the weak, however, is matched by a corresponding concern among the large and powerful for recognition of their superior status. These wish for various kinds of distinction to be maintained. Though the term "Great Power" is no longer much used (at least in the precise sense previously employed), the concept of "superpower" is similar in effect. Though China publicly denies any desire to be recognised as a superpower, she does not conceal her wish to enjoy a respect appropriate to her size (for example in her adoption of the role of aid-giver, despite her own economic backwardness, her refusal to be upstaged by the Soviet Union or Japan and her determination to teach her contumacious neighbour Vietnam "a lesson"). There is intense pressure among the larger and more powerful states to enjoy the privileges of permanent membership of the Security Council: Japan, Brazil and other states lobby openly to be accorded that status. There is competition (among continents as well as among individual states) for other international positions: to provide the next Secretary-General of the UN, to secure senior posts within the organisation, to provide the director-generals of specialised agencies and the chairmen of prominent committees. Among smaller groups similar contests can be seen: Italy seeks equality of treatment with France and Germany within the EEC; Argentina with Brazil in Latin American institutions; Pakistan with India in South Asian affairs; Iraq with Egypt, and Syria with Iran, in Middle East bodies. Among developing countries generally there is competition for leadership of the Non-Aligned Movement or of the Group of 77.

There is also competition, as in earlier days, over levels of armaments. Again this in part reflects genuine apprehensions concerning defence needs. But once more it is to a substantial degree an expression of the desire of governments, and especially of their armed

10. This was the final outcome of prolonged disagreements about representation on the UN committee set up to consider north–south economic relations in 1975–6.

forces, to secure high national status. The desire to acquire nuclear weapons reflects at least as much a desire to acquire the *standing* of a nuclear power as to acquire the defensive capability that such weapons afford (Britain openly admits that she needs such weapons partly to secure a "place at the top table"). Existing nuclear powers compete to build warheads and missiles of ever-increasing size and complexity, or "strategic defence" systems of ever-increasing cost, as much for reasons of prestige as of defensive needs. Middle-sized powers seek to acquire supersonic aircraft, new radar scanning devices or air-to-sea missiles for similar reasons. So rivalry takes place at many different levels. While the rapidly rising cost of modern weapons, and their ever-increasing sophistication, means that only the richest and largest states can compete at the highest level, every state continues to compete, often with particular neighbours and rivals, at its own level; a competition which is at least as much about status as it is about military power.

But there are also new forms of competition hardly known in earlier days. One of these, as we saw earlier, is economic competition. The desire for economic development is not exclusively competitive. It is of course desired for its own sake. But it now acquires a strong competitive element. The very word "development" has a *comparative* meaning: it denotes being like a developed state, a condition to which nearly all poor states aspire. "Growth rates" are continually compared, and become a matter for envy or self-respect. Standards of living, now more visible than ever, with better communications and better statistical measures, are seen nearly always in relative rather than absolute terms. Governments are judged by the number of steel mills, hydro-electric dams or nuclear power stations they can boast. These are the status symbols of the contemporary age, which every country of the world competes to display. Keeping up with the Joneses in international society means above all keeping up in visible demonstrations of affluence of this kind.

As in smaller societies, however, there is no exclusive measure of status. New ways of measuring a state's performance begin to be employed, more varied than in most earlier ages. Though the dominant élite may think mainly in terms of military power or economic development, other groups become concerned about different types of attainment. Some will see the establishment of good social services or an effective health system as an important standard of achievement: so Scandinavian countries may be admired for their performance in this respect (while conversely the US and Japan, for all their economic achievements, may in this respect be rated badly). Others attach importance to environmental standards: so Britain may win credit for clean air and clean rivers, and lose it for acid rain. Cultural attainment will be seen by some as a source of status: so the winners of piano competitions, film festivals, Oscar awards, literary prizes, secure glory for their countries as well as for themselves. Scientific achievements can have the same effect: countries are compared in terms of the number of space shots they have undertaken or Nobel prize winners they have provided, and the discoverers of a cure for cancer will win glory not only for themselves but for the countries from which they come. Sporting victories can be (as in ancient Greece) a source of pride and satisfaction for those states which are successful. In all these ways a nation's status can be secured in international society from a much wider range of achievements than was normally the case in earlier times.

Because of this variety of standards, a state (like individuals in smaller societies) does not occupy a single ranking within the social hierarchy. It may be admired in one respect and condemned in another. A state may be afforded top place for its military power but condemned for the inequalities in its society; it may be admired for its scientific achievements but condemned for its poor record on human rights; applauded for its growth rate but detested for its undemocratic system of government. And so on. This may have the effect that every state can pride itself on its attainments in one respect or other; and can (like individuals in smaller societies) console itself for its lack of respect on one count by its widely admired performance on another.

Yet for all this variety of measurement the hierarchy of power continues to be the most fundamental of all. For it is the measure on which many of the others are in the final resort dependent. While military power may depend on economic success, there can be no economic performance at all by the country that cannot defend itself. A "major" or "first-class" power, today as in earlier days, does not mean one with a high cultural, educational or scientific level, nor even one that provides a high level of material well-being for its people. It means a state of great military power. So Japan, having gratefully opted out of the military race in the aftermath of war, is later constrained to re-enter it, without any visible threat to her security, because her leaders see it as a significant source of status. China for all her poverty, covets nuclear weapons. So long as warfare remains a normal activity among states, military capacity will continue to be an important measure of status among them. Only in so far as that danger declines will a different standard of measurement, reflecting a different value-system, come to be more widely used for determining the respect to be accorded within international society.

CONCLUSIONS

In different international societies, therefore, differing criteria of status have been established. The measure used is one of the principal factors characterising each society. It establishes a standard of desirable achievement, and so of desirable behaviour by states. It is thus a measure of the society's values. A militaristic type of international society will attach high status to a state that excels in military prowess. A society which values colonisation will lend status to the state which is most successful in that venture. A society which is deeply concerned about economic achievement will attach high status to the state which succeeds in economic terms. And so on.

Each international society will establish status *symbols* appropriate to the differing criteria they use. So the main status symbols in the society which reveres military success will be the triumphal arch, royal insignia and the amount of territory conquered. In the society which accords high status to imperial power, the symbols of status are the panoply of vice-regal splendour, royal durbars and the roll-call of colonies acquired. In a society where high status is accorded to economically successful states the symbols of status may be the parity of the currency, the volume of export markets won or the rate of growth. If an international society were to come about where high status was attached to the level of culture attained, the appropriate status symbols might be the proportion of the population who attend university, the number of world-famous poets, painters or composers a country has produced, or the number of concert orchestras and art galleries it can boast.

Status systems are important because they may not only *reflect* valuations, and so motivations, but *create* them. The fact that a particular type of state is accorded honour within a particular society may lead other states to adopt similar policies. The fact that John of Bohemia won glory for himself by his successful chivalric exploits encouraged other princes and knights of the age to seek similar glory by similar means. The fact that Britain and other countries won prestige by the possession of a world-wide empire meant that the states newly emerging at that time – Germany, Italy and Japan – were inspired with the ambition to win comparable status by comparable methods. The fact that Japan is so widely respected for her economic performance over the last forty years has inspired countries emerging to independence – such as South Korea and Singapore – to hope for similar international regard by similar success.

The measure of status established in each society is thus a reflection of its value-system: in other words of its underlying ideology. The criteria adopted in measuring status are implicit in the beliefs and attitudes of each ideology. Conceptions of status, therefore, are unlikely to change without a change in the underlying ideology itself. Here too, as in the case of motives and roles, it is the ideology which is ultimately the decisive factor. It is this which will determine aspirations, ambitions and actions alike; and, in influencing these, it will influence also the conceptions which are held concerning the kind of state, and state activity, that are most to be admired and imitated.

9 Conflict

CONFLICT IN SOCIETY

There is no society without conflict. Because the desires and beliefs of individuals never coincide, there must sometimes be disagreements among them. Because interests diverge, there must always from time to time be disputes. Societies differ, therefore, not in the fact of conflict but in the *type* of conflict that occurs, and in the way it is expressed and regulated.

The most frequent source of conflict is competition for scarce resources: wealth, land, status, authority, influence or affection. Because there is not enough of any of these for all to have as much as they want, each must be shared. Conflict occurs, in the first place, about how they should be divided; and, in the second, about how disputes on such questions are to be resolved.

Since, as we saw, individuals belong to many different societies, each is involved in many kinds of conflict. Conflict occurs at different levels: in the family, in the neighbourhood, in a national political system and in the world as a whole. The individual is involved in different degrees at each of these levels.

Some of these conflicts are internal – within the group – and some external. While conflicts within the group will divide and weaken it, external conflicts – conflicts of the entire group with another group – may unite and strengthen it. The solidarity and cohesion of a family may be destroyed by the disputes which divide its members; but they may be strengthened by a conflict between the family as a whole and that of a neighbour. The unity of the work-force in a factory may be weakened by divisions among the different unions to which they belong; but may be re-established by a dispute with the factory's owners. Conflict at one level may therefore help to bring about cohesion at another. Conversely if conflict within one group is sufficiently acute, despite its members' common interest against another, then it may be exploited by groups which are better able to resolve their own divisions. In other words the capacity to engage effectively in conflict at one level may depend on the capacity to resolve it at another.

Individuals not only belong to different societies – local, regional, national and international – but to different groups within each society. Each society and group may be involved in conflict with other groups or other societies. Individuals may have to choose what position they will take in each of these conflicts. And because most of their interests today are collective interests (pp. 117–18 above), they sometimes have to choose between the different collectivities to which they belong: between family or trade union, between trade union and enterprise, between class and profession, between state and international organisation.

The social significance of conflict depends on the means used to resolve it. Though conflict at each level must always be divisive, the *extent* to which it divides will depend on how far mutually acceptable procedures can be found for resolving it. Because conflict weakens a society, each society will seek to establish means for resolving it which will reduce its destructiveness. Most members most of the time will be willing to make use of those procedures. Only where a sufficient number, exercising sufficient power, find them wholly unacceptable, will the entire system for conflict-resolution which society has established come under challenge (for example in revolution).

Within most national societies some fairly generally acceptable means for resolving conflict have usually been established. Today it is above all *between* societies – that is, within international society as a whole – that no effective system for conflict-resolution exists. In that society conflicts continue, in many cases, to be settled by the time-honoured arbitrament of war. In that society, therefore, above all conflict continues to threaten the integrity and viability of the social organism as a whole.

CONFLICT IN INTERNATIONAL SOCIETY

In international society as in all others, some conflict is inevitable. There too the desires and beliefs of states can never be identical. There too interests diverge. There too competition takes place for scarce resources: trade, territory, status, security, influence or goodwill. And there too, because each of these is insufficient to satisfy the demands of all, conflict occurs both over how they should be divided; and over what principles should determine that division.

Some of the conflict in international society is among individuals: two cousins living in different countries may dispute the inheritance of property. Some is between groups: companies based in different states may compete in take-over bids; international unions may undertake strike action against a trans-national corporation operating in several countries. But by far the most serious type of conflict occurs between states. These dispose of resources and means of destruction far greater than are ever available to individuals or groups. Their conflicts, moreover, determine the interests of the individuals and groups which belong to them; and, by their destructiveness, have a decisive effect on the welfare of both. For this reason it is the conflicts of states that are of greatest significance in the operation of international society.

Conflicts between states, like those of individuals in smaller societies, result often from a conflict of interests. A state with a developed manufacturing industry has an interest in open markets, which may conflict with that of a less-developed state in the protection of its infant industries. An oil-producing country has an interest in high prices for oil, which conflicts with that of consumer states, both rich and poor, in low prices. A militarily powerful state has an interest in ensuring that neighbouring regions do not come under hostile influence: an interest which may conflict with the interest of other countries in that region in retaining their political independence. Most simply of all, one country may have an interest in the recovery of territory which once belonged to it, which conflicts with that of another in retaining it under its own control.

For the most part in conflicts of this kind individuals identify with their own state. As we saw earlier, the interests of individuals increasingly become collective interests (p. 117 above). And, among the collective interests they share, that of the state is seen as the most important. Their welfare increasingly seems to depend on the success of their own state – in winning trade abroad, in raising oil prices, in increasing its rate of growth, in promoting its own power – rather than in the success of themselves individually, or of their occupation group, or even of their class. Increasingly individuals see the interest of their state as their own. And increasingly the conflict of interests between states creates a related conflict of interests between the individuals which belong to them.

The social consequences of conflict among states depends, as in smaller societies, on the way they are resolved. If the conflicts – about trade, oil prices, the political independence of neighbouring states or disputed territory – can be resolved, through negotiation, mediation or arbitration, their social effect may be limited: like the effect of a dispute among neighbours in smaller societies which is resolved through the law-courts. But at the international level the procedures which lessen the impact of conflict in smaller societies are not available; or, if they are, are seldom used. At the international level it has generally been seen as normal that a conflict should in the final resort be resolved by force. Within international society, therefore, conflict plays a much more disruptive part in social existence than it does in most other types of societies. The consequences of conflict are also greater, both in terms of the immediate effect in violence, suffering and loss of life, and in the longer-term effects, in creating insecurity, instability and mutual antagonism, than in societies where alternative means of resolution are habitually employed.

Conflict in international society, as elsewhere, is socially derived. It is society that teaches what things are worth disputing about. Conflict has thus resulted from different types of issue in different ages.

The questions which give rise to conflict at any one time depend on a number of factors. But they depend above all on the aspirations and attitudes of the dominant élites within society.[1]

In the late Middle Ages in Europe, for example, the matter of principal concern to the rulers and their followers was dynastic power. The main cause of international conflict, therefore, was the competition for thrones: both among those who already held them and those who sought to acquire them. Of the wars which took place in the two centuries before 1559, by far the greater number, and all the more important ones, concerned this question. It brought about 120 years of war between the French and English kings for the throne of France; nearly a century of war, in five or six separate conflicts, between the houses of Aragon and Anjou for the throne of Naples; thirteen wars in fifty-five years between Hapsburg and Valois for rulership in Naples, Milan, Burgundy, Guelderland, Cleves, Navarre and other places; and recurrent conflicts between Sweden and Denmark, Hungary and Bohemia, Poland, Lithuania and Russia for the thrones of one or other of them. Altogether, of the international wars in Europe at that time, the vast majority concerned the question of succession.[2] Most of the civil conflicts of the age – the Wars of the Roses in England, the frequent wars between the French kings and

1. For a much more detailed account of the changing character of war and the disputes about which it is fought, see Evan Luard, *War in International Society* (London, 1986) esp. chap. 3.
2. For details, see ibid., pp. 25–6.

their nobles, the struggles of central European rulers with powerful subjects – equally concerned dynastic rights, or the rights of rulers over particular regions.[3] *Control* over territory was not the issue in such conflicts: in most cases local and traditional institutions were left unchanged whatever the outcome of the dynastic conflict. The subject in dispute was simply the *right* to rule. A small number of wars, especially those of the Hanseatic cities, concerned economic questions. An equally small number, for example the wars against the Hussites, concerned religion. But overwhelmingly the conflicts of the day reflected the major preoccupation of those then in power: the competition among the rulers and their immediate supporters concerning dynastic rights.

In the age that followed, from 1559 to 1648, the principal subjects of dispute changed. A large proportion of the conflicts, both between states and within them, concerned religion. This was now the question which mainly preoccupied the leading figures of every state: rulers, politicians, church people and the mass of the population alike. Of the forty-nine principal European wars of the age, twenty-five were related to religious issues.[4] Because it was everywhere taken for granted that there should be only one religion in each state – un roi, une loi, une foi, as the French put it – one faith could only be practised at the expense of another. Once again competition was the basis of the conflict: just as, before, two claimants had fought for a single crown, now two religions fought for the right to practise their cult, a right which it was believed could not be shared. For many the motive was seen as largely defensive. Catholics fought to defend the true faith against heretical reformers; Protestants to defend the right to practise their own religion against those who sought to deny it. At the same time, since each believed their enemies were guilty of mortal error, they saw themselves as fighting for truth, the only valid religion, an exclusive god that could admit no other. There continued to be wars over succession; but in this case too, since the ruler could in most places determine what faith was to be practised, the real issue was in many cases religious. Even territorial disputes were fought partly in the name of religion: so Hungary was contested between Christian emperor and Muslim Turk, the Ukraine between Orthodox Russia and Catholic Poland, Baltic territories between Protestant Swedes and Catholic Poles and Germans, Bohemia between

3. Ibid., p. 26.
4. Ibid., pp. 38–9.

Protestant elector and Catholic emperor – to secure those territories for a particular faith as much as for a particular ruler or state. In the age of sovereignty that followed, the main source of conflict changed again. In the entire period hardly a single war was fought about religion. There were a number about trade and trading rights, especially among trading states, such as the United Provinces and England. But for the most part the conflicts of this age were about a single theme: the "balance of power" among competing sovereign states, each seeking to strengthen the basis of its own power by the acquisition of strategically important or otherwise desirable territory and to prevent any undue accretion of power by other states. Power was now seen as the finite resource for which states had to compete to have their share: so a publication in England extolled the virtue of a balance of power policy under which "when any potentate has arrived at an exhorbitant share of Power", the rest should "league together in order to reduce him to his due Proportion of it".[5] The power and prestige which states sought was often seen in territorial terms. So France fought to acquire the "gates" of the country to the south-west, south-east and above all north-east; Prussia to swallow the smaller states which divided her scattered territories; Russia to advance to the Baltic and Black Sea; Austria to secure her position in Hungary and Italy; Britain to win strategic positions in the Mediterranean and beyond. For some an important part of the competition was a struggle for colonies and trading posts in trading areas beyond the seas: the Caribbean, Canada, West Africa and above all the Indies. Even the wars of succession were now fought in the interest of states rather than of ruling families. Often they were fought to *prevent* a succession rather than to secure one – because it was believed that the succession would give undue power to a particular state; the wars of Spanish, Austrian, Polish and Bavarian succession were all fought for this purpose (and all succeeded, wholly or partially, in that end). Because it was a struggle of all-against-all, there were few long-term partnerships. Allies were changed with breathtaking speed; and could frequently be abandoned in mid-war if the opportunity for a separate peace on favourable terms presented itself.[6] The conflicts of the age, in other words, were no longer those of rulers, nor of religions, but those of *states* struggling among each other for power and pre-eminence.

5. *Europe's Catechism*, published in England in 1741.
6. See Luard, *War in International Society*, pp. 49–50.

In the following age the basis of conflict changed again. It was no longer a competition between states but between nations. For the first time populations began to identify themselves with the struggles in which their rulers engaged them. They acquired a sense of nationhood which was expressed not only in national pride but in national competition. That sense of nationhood was acquired not only by the people of existing states, but by populations of similar language, culture, history or race who were scattered among different states (as in Italy and Germany), or living under foreign rule (as in the Ottoman, Austrian and Russian empires). Here there existed an automatic conflict between the "legitimacy" claimed by the existing sovereign power and the aspirations of the minority concerned to a separate nationhood. One effect is that in this age, unlike the previous one, a number of the principal wars began as internal conflicts: usually nationalistic revolutions leading to external intervention by other powers.[7] But nationalist fervour was as great among existing states as among the minorities deprived of nationhood. It was expressed in the competition for colonies: in South-east Asia, Africa and elsewhere. It was seen in periodic arms races: between France and Germany in land forces before 1870, between Germany and Britain in naval forces before 1914. It was seen in the bitter struggles for dominance in particular areas: between Prussia and Austria in Germany, between Germany and France on the Rhine, between Russia and Austria in the Balkans, between Britain and Russia in Asia, between Russia and Japan in the Far East, for example. In demanding further colonies, a "place in the sun", and above all "world power", the leaders of Germany were only expressing more openly ambitions that were held by many of the nations of the day. But there was only a limited supply of "world power" to be had. This was now the main asset in short supply. The states that were declining would not voluntarily concede it to those that felt they had a claim to more (such as Germany on one side, or Serbia on the other). And ultimately its distribution could be determined therefore, many believed, only by armed conflict.

After 1917 the main source of international conflict changed again. Nationalist ambitions and rivalries remained powerful for a time, especially before 1945. But they were increasingly overlaid and influenced by a new source of competition: that between ideological faiths. This was a conflict, like that of the age of religions, which was

7. Ibid., pp. 54–8.

essentially trans-national. It took place within states as much as between them, and each ideological alliance could expect to find supporters among the peoples who lived within the other. The conflict was fought out in the first place mainly within states. Thus most wars began as internal conflicts and only subsequently became more or less internationalised. The competition was for political power in many different states scattered across the earth. This was now the resource that could not be shared, and which must therefore be contested for. The shrinkage of distance meant that none could remain indifferent to the outcome of each individual struggle, so that all came to be seen only as components in a single, world-wide competition. This ideological contest, though genuine and sincere, became inextricably intertwined with a struggle for power between the most powerful states of each alliance. Political power in particular areas was demanded as much in the interests of strategic security as of ideological conviction. The control that each side demanded was only indirect. Territorial expansion, colonial power, national prestige, these now ceased to be significant aspirations or sources of competition. The contest was for political power for ideological allies in other states, often seen as the means of external influence, and ultimately of military security. Some wars still resulted from other causes: from other kinds of political instability, frontier disputes or the demand of minorities for autonomy or independence. But the dominant conflict of the age, and the one which it was feared could bring about the most costly military confrontation of all, was that which resulted from the competition for ideological domination.

International conflicts are not of course confined to those about which wars are fought. There are many important sources of dispute about which wars are never, or rarely, fought. In the modern world, for example, there are serious disputes on trade, investment, debt, financial policy and many other issues which never lead to war. This does not prove that the issues are not important: as we saw earlier, north–south economic conflicts are among the most important of the modern world. But in general it is a reasonable assumption that the issues about which states are willing to go to war are among those that are of most immediate importance to them. The changing issues about which wars are fought, therefore, give an idea of the conflicts which have appeared most important in each international society.

They have mattered, that is, to those who have controlled the destinies of states in each period. So it was the dynasts and their immediate supporters who cared most about dynastic questions in the first of these periods. It was the rulers and the church leaders, together with the believers in minority faiths, who cared most about religious questions in the age that followed. It was the monarchs and their great ministers in the age of sovereignty who were most concerned with promoting the power and prestige of their own state. It was middle-class nationalistic movements which were most concerned over questions of national pride and national independence in the age of nationalism. And it is the political leadership of states, in east and west alike, who care most about ideological questions and the outcome of political conflict in other states in the modern world.

Such issues have not mattered only, however, to the leaders. In each age, leaders (as we saw in Chapter 5) establish an ideology which affects the way of thinking of the bulk of the population. It is for this reason that ordinary people felt themselves personally involved in conflicts over dynastic power in the late Middle-Ages; over religion in the late sixteenth and early seventeenth centuries; over the power of their own states in the age of sovereignty; over nationalistic competition in the nineteenth century; and over the ideological struggle of the modern world. It is in this way that the conflicts which have mattered most to particular groups have been made into the conflicts of states and nations and peoples: the principal conflicts dividing international society in each age.

CONFLICT IN CONTEMPORARY INTERNATIONAL SOCIETY

Let us look now, in rather greater detail at the main form which conflicts take in the modern world society.

In every age the form taken by international conflict depends on the principal source of *loyalty*. When the main loyalty was to dynasts, it was the competition of dynasts which dominated the international scene. When the most important loyalty was to contending faiths, it was the rivalry of faiths which became of more importance. When the principal loyalty was to sovereign states, it was the struggle between states which dominated. And so on. In the modern world the main loyalty is no longer to ruler, to state or even to nation, but to political ideas; and what most concerns people is the victory or defeat of these ideas. This battle differs from earlier types of international conflict – for example those of the age of sovereignty –

in that it is not inherently an international struggle: one between states. It is conducted originally and primarily within the domestic political system. Loyalty to political ideas, in other words, is expressed in the first place in the demand by citizens for political change within their own states. Increasingly, however, in a shrinking world, they extend these demands also to other states as much as to their own. The political organisations which formulate and articulate them in their own state are closely linked with others putting forward similar demands elsewhere. Thus the conflict that begins within states – between right and left, fascist and communist, Stalinist and socialist, liberal and authoritarian, secular parliamentarian and Islamic fundamentalist – spills out in a wider political conflict in the world as a whole.

Because each of these ideas has been triumphant in particular states and groups of states, the battle becomes closely associated with the conflict among states. Particular countries become identified with the cause of particular ideas. States come to be labelled in this way: no longer as monarchies or republics, Protestant countries or Catholic countries, national states or multi-national states, but as "communist" or "democratic", Marxist or Maoist, revolutionary or conservative. This transforms the nature of international alignments. Because the world is divided on the basis of a political confrontation, alliances correspond with political attitudes. Ideology has never previously played much part in determining such groupings. Though, for a brief period in the mid-1830s, the states of Europe were ranged in rival political alliances, conservative and constitutional, each was soon disrupted by traditional national rivalries (with France against Britain in Egypt, Austria against Prussia in Germany for example) and even during the French revolutionary wars, the most overtly political conflict before 1917, Austrian monarch and Russian tsar found no difficulty in making common cause with the French revolutionary forces when it suited their national purposes. In the contemporary world, however, political alignments among states are governed almost exclusively by political sympathies. The conflict between ideas, in other words, is as powerful in the international society as in the national in determining political actions.

This reflects the character of those who control power in each state. Power is no longer held by hereditary rulers, nor by entrenched aristocracies, nor even by a traditional ruling class, but by politicians, party leaders who have won power because of their successes in the political struggle within states (p. 109 above). Having won power in such a contest at home, it is not surprising that they proceed to extend the conflict beyond their frontiers; or that they should judge other states on the basis of their political character. Those who are accustomed to a battle of right against left, or left against right, within their own states are naturally inclined to see the international political scene in similar terms. The political struggle in which they engage at home is fought out equally in the international arena. And the political enemies, the upholders of alternative doctrines, who they once found only at home, are now found equally in other states. International conflict becomes political conflict.

This means that the *issues* of international conflict become similar to those of the domestic political arena. The demands that have been made for centuries within states are now increasingly applied to other states. What should be the basis on which power is held? In what sense should governments be responsible to their peoples? What should be the balance of private and public power within the state? Is political equality or economic equality more important? What kind of human rights ought to be respected by every government in all states? These questions, which have been the stuff and substance of political conflict within states for so long, now come to be demanded equally vociferously between them too. Political parties and movements associated with particular postions on these questions now operate internationally. The political debate, which was once seen as a debate to be conducted separately within each individual state, now becomes one to be conducted within international society as a whole.

It is a battle conducted by individuals and groups as well as governments. But it is *governments* which feel particularly concerned to influence the political process in other states. It is they which believe themselves best placed to exercise that influence. It is they which are best able to determine which political faction elsewhere shall survive or be overthrown: by their decisions on the provision of economic assistance or political support. It is above all the largest powers of all which are most concerned and best able to exercise this influence. It is they which are most inclined to identify their own political interests with the success of particular ideological factions in other states; and it is they, therefore, which most often intervene to affect the course of the political struggle elsewhere.

There is thus a complex interrelationship between the interests of a particular set of ideas and the interests of the powers with which they are most closely identified. In some states a political doctrine rules not because it is the one that has been chosen by their people but because it is the one favoured by the superpower with which it is associated. To protect the governments which they support, each superpower makes increasingly heavy commitments, in economic assistance, military hardware and political support. The more precarious the position of the government assisted, the greater the external support needed to keep it in power (for example in Vietnam or Afghanistan, Pakistan or Ethiopia, El Salvador or Poland). But at the same time the more precarious their position the more deeply the external power is dragged into the quagmire of local politics. Thus mutual dependence is increased all the time. And the commitment which may once have been made to a great political cause may increasingly become a commitment to hold in power a corrupt faction or a dictatorial ruler, valued for their loyalty to a particular alliance rather than their genuine commitment to a particular political ideal.

The political conflict is fought out in practice mainly in the marginal areas of international society, where at present neither side prevails. In some regions, especially those in the immediate vicinity of superpowers, there is little political change, and little prospect of change. One ideology or the other is firmly in control and their opponents have little hope of overturning them. So it is elsewhere that the struggle is conducted: outside Europe and North America, in the third world countries across the world. It is here that political systems are most unstable, and the opportunity to win a victory, by coup or counter-coup, is most appealing. By such means success in both contests at once, between political ideas and between superpowers, can be won at relatively insignificant cost.

As in the age of religion, the objective in the contest is often primarily defensive. Though each side would like to win over new areas to its own cause, what they most want is to prevent the other from making any further advances, especially in areas close to home: to avoid losing Hungary or Czechoslovakia or Afghanistan to the opposing forces, to prevent Cuba, the Dominican Republic or Nicaragua from going over to the enemy. In such cases the conflict among the superpowers comes to prevail over the conflict of ideas. In those areas political weapons alone are not enough: if necessary military means also must be employed.

Not all international conflict in this age is ideological, even in appearance. There are other divisions and disagreements that are equally important, even if they lead less often to military clashes: above all the conflict resulting from inequalities in wealth and welfare among the peoples of different states. This too mirrors a conflict that takes place even more intensively within states: the conflict that has existed from time immemorial, between rich and poor, advantaged and disadvantaged propertied and propertyless. That conflict is now increasingly seen in international rather than in purely domestic terms. The inequalities between states are now much greater than those that exist within them. More importantly, those that exist between states are now, with the improved communications of the modern world, as *visible* as those within them. Whatever the reasons, the struggle between class and class, the struggle to transform institutions and establish a fairer economic system, the struggle for redistribution through transfers of wealth from rich to poor, is now one which takes place at the international as much as it does at national level. This is the contest which, because it concerns material conditions, often appears, to many individuals and states in international society, the most important.

Unlike the conflict between political ideas, however, it is one that is not fought out through armed force. This is partly because the states which most seek change – the poor – do not command a superiority of armed power; and partly because, even if they did, a simple act of force would hardly bring about the kind of changes which they demand: the aid and trade policies of rich states, the transfer of technology, the stabilisation of commodity prices, the practices of the IMF and the World Bank, none of these could be easily influenced through an act of force, even if successful. Moreover the conventions of the day, while they permit or at least tolerate, intervention for political purposes, do not accept the legitimacy of military action to procure economic ends. Even the rich and powerful therefore do not intervene to influence the economic policies of other states: to enforce the repayment of debts or resist the nationalisation of assets. This conflict, therefore, intense though it is, is fought out by political rather than by military means; by negotiation rather than by compulsion; by conference rather than by coercion.

These two therefore – the struggle between political ideologies and the struggle between rich states and poor – are the characteristic international conflicts of the age. Both were scarcely to be found in any earlier international society; certainly not in the organised forms in which they are found in the modern world. Both have been long experienced at the domestic level. Now they are as intense between states as within them.

They do not exhaust the kinds of conflict which occur in the modern international society. Some that were familiar in earlier ages are still to be seen. Conflicts over territory still take place, though now only in restricted border areas, and mainly among newly independent states. For a number of years there were conflicts over the liquidation of colonialism, but these are now almost exhausted. There are conflicts over demands for independence by minority peoples: but these rarely receive support from outside states (as they did so often in the nineteenth century) and so remain limited in scope. There are riots and revolts and civil wars which are not ideological in the sense here described; but these too have little international impact. There are interventions by particular states in areas beyond their borders: for example by China, Israel and South Africa in neighbouring states; but most of these are essentially local conflicts, affecting particular states and particular localities, rather than those of international society as a whole. The pervasive conflicts, those that affect almost every state to some extent, those that mobilise the passions of individuals across the world and influence the actions of states, are those between political ideologies and those between international class interests: between east and west and between north and south. It is they that represent within this age the fundamental divisions of belief and interest and so the principal source of conflict in international society.

CONCLUSIONS

As we saw earlier (p. 27), a number of social thinkers from the earliest times have emphasised the role of conflict in society. Without positively welcoming its universal character, they have believed that it was an important factor in all human existence, determining political change and social evolution. Han Fei-zu, Machiavelli, Hobbes, Marx and a number of more recent writers have all held it to be a central feature of social life (though arriving at quite different conclusions about the kind of social institutions which were consequently made necessary). In contrast other social thinkers, as we saw in Chapter 1, tended to stress co-operation and stability as essential characteristics of social life, and saw conflict as an occasional and regrettable aberration.

That argument is a somewhat sterile one. The concept of "conflict" is vague and imprecise. It can take many forms, of widely varying nature and degrees of intensity, ranging from a difference of opinion to an armed struggle. Generalised statements about "conflict" in the abstract, whether relating to its prevalence or to its desirability, can thus have little meaning unless they specify precisely what kind of conflict is intended. If such general statements have any value at all, it would seem more sensible to suggest that, while some degree of internal stress is a likely and probably a desirable, feature of most social institutions, an excessive amount, and especially the kind which takes the form of armed conflict, is likely to have damaging and destabilising effects on the quality of life of all or most of society's members.

In international society the prevalence of hostile relationships is immediately evident. Conflict is seen not only in widespread tensions and antipathies among the members of society, but is regularly expressed in armed combat. Even in this case, however, the degree of conflict varies widely. There exist large areas of international life in which conflict – even non-warlike conflict – plays a relatively minor role. For the most part states – and groups and individuals of different states – are able to reach accommodations relatively amicably on the issues which divide them. Governments do not quarrel violently about the arrangements for postal services or telecommunications between their countries, nor about air travel and other communication services (though they may strongly *disagree* about such questions). States, groups and individuals are able to undertake large volumes of international trade and investment without serious altercation. Cultural relations, sporting engagements, travel and tourism, by far the most frequent transactions of international society in normal times, are carried out for the most part in a relatively harmonious atmosphere.

Violent conflict therefore affects only particular types of international relationships, and those only at particular moments. Nor does it affect all states. Particular states have been able to maintain peaceful relations with all others over very many years. Switzerland has not been engaged in external war for nearly two hundred years, and Sweden for nearly as long. Particular groups of states have been able to remain on friendly terms for equally long periods. The US and Canada have never throughout their history been engaged in war against each other. Even the countries of Western Europe, which only forty years ago were engaged in ferocious and highly destructive conflicts, now undertake relations which, though not without occasional friction, are generally co-operative.

Since conflict is to be found in every society, need it be a matter of concern that it is to be found, even if in an especially intense form, in international society? Conflict is seen by some as a necessary stimulus to change and development, the source of progress, or at least the means by which differences – in viewpoint, situation and interest – have to be resolved. A society without conflict, it can be argued, would be a stagnant society which, though it might avoid the friction and destruction which internal disputes often cause, would do so only at the cost of becoming an ossified and unchanging structure, no longer capable of constructive evolution.

But even if it is true that conflict of some kind is both necessary and desirable, this does not prove there is a need of *armed* conflict, in international society any more than any other kind of society. It might be argued that armed conflict is necessary in international society to fulfil certain necessary social functions: the righting of wrongs, the securing of justice, the achievement of deeply rooted aspirations (for example self-determination or the overthrow of an unjust government) which cannot be achieved by other means. It is doubtful, however, whether this argument can be sustained. First, it cannot be said that all wars, or even most wars, are undertaken to secure such admirable objectives: many are waged (however they may be described) to achieve particular *national* objectives, such as the recovery of territory, retaliation for a grievance, or the protection of security interests. Second, it would need to be shown that, even where they are fought for such ideals, the goals in mind could not be achieved in any other way than by war: which is not always the case. Third, even if a war is undertaken for such a purpose, there is no assurance that it will succeed: there is no law that the side which has the greatest justice on its side, or the higher moral aspirations behind its efforts, is the more likely to prevail. Fourth, even where it does succeed, it would still be necessary to demonstrate that the value of the benefits won more than outweighs the heavy cost involved in winning them. Finally, if war is tolerated for some purposes, it will in practice be undertaken for many others.

To justify armed conflict it has always been thought necessary to show that the benefit it procures outweighs the costs it entails. In earlier ages that reckoning (as the theological proponents of just wars in the Middle Ages recognised) might conceivably lead to a decision in favour of war. In recent times, it is almost impossible that such a conclusion could be, at least in relation to a major war, a rational one. The possible costs of armed conflict have become so heavy – even if, as is likely, nuclear weapons were to be avoided – that it is difficult to maintain that the benefits it can bring can ever outweigh them. The direct losses, in terms of human lives lost and property destroyed, have, in the wars of the past century, been enormous. The indirect cost to international society, in terms of the bitterness, resentments and divisions brought about (leading to a greater likeliness of war in the future) are almost as great. The consequences for the entire society, whatever they may be for individual states and groups, are therefore almost entirely negative. It cannot, for example, be reasonably claimed that the technological progress which results from military competition more than compensates for the destructiveness of war. Nor can it be said that war promotes the survival of the fittest, either among nations or among individuals. So far as individuals are concerned, it is the bravest and best, rather than the weakest, who are most likely to be eliminated; while among nations it is only the most warlike or militarily efficient that are selected (and even this in many cases does not occur, since victory goes to the state with the most, or most powerful, allies rather than that which is most powerful or best-organised).

Thus *armed* conflict is likely to be always a divisive and destructive force. Since this is increasingly recognised, it may not prove to be a permanent feature of international society (it has already been virtually eliminated from the more developed parts of the world where there has been no significant war for forty years). Conflicts of *other* kinds, however, will inevitably remain an important feature of international social life. Political conflict, not only between states and groups of states, but between interest-groups, economic classes, ideologies, will be fought out at least as intensively as are similar conflicts fought out within states. Indeed, as communciations improve, the international political system may increasingly resemble that which exists within states. The link between groups of similar ideas or similar interests may continually increase and become more significant than the links existing between all who live within a particular state. Such groups may become engaged in a common struggle to promote particular rights or beliefs in many different countries simultaneously. In this way the political process may increasingly become trans-national, rather than national. Instead of being concerned with what policies should be pursued within a national state, political conflict will concern the policies to be pursued internationally: within the IMF (rather than the Ministry of Finance); by the World Bank (rather than the Ministry of Development); by the International Labour Organisation (rather than the Ministry of

Labour); by the Food and Agriculture Organisation (rather than the Ministry of Agriculture). The fundamental divisions of interest will increasingly be seen as those that exist within world society as a whole, rather than in particular states: between those with access to resources internationally and those without it; those who control international economic power and those who are controlled by it; the rich and the poor, the powerful and the powerless, internationally rather than nationally.

It is this type of conflict – not armed warfare – which can be regarded as an inevitable feature of every society. Even if the economic divisions which at present underlie political conflicts, between states as within them, are eventually reduced, conflicts of other kinds will remain: over social, political, environmental and other questions. Differences over such matters may increasingly replace the geographical divisions which have so often been at the root of international conflict in the past. In most ages conflict has been primarily among distinct geographical units, states and groups of states. As exclusive loyalty to the national state declines, as international consciousness increases, as the capacity to combine with members of other states is enhanced, the geographical basis for conflict may be progressively reduced. Conflict in international society may then increasingly resemble conflict in other societies. It will become a struggle among those of differing beliefs, interests and attitudes, each seeking to impose their own conception of desirable social arrangements, or of the degrees and types of change or stability they favour on society as a whole: international society.

10 Norms

SOCIAL NORMS

No society exists without some rules to govern the behaviour of its members. Where no such rules exist, where conduct is based entirely on individual desire and competitive instinct, there may be interaction of a kind, but there is no society. The essential characteristic of a society is that regular interaction within it has created expectations among its members concerning their conduct towards each other. These expectations create *norms*: patterns of conduct regarded as desirable, or at least normal, in particular circumstances.

We distinguished earlier four types of social norm (p. 61) above): practices, *ad hoc* procedures and habits of interaction, adopted among two or more parties and establishing firm expectations about their behaviour in particular situations; conventions, forms of behaviour approved among a wider society and enjoying an authority independent of the immediate advantages to be derived by the parties; morality, possessing a more deeply imbued authority and sometimes supported by religious sanctions; and law, a more detailed and explicit code than any of the others, enforced by public law and order agencies. Each of these categories could be further subdivided, according to the areas of conduct which they influence. So there may be specialised norms relating to business conduct; others concerning social etiquette; others relating to sporting encounters; and so on.

As we saw earlier (p. 62), each type of norm is associated with a particular kind of sanction. But perhaps more significant than the type of sanction is the degree of compulsiveness which the norms possess for each individual: how far they appear as absolute obligations, as general rules which should normally be observed, or merely as mild recommendations which may or may not be complied with. This depends not only on the kind of sanction available but on the *sense* of obligation felt by each person. Thus though parking rules are a legal obligation, backed by all the sanctions of the law, individuals may feel less of an obligation to obey them than they do to heed certain rules of etiquette backed only by the force of social convention. It may seem more important to some not to flout the rules of their club than to obey the Ten Commandments.

All these different kinds of norm perform a certain social function. First, all provide an element of *predictability*. The probability that the norms will be complied with reduces the uncertainties that would otherwise surround many social encounters. Second, they establish *restraint*: by requiring one form of conduct, they exclude another (the wholly self-interested activity which might otherwise occur and could breed conflict or coercion). Third, they establish *standards*: measures for judging the behaviour of others and adjusting one's own: so those that fall below the standard are condemned and those that rise above it are admired.

Norms are therefore, by definition, socially derived: that is they are in origin external to the individual that is influenced by them.[1] They are the means by which a "society", that is groups of people, usually spread over several generations, secure from their members a particular type of conduct that conforms with social requirements. The norms, especially if acquired by the individual in early years, may become "internalised", so that they appear to be *personal* convictions or commands of the conscience. But this does not alter the fact that they are in origin rules imposed by the group, to promote the purposes of that group.

How does this inculcation take place? Sometimes it occurs through direct instruction. The child is explicitly taught: do not speak with your mouth full. In other cases the norms are acquired by more indirect means: the value-standards of a society as a whole *imply* adherence to particular kinds of rules: so the injunction to love your neighbour as yourself by implication creates the obligation to give money to help the starving in Africa. In other cases – perhaps the majority – the norm is established mainly by *example*. It is through imitation that the desired type of conduct is acquired: children learn to restrain temper tantrums and moderate their voices because they see that their parents and other adults around them have done so and wish them to do likewise.

---

1. For this reason it is impossible to accept the statement of Bates and Harvey (in *The Structure of Social Systems*, New York, 1975, p. 250) that "If a single person has a norm with which no one else in the entire world agrees, nonetheless that idea is normative for him." An individual may have a firm conviction of what he should do in certain circumstances, but this does not represent a "norm" (certainly not a social norm in the sense used in this chapter), if it is contrary to what all others believe he should do. The essence of the norm, as the derivation of the word implies, is that it is a rule accepted as normal by a group.

However acquired in the first place, each kind of norm is continually reinforced, not only by their characteristic sanctions – inconvenience, disapproval, the pangs of conscience or the enforcement of the law – but by the reciprocal actions of others. Because the type of action demanded is the "norm", in that it is expected by others, it is greeted with approval and with appropriate counter-action; while action contrary to the norm will evoke dismay and disapproval, and so be deterred. Even if other forms of sanction also exist it is usually the sanction of public opinion which above all secures conformity with the code.

Norms, therefore, as the name implies, denote essentially the behaviour seen as normal; what is expected, or (in some cases) demanded even if not expected. They represent the cement which holds society together by protecting it from violence and vagary, the arbitrary and unpredictable. They are thus the essential condition of social existence. For while a society can exist without central authority, without an established legal code, without an acknowledged ruler, parliament or police force, the basis for social life does not exist without mutually consistent expectations to guide behaviour.

NORMS IN INTERNATIONAL SOCIETY

Norms of behaviour have had an important role to play in international as in other societies. Here too there is a need of predictability to reduce the uncertainties and instabilities of a wholly unregulated existence. Here too there is a need of restraints on the anti-social and disruptive conduct which might otherwise characterise the relationships of states. Here too there is a need for standards, measures for judging the behaviour of other states as well as one's own, which reflect the requirements of the society as a whole rather than of any individual state.

Some such conventions have existed among states since the earliest times. For example, to ensure a system of reliable communication it has been in the interest of all that those entrusted with the transmission of messages from one state to another should be assured of safe passage. Thus among the earliest rules of international behaviour to be established was that against the killing of heralds and messengers. This was a clearly established rule in both the two earliest societies of states of which we have knowledge: those of ancient China and of the Greek city-states. That the rule was one that was important in

China, and was generally observed, is shown by the reported case when a deliberate violation of the rule – the killing of an ambassador – was undertaken as a means for provoking war; as well as by the more complex strategy adopted in another case when an ambassador was sent, without permission, across the territory of another state in the expectation that he might be put to death so as to justify retaliation against such action.[2] The fact that retaliation was believed justified in such circumstances is an indication that the rule was normally observed. In late medieval Europe heralds were granted safe conduct in war and it was a gross breach of the chivalric code to violate such immunity. When the first diplomatic contacts began among the newly emerging states of Europe, the rule was made more explicit. An established code emerged concerning the treatment to be accorded to ambassadors, whether resident or visiting. It came to be accepted that to strike or injure an ambassador was an offence punishable by death. An ambassador could not be sued in the courts, nor could legal action be taken against him for debts, even though they were contracted before the beginning of his embassy. He was exempt from all taxes and customs duties, and all authorities were bound to protect and assist him in every way. These immunities applied not only to the ambassador himself but to all regular members of his suite. As time went on, an increasingly elaborate code began to be elaborated laying down the treatment to be accorded to the different ranks of envoy which were recognised. The rules were extended and refined over the years and were codified in the Treaty of Vienna of 1815 and especially in the Protocol of Aachen of 1818. Despite all these efforts, though the general principle of diplomatic immunity was universally accepted, the treatment offered was not uniform and disputes continued to take place concerning the precise privileges to be accorded, making necessary yet a further codification in recent times (p. 215 below).

Another question on which there was an evident need for agreed principles among states in all societies concerned truces and other understandings in time of war. Among the Greek city-states, for example, one of the earliest rules was that a truce should be observed during the celebration of festivals. Oracles, shrines, festivals and games, such as the Olympic games, were to be guaranteed against attack. When Aegina failed to observe a truce during the festival in

2. R. L. Walker, *The Multi-State System in Ancient China* (Hamden, Conn., 1953) p. 24.

Potideia in 506 BC, this was sufficient to cause her ally Sparta to withdraw support from her. It was an absolute rule in any war that a truce should be observed during the Olympic games. Detailed rules concerning truces were also developed in the society of states which emerged in medieval Europe. Under traditional "just war" doctrine, truces should automatically be observed on holy days, Sundays, even (in some views) during weekends, that is from Friday to Sunday inclusive. In addition truces were instituted to secure the settlement of a war: thus the pope helped to bring about a truce between England and France during the Hundred Years War in 1435 and his representative presided at the peace talks which followed. Throughout the sixteenth and seventeenth centuries, it was normal for a war to be interrupted by long periods of truce: for example there were almost as many years of truce as of war during the protracted struggle between Sweden and Poland from 1600 to 1660. Such truces, however, were normally agreed only between rulers, so that if one ruler died, the truce expired or had to be renewed. In later ages the suspension of a war through agreements of this kind became increasingly uncommon, though battlefield truces continued to be negotiated to allow the gathering up of the dead and wounded. It increasingly became the convention that a war would be fought, without respite, to its conclusion. The nearest to a conception of a truce was the armistice, an agreement for a cease-fire pending the negotiation of a final settlement.

In some societies rules were developed concerning the protection of particular *places* from the ravages of war. In ancient Greece temples were regarded as inviolate and beyond the scope of war and for this reason were sometimes used as places of refuge by those fleeing their enemies. Thucydides records how Boeotia complained against Athens that "the Athenians had done wrong and transgressed against Hellenic law since it was a rule established everywhere that the invader of another country should keep her hands off the temples in that country".[3] There has been a general sentiment in favour of sparing religious buildings in other societies. But these have, especially in the ages of religious conflict, often been disregarded – during the Thirty Years War Magdeburg was ravaged by imperial forces, because it had become the symbol of Protestant faith throughout north Germany, while in England and Ireland Cromwell's forces took delight in desecrating Catholic churches in the places they occupied. In

3. Thucydides, *The Peleponnesian War*, vol. IV, p. 97.

any case the tradition of respect for church property and ecclesiastical figures progressively declined. Imperial forces sacked Rome and imprisoned the pope in 1526–7; the papal states were not spared the ravages of successive wars in Italy; while Louis XIV had no compunction in invading the papal territory of Avignon and seeking to coerce the pope on questions in dispute between them. During the eighteenth and nineteenth centuries, when it was generally held that war was an activity that should be confined to the military, there was some attempt to avoid damage to civilians, and the bombardment of "open cities", unfortified places inhabited by civilians, was generally prohibited. This too, however, is a convention that has been progressively eroded over the past century and in the two world wars the bombing of cities and the destruction of civilian houses became normal, and in some cases the deliberate object of policy.

In most societies other rules have been developed, designed to reduce the destructiveness of war. In ancient China wars were supposed to be conducted in such a way as would avoid unnecessary loss of life, even among soldiers: battles were so far as possible to be won on the basis of tactical manoeuvre alone. In ancient Greece, though wars could be conducted with great severity, there was at least an attempt to spare women and children from its ravages. Even when Athens meted out her savage punishment on the people of Mytilene for declining to join her cause, sentencing all the island's menfolk to death, she contented herself with selling the women and children into slavery. Members of the Amphictyonic League undertook that they would not raze cities or cut off water supplies. In medieval Europe the rules of "just war" held that not only women and children but members of most civilian occupations – for example, clerks, monks, friars, pilgrims, travellers, merchants and peasants – should be spared in war.[4] The effect of such injunctions was reduced by the fact that they were confined to Christians. Almost any treatment was thought suitable for Muslims and other heretics. For example, though the Third Lateran Council prohibited the enslavement of Christian prisoners, Muslims continued to be freely enslaved (as Christians were, even more extensively, by Muslims). The restraints of the rules of chivalry were similarly confined to knights and gentlemen only. In any case these injunctions did not prevent considerable brutality in many of the wars of the age,

---

4. J. T. Johnson, *Just War Tradition and the Restraint of War* (Princeton, N. J., 1981) p. 127.

especially religious wars such as those against the Hussites, the wars in Hungary and above all the Thirty Years War. Only from the late seventeenth and eighteenth centuries did there begin to be some attempt to mitigate the worst brutalities. "Cartels", agreements between commanders, were reached, covering such matters as the exchange of prisoners, ransoming and the levying of contributions in occupied territory. Agreements were sometimes reached for the protection of the sick and wounded when a besieged city was given up and for the safeguarding of hospitals. In a few cases poisoned projectiles and missiles of tin or other material were banned.[5] In the following century there was a more systematic attempt to negotiate *multilateral* agreements governing such questions: for example concerning the treatment of prisoners and the injured (1864) and on the conduct of war generally (the Hague Agreements of 1899 and 1907). Gradually such agreements became more detailed and comprehensive in their scope. However, as the actual practice of warfare became, with more powerful weapons, more destructive and above all less discriminating, the norms established were nearly always overtaken by events (p. 220 below). The consequence was that despite the new agreements, the total suffering in war was far greater in the conflicts of the twentieth century than at any earlier time, and certainly affected a far larger number of civilians, including women and children.

One type of rule introduced in many societies to reduce the destructiveness of war has been the banning of particular weapons. In medieval Europe, for example, there was an attempt to outlaw the crossbow, which the Second Lateran Council in 1139 forbade as "deadly and odious to God". The injunction seems to have had little effect on the actual practice of war however: the crossbow continued to be widely used. In the same way, the attempt during the eighteenth century to secure a prohibition of projectiles made of metal other than lead, poisoned projectiles and irregularly shaped missiles appears to have been ignored.[6] In the nineteenth century there was a more intensive effort to ban weapons or methods of war regarded as unnecessarily destructive or indiscriminate. Thus an agreement was

5. Sir G. Clark, *War and Society in the Seventeenth Century* (Cambridge, 1958) p. 86.
6. Ibid., pp. 86–7. Other proposals were for a ban on the bombardment of cities and of red-hot balls, bombs and other destructive missiles. However, the "attempt to humanise the laws of war had no direct effects that we can trace" (ibid., p. 87).

reached to prohibit the use of the dum-dum bullet; while the Hague Convention outlawed the poisoning of wells (which could cause death to civilians as much as to the military). Unfortunately prohibitions of this kind were rarely able to foresee the weapons, often far more destructive, that were to be developed and used in future conflicts. Thus the banning of the poisoning of wells and the dum-dum bullet did not prevent the use of poison gas, the bombing of cities from the air and the use of naval raiders and submarines against civilian shipping in the First World War. The 1925 Convention prohibiting the use of poison gas (already regarded by many military commanders as unusable) did not prevent the use in the conflict that followed of saturation bombing and nuclear weapons, each causing hundreds of thousands of civilian deaths. Though the effort to civilise war by the prohibition of particular methods may have been sincere, therefore, it was never able to overcome the determination of every government to develop new and yet more powerful weapons which, they hoped, might bring them victory in the conflict to follow: weapons which were often indiscriminately used.

Another type of rule required by every international society concerns treaties and their enforcement: without some mutual confidence that such agreements are likely to be observed, there would be no point in concluding them at all. In ancient China the signing of treaties was surrounded by religious ceremonies of various kinds, designed to increase mutual trust that their terms would be observed.[7] Even so they were in practice widely broken if state advantage demanded it.[8] In ancient Greece treaties were often accompanied by sacred oaths under which the parties pledged themselves to keep its terms. Thus the cities that were party to the Thirty Years Truce in 446 bound themselves to keep the treaty by religious oaths; and copies of the agreement were inscribed at Olympia so that they could secure divine authority and sanction. When Elis and Heraea made an alliance they agreed that if it should be broken they would pay a fine to Zeus. In medieval Europe, likewise, treaties were not only

---

7. Cf. Walker, *Multi-State System*, p. 82: "The representatives participated in a very solemn ritual in which an animal – usually a calf – was sacrificed at some holy spot outside the walls of a city. The left ear of the sacrificial victim was cut off and it was used to smear with blood both the documents bearing the articles of agreement and the lips of the principals. One copy of the document was buried with the sacrificial beast and each of the signatories kept a copy."
8. Ibid., pp. 82–4.

signed and sealed but often confirmed by a sacred oath, under which the parties committed themselves to the judgement of God and the church should they violate the treaty.[9] Even so, many rulers observed the terms of a treaty only so long as it was in their interests to do so. Most probably agreed with the advice of Machiavelli that "a prudent ruler ought not to keep faith when by so doing it would be against his interests and when the reasons which made him bind himself no longer exist". But because a widespread violation of treaties would create a state of anarchy which was in the interests of no state, it came to be increasingly accepted that commitments in treaties should be regarded as binding: *pacta sunt servanda* (though even in this case the prudent reservation was often added, *sic rebus stantibus* – circumstances remaining unchanged – an escape-clause almost as comprehensive as Machiavelli's). Respect was especially demanded for multilateral treaties, such as the Peace of Westphalia and the Treaty of Vienna, which were seen by many as establishing a "public law" of Europe, from which no individual state could unilaterally release itself. For some at least it became a matter of honour that a state should be seen to abide by the pledges to which it was publicly committed. Rules and traditions began to develop about how far treaties bound successor governments, the circumstances in which they could be revised or revoked, and how conflicts between the terms of different treaties were to be resolved. An international law of treaties, in other words, began to emerge.

Rules were also required in various specialised areas. Wherever the shipping of different states has come into contact, there has been a need for rules concerning navigation. In Greece this purpose was served by the Rhodian sea law, which acquired general acceptance among the city-states. Similarly in medieval Europe the Rolls of Oleron, originally developed, for the same purpose, for the island of that name and subsequently adopted by the Barcelona traders, became finally the basis for maritime rules which were adopted throughout the continent. There were attempts to arrive at understandings concerning other maritime questions, including the degree of control a state could exert in the areas immediately off its coast, rights of navigation in straits and other questions.

9. The parties would, however, sometimes seek escape from these pledges by demanding a dispensation from the pope: for this reason Louis XI and Charles the Bold had to pledge themselves in their treaty of 1476 not only to the terms of the treaty but to refrain from seeking a dispensation from their oaths in this way.

Rules governing commerce, the principles of fair trading and settlement of disputes, have equally been necessary. Among the Greek city-states treaties were concluded among members of the same alliance, and sometimes more widely, setting out the rules to be applied on such questions. In late medieval Europe, commercial rules were set out in the laws of individual states and later in bilateral treaties, such as the famous Intercursus Magnus between England and Burgundy of 1495. In the following century such treaties became more common. In 1606 France and England concluded a treaty "for the safety and liberty of commerce", providing for the public advertising of tariff rates, a limitation on internal taxes and reasonable treatment for the merchants of the other state. Gradually a new principle, that of non-discrimination, began to be widely recognised: it was expressed in "most-favoured-nation" clauses, under which states undertook to give another state treatment as favourable as it granted to any other. This led, by the end of the nineteenth century, to the establishment of a generally non-discriminatory system, except in colonies where discrimination (including sometimes the total reservation of all trades to the home country) was still widely employed. But there continued to be many disputes on commercial matters, on the treatment accorded to the merchants of one country in the territory of another, on the principles governing taxation and tariffs, and especially about the way in which commercial disputes should be resolved; and a general codification of the rules governing international trade had to await a later period.

International societies also require rules defining the degree to which one state can intervene in the affairs of another. Among the states of ancient China there was a rule that a state should not attack another in the year that a revolution had occurred there: a provision undoubtedly intended to limit intervention in the affairs of other states. The multilateral agreement reached among twelve of the principal states in 562 BC provided that none of them would "protect traitors" and "shelter criminals" – that is give asylum to rebels from another state: an indication of the general desire to prevent one state from abetting sedition in another. Such rules were made necessary because the rulers of the age "appreciated the value of supporting claims to power in another state" so that "use of satellite parties and puppet regimes was one of the most important strategies of state expansion".[10] Similarly in Greece, in a system of ideological conflict,

10. Walker, *Multi-State System*, p. 86.

with two superpowers each closely associated with a particular political system, intervention was widely practised to support rival political factions and there was a concern to limit this practice. It was generally accepted that, if a colony revolted against its mother country, no other state should intervene: this was the argument strongly used by Corinth against Athens at the beginning of the Peleponnesian war.[11] In practice external involvement in civil wars tended to be denounced when practised by the other side, but justified when practised by one's own (in other words the situation was exactly as today). But the sense that all states should decide their own affairs for themselves found expression in the widespread demand for "autonomy"; paradoxically intervention, especially by Sparta, was sometimes in the name of "autonomy" (once more not unlike the situation today when external powers claim they intervene to establish a "genuinely representative" government). In medieval Europe a justification for intervention was provided by the dynastic principle: if only a claim to succession could be found, a foreign ruler, it was widely held, had the right to prosecute the claim with whatever local support could be found. Increasingly, however, from the early sixteenth century this justification was challenged: François I was widely condemned for his interventions in Guelderland and Navarre, which sparked off the Hapsburg–Valois war of 1521–5. During the age of religion a new justification for interference in other states emerged: a need to assist co-religionaries elsewhere. Even if agreements to the contrary were reached, as sometimes occurred, they were rarely observed. Thus Elizabeth was pledged, under the Treaty of Cateau-Cambrésis, to non-intervention in Scotland, but violated the undertaking in the following year. There was no more surprise that Spain intervened to assist Catholics in France than that England and the Palatinate intervened to assist Protestants in the Netherlands. Even the writings of international law reflected this assumption of religious solidarity: thus Gentili supported the right to send aid not only to an ally but to any people similar in religion, blood or race which was involved in conflict. A rule of non-intervention became more strongly established in the age of sovereignty which followed (since intervention violated the central principle of sovereignty) but was still not always obeyed: Louis XIV sent help to rebels in Hungary

11. Thucydides, *The Peleponnesian War*, vol. i, p. 41. Athens assisted Corcyra, Corinth's colony, against her mother country and this was the chief *casus belli* of the Peleponnesian War.

and Ireland, while France, Sweden and Spain all gave assistance to the Stuart pretenders at different times between 1715 and 1745. In the nineteenth century, however, a new justification emerged for intervention: the need to give support to a national revolution in some other state. So Russia intervened to help Greeks and Bulgars against Turkey, France to help Italians against Austria, Prussia to help Germans against Denmark and so on. Conversely supporters of the old order believed that intervention *against* revolutions was justified: so Austria intervened to prevent revolution in Italy, France in Spain, Britain in Portugal, Russia in Hungary and Prussia in the German states. In practice it was rather national interests than ideology which determined whether or not intervention took place; but it remained frequent, above all by the "powers", which had constituted themselves as international policemen in this age. Though international lawyers tended to demand neutrality among outside states in civil wars, this had little influence on the actual practice of governments; and the failure to establish clear-cut rules on the matter was to prove of even greater significance in the new age of ideology which emerged at the end of the First World War.

Principles were also required to determine what action could be taken to protect human rights in other countries. Throughout the centuries concern to undertake such action conflicted with the equally strong concern to maintain the independence of each separate state. In China the tradition emerged under which the rulers would grant political asylum to refugees from another state, a tradition which frequently overrode the obligation to heed the requests of neighbouring rulers for their return.[12] A similar concern for individual rights is reflected in the tradition among the Greek city-states that a refugee could find sanctuary in a temple: thus when the Spartans almost starved to death Pausanias, who had taken refuge in a temple, this was regarded by many as a heinous offence and was used by the Athenians as one of their justifications for the Peleponnesian War. In Europe in the later Middle Ages sanctuary was frequently given to refugees, political or religious, from other states, and often there was widespread sympathy for these: as for the Protestants expelled from France in 1685, who found refuge in England and the Nether-

---

12. Walker, *Multi-State System*, pp. 90–2. As time progressed the interest of the rulers in suppressing rebellion had the effect that the right of asylum was increasingly overridden by extradition treaties and other undertakings (such as the multi-lateral agreement of 562 BC) providing for the return of "traitors" or "criminals".

lands. But the need to establish more general international principles concerning human rights questions arose first in the late eighteenth century in relation to the practice of slavery. Even then the powerful tradition of sovereignty limited the scope of the action it was thought possible to take. For a long time concern was concentrated not on the institution of slavery itself but only on slave-trading. Whether or not slavery itself should be abolished continued to be regarded as a question that was to be decided by each government individually, so attention was focussed only on the trade which supplied the slaves. Even here concern for sovereignty had the effect that it was for long seen as a matter for each government to deal with individually. Towards the end of the nineteenth century, however, the problem had come to be seen as an international one: a multilateral agreement was then signed by which European states agreed not only to abolish the trade but to allow mutual inspection of ships to ensure that the agreement was being observed. Concern on human rights questions was seen in other questions, and slowly there developed a willingness even to disregard traditional rights of sovereignty. In 1833, for example, the British and French governments protested to Russia about the way in which she put down the Polish rebellion in that year. The revolt in Bosnia and Bulgaria in 1876 against Turkish oppression evoked a similar concern about the rights of the peoples of those areas. And by the end of the century international commissions had been established to examine the situation of Africans in the Congo and Armenians in Turkey.

The most important rules required by an international society are those concerning war and the conditions which justify it. In almost every society some rules on the question have been established. In ancient China there was, for example, a rule that one state should not attack another in the year in which its ruler had died, nor one having a ruler of the same surname (seen as a form of domestic conflict). More generally the philosophers of the day, such as Mencius and Confucius, preached the need for peaceful policies and denounced the warlike character of many rulers of the day. Confucius believed that if a truly virtuous ruler came to power and followed the doctrine of benevolent government which he preached this would not only bring peace to his own land but to others as well. Such teachings, though frequently disregarded, may have served to spread the idea that foreign policy should be conducted according to recognised principles. In Greece, though the rules were imprecise and often disregarded, there was a general presupposition that a state should not engage in unprovoked aggression. "Hellenic law" laid down certain rules about the conduct states should employ towards each other; and it was the aggressive policies of Athens which eventually aroused the Spartan league and other states against her. In medieval Europe "just war" doctrine sought to lay down the rules which should govern the initiation of war, though they left plentiful justifications for those who needed them. Thus it was said that the intention of war should be to promote good against evil; that war should not be waged out of revenge; nor for the sake of power alone. Since attacking states could always convince themselves that their motives were just, it is doubtful whether these rules, if they were considered at all, had much influence on state actions. In the age of religion, likewise, war could be shown as justified, and even honourable, if it was designed to defend or promote the true faith against sinful heretics. Legal writers, such as Grotius, sought to define more precisely the circumstances in which war was justified, but none suggested that it was always wrong, and all left a large number of reasons which could be used to show that a war was "just". In the seventeenth and eighteenth centuries such justifications were neither demanded nor used, since it was generally believed that state interest was sufficient explanation and vindication of a war, especially if it could be said to promote the balance of power. So Frederick the Great wrote that "aggressive wars, though detestable if waged for inadequate reasons, are justified if made necessary by the real interest of the state".[13] In the nineteenth century too, though major war became less frequent in Europe, it was widely believed to be justified in defence of national "honour" or vital national interests, or to succour national revolutions elsewhere. Even the treaties of arbitration which were increasingly signed at the end of the period, habitually excluded questions of "vital interest" or the "honour of the state": these, it was held, could if necessary be settled by the time-honoured remedy of war.[14]

So a variety of principles designed to govern the behaviour of states have been established in different societies. The fact that conflicts on many such questions, and even war itself, have continued to occur in all these societies is no indication that the norms have been without influence. Until the present century war has never been contrary to the rules of international society. States have often

13. Quoted in G. P. Gooch, *Frederick the Great* (London, 1947) pp. 3–4.
14. For a survey of the evolving beliefs about the justifiability of war over recent centuries, see Evan Luard, *War in International Society* (London, 1986) chap. 8.

consented to abide by most of the conventions established, even when they have reserved the right to make war in the final resort. It has normally been more convenient to keep the rules in most respects than to tolerate a total disorder among states. In this sense there has never existed, as is sometimes suggested, a state of "international anarchy".[15] The members of international society, like those of smaller societies, have found it useful to establish rules of co-existence which would at least reduce the uncertainties and inconveniences of a wholly unregulated interaction.

NORMS IN CONTEMPORARY INTERNATIONAL SOCIETY

In the contemporary international society the scope of the norms devised to govern international behaviour has been significantly widened. As communications have improved and contacts become greater, the code required becomes more extensive and more complex. An increasing range of international actions become subject to the influence of socially derived standards.

In a number of specialised areas existing norms have been clarified or new ones developed. The rules concerning diplomatic privileges and immunities, disputed for centuries, have been laid down more definitively than ever before, in the Vienna Convention of 1961, to which virtually every state in the world has acceded, and in subsidiary conventions concerning more detailed questions (such as consular relations, special missions and the protection of internationally protected persons). The law governing the use of the sea, another long-standing subject of dispute, has been codified in substantial detail in conventions in 1958 and 1960 and, more comprehensively, in the Law of the Sea Convention (opened to signature in 1982):

15. Cf. Hedley Bull, *The Anarchical Society* (London, 1977) p. 42: "At no stage can it be said that the conception of the common interest of states, of common rules accepted and common institutions worked by them, has ceased to exert an influence. Most states at some time pay some respects to the basic rules of coexistence in international society, such as mutual respect for sovereignty, the rule that agreements should be kept, and rules limiting resort to violence. In the same way most states at most times take part in the working of common institutions: the forms and procedures of international law, the system of diplomatic representation, acceptance of the special position of great powers, and universal international organisations."

although a part of the latter text is controversial, its formulations of the law on many issues previously disputed is now almost universally accepted. Humanitarian law, especially the law relating to the conduct of war, the treatment of prisoners, guerrilla operations and other questions, has been codified in successive Geneva conventions and protocols.[16] The law governing international trade and trade disputes has been progressively elaborated and clarified by the UN Commission on International Trade Law (UNCITRAL), a new body set up for the purpose. A wide range of agreements, concerning transport, communications, environmental questions, health, labour standards and many other questions, have been negotiated within the specialised agencies of the UN. More significant, new procedures have been established for framing the rules in previously controversial fields. The International Law Commission was set up in 1945 for the express purpose of examining areas where the law is in dispute or where no law exists, and for proposing new texts (as it has done, for example, on the law of treaties, the law governing international waterways and other issues). Finally the International Court of Justice, through judgments which it reaches on the cases submitted to it, has established a body of case law determining the principles to be applied in various disputed areas (for example maritime boundaries).

Even on the most vital and controversial issue of all, the right to make war, there has been some attempt to develop more clear-cut international rules. Until 1914, as we saw, it was generally accepted that every state had the right, if it so wished, to make war to promote essential national interests. After the First World War, a series of commitments were undertaken designed to limit and define that right. In the Covenant of the League of Nations the majority of states committed themselves to "respect . . . the territorial integrity and existing political independence" of other members of the organisation and to join in preserving these against any threat from other states. Under the Kellogg Pact of 1928 almost every state of the world formally renounced was as an act of policy (though it was made clear, by the US Secretary of State himself, who had inspired the pact, that this did not exclude war in self-defence, including "the defence of national interests and policies".[17] Under the UN Charter of 1945 member states, which eventually included virtually the whole inter-

16. The last was that of 1977 laying down rules concerning guerrilla warfare, the protection of civilians and other questions.
17. J. T. Shotwell, *War as an Instrument of National Policy* (London, 1929) p. 211.

national community, undertook to refrain from the "use or threat of force". There were subsequent attempts to spell out more precisely the content of these abstract commitments. In 1970 the UN General Assembly passed a declaration setting out the "Principles Governing Friendly Relations among States", a detailed set of rules which had been negotiated in the legal committee of the Assembly for a number of years; and in 1974 it endorsed a new carefully worded definition of "aggression", which had been formulated by the same committee. Such commitments did not prevent wars from continuing to take place, though these were now less often in the form of direct territorial aggression; but they did reflect the increasing concern to establish, more unequivocally than in early international societies, the principles governing the use of force by states, and to condemn outright attack by one state against the territory of another. "Aggression", for example was now almost universally held to be contrary to the accepted principles of international society, even if there continued to be widespread disagreement about what actions that word implied.

These legal formulations reflected changing public attitudes. Public opinion generally, which is ultimately more important than legal instruments as an influence on the behaviour of governments, was increasingly hostile to the unrestricted use of force by states. The horrors of two world wars created a revulsion against the deliberate use of war as an act of policy. It was widely condemned as an aberration, an immoral crime, or a "great illusion", which, it was said, would bring no benefits even to the victors. War for territorial purposes, the traditional aim of most wars in the past, in any case was increasingly irrelevant to the concerns of the age. The demand for territory was, after 1945, non-existent among developed countries; and usually concerned only marginal border areas among newly independent developing countries.[18] Territorial aspirations were irrelevant to the main concern of an age of ideological competition. In such age what was mainly desired was the victory of a political creed: especially to prevent governments of opposing ideology coming to power in other states, above all strategically important states, and if necessary to intervene, whether overtly or covertly, to bring that about. For that purpose war remained widespread and would still usually carry considerable public support.

Thus though "aggression", the clear-cut use of force against the territory of another state, was now generally condemned (and only

18. See Luard, *War in International Society*, pp. 125–6, 172–3.

very rarely occurred), other uses of force were still widely condoned. In an ideological age most wars were civil wars. Not only was the initiation of such wars *within* states seen as a legitimate means of securing political objectives, especially in countries where no alternative means of political change existed; intervention from outside to affect their outcome was equally often tolerated or approved. The force being assisted could always be claimed as more "democratic" than the government against which they were fighting. Defence of an ideological faith, the need to overcome an ideological enemy, and to prevent him securing successes in new areas, appeared to many an ample justification for forcible intervention in civil wars elsewhere. On this, the most popular use of force in such an age, no clear rules existed. International law had traditionally held that where civil war became acute external powers should recognise a situation of "belligerency" and offer no help to either side. But in an ideological age this was no longer an acceptable option and was rarely even seriously proposed. Many held that assistance to a government seeking to defend itself against rebels was legitimate, whether or not it had been democratically elected. Others held that assistance to rebels was also legitimate if their cause was just. In practice most governments, including both superpowers, were willing to justify the dispatch of assistance to both governments and rebels, so long as they were fighting for their own ideological cause. So the US denounced Soviet aid for rebels in Greece, South Vietnam, Angola and (indirectly) El Salvador, but herself assisted rebels in Guatemala (1954), Afghanistan, Angola and Nicaragua. The Soviet Union denounced assistance to recognised governments in Greece, Lebanon (1958), Vietnam and other cases; but herself intervened to assist the governments it recognised in Angola, Mozambique and Afghanistan. China denounced US intervention in Korea, but herself intervened in Vietnam. India denounced great power intervention in some areas but herself intervened in Hyderabad, Goa and Bangladesh. Intervention was sometimes undertaken in covert form, through intelligence agencies, training missions and the secret supply of arms. But during the seventies and eighties assistance of this kind was provided increasingly openly and unashamedly (as when the US sought funds from Congress to arm rebels operating against the territory of Nicaragua from a foreign state). This then was the use of force most widely resorted to in an age of contending ideologies. But on that practice, leading to the loss of millions of lives in Vietnam, Afghanistan and many other countries, there were no accepted rules; and the International Court's ruling (on Nicaragua) was ignored.

There were other ways in which the rules concerning the use of force were ambiguous. It was sometimes held that force was justified to protect a country's nationals when they were under threat in another state; but since, in the modern world, there are nationals of every state in almost every other one this was a justification which could be brought into use in almost any circumstances (such as Britain's attack on Egypt in 1956, or the US intervention in the Dominican Republic in 1965). Or an intervention could be said to be undertaken as a result of an invitation from within the state concerned, another condition usually not difficult to fulfil (used for example by the Soviet Union when she intervened in Czechoslovakia in 1968, and by the USA in relation to Grenada in 1982). Or it could be said to represent "anticipatory self-defence" (as claimed by Israel in the Six-Day War). Or it could be said to be undertaken "to restore law and order" (as the Soviet Union said about Afghanistan); to remedy an "injustice" (as said by India about the invasion of Goa and by Iraq of her attack on Iran); to promote self-determination (Pakistan's attack on Indian-held territory in 1965); to reunite a divided people (Somalia's attack on Ethiopia in 1977); and so on. There was no shortage of justifications which could be put forward and which were, by some at least, widely accepted. A simple prohibition of "aggression", however ingeniously defined, was not sufficient to deter such action. Few states, in resorting to force, declared that their purpose was to commit aggression. More detailed principles were therefore now required if the uses of force which had become most popular were to be prevented.

The continued effort to ban or limit the use of particular weapons suffered from the same difficulties. As in earlier ages, sporadic revulsion against the use of particularly inhumane weapons or methods of war occasionally stimulated the demand for a ban; and sometimes international agreements to that end were drawn up. But these related nearly always to the weapons which had proved most destructive in the past, not those that were to be the main threat in the future. Just as the agreements reached before the First World War prohibiting the poisoning of wells and the dum-dum bullet had no effect in restraining the use of poison gas, the sinking of civilian ships and the bombing of towns which took place in the holocaust which followed, so the agreement reached, among some countries at least, for the prohibition of poison gas in 1925 did nothing to prevent the use of rockets, fire-bombs, mass bombing raids and atomic bombs, causing hundreds of thousands of civilian deaths in the subsequent conflict. Agreements for the banning of weapons of mass destruction in the Antarctic, on the sea-bed and (in theory) in outer space, had no effect in reducing the vast stockpile of atomic weapons that had been accumulated in the places where they were actually deployed. Chemical weapons and nerve gases were denounced in principle by many states; yet in practice large stockpiles were retained, and there was little compunction in using napalm to burn women and children alive in Vietnam, or to use poison gas causing excruciating death in the Gulf War. Thus though a few weapons of the past were at least theoretically prohibited, for the new and improved means of destruction now devised, the hydrogen bomb with a thousand times the destructive power of the Nagasaki bomb, the multiple, independently targetted re-entry vehicle (multiplying the destructive power of each nuclear-armed missile), the neutron bomb (designed to kill people rather than damage buildings), laser weapons, electronic cannon and all the other new means of destruction which modern science was able to devise, there was not even an attempt at limitation, let alone a ban. Even when, rarely, an agreement was arrived at, as in the case of anti-ballistic missiles, there was little hesitation in jettisoning it (or redefining it, which amounted to the same thing) when it was thought possible to develop a "strategic defence" system against incoming missiles (which it had been the purpose of the treaty to outlaw). The fact was that, though governments were occasionally willing to agree measures of marginal restraint in marginal areas, as soon as they believed that by abandoning those measures and developing new weapons they could secure an advantage, none would forgo that opportunity.

There were somewhat similar weaknesses in the attempt to develop international principles governing the protection of human rights. Here too there were hesitant efforts to develop new norms: principles that all governments would agree to apply, even within their own territories, concerning the treatment of their own populations. The unimaginable crimes committed against Jews in Germany stimulated an effort to lay down in unambiguous terms the rights which every individual human being had a right to enjoy wherever they might live. A Universal Declaration of Human Rights, and a number of covenants, conventions and other instruments of a more specialised kind, were formulated. Unfortunately, though it was often possible eventually to agree on a form of words, it was less easy to agree precisely what they meant: in other words what precisely were the obligations it imposed on governments. Although almost every government signed the Universal Declaration, even the most elementary rights it contained continued to be violated by many of those which had done so. There were differences of view concerning the relative importance to be attached to civil and political rights on the one hand, and economic and social rights on the other. There were differences concerning which rights were "fundamental", and which only optional. Above all there were deep disputes about the role which international bodies might play in seeking to protect such rights: if there was little agreement about the precise nature of the rights which should be enjoyed, there was still less about the degree to which international bodies could intervene – for example in South Africa, the Soviet Union, Chile or Iran – to ensure that they were being enjoyed. Here too, therefore, the attempt to establish an agreed body of international norms, and a system to ensure they were being observed, was far from being achieved.

Even in this field a few advances were made. Slavery was virtually abolished. Minority peoples in most places began to secure somewhat better treatment. Serious religious discrimination became less common. Even those governments which held parts of their population in considerable subjection, such as those of South Africa and the Soviet Union, were sometimes induced to make marginal adjustments (for example in their treatment of African workers and Jews respectively) in response to external pressures. Even though, therefore, no system of enforcement of the rights demanded could be established, world opinion increasingly ensured that no government could be totally oblivious of the principles which were now widely accepted.

During this period, therefore, there was some evolution in the character of the international norms established. In quantitative terms, at least, there were a larger number of generally recognised rules than ever before; and, at least in the less controversial areas, there was a greater readiness among states to abide by them. More than ever before too the rules were seen as universal, applicable to the whole world community: there was no longer a separate set of rules for Europe, Africa or Latin America, for more or less "advanced" societies. Unfortunately, however, in the areas which mattered most – above all those relating to questions of peace and war – the rules often remained ambiguous and subject to conflicting interpretation (if indeed there were any rules at all). On such matters governments were either able to persuade themselves that their actions were consistent with the rules; or they could deny that any widely accepted body of principles existed. In an age of contending ideologies there was often disagreement about the norms that were applicable, and a widespread unwillingness to accept the relevance of principles upheld by those of opposing political viewpoints. While, therefore, there was a growing recognition that in a shrinking world agreed principles of interaction were required, there were no agreed procedures for establishing those principles. Still less was there agreement on the principles themselves.

CONCLUSIONS

The process by which societies evolve norms of conduct is complex. Even in domestic societies norms are not usually *created* by a deliberate decision. They emerge gradually out of the experience of the society, the recognition that certain rules are necessary if society is to be able to operate effectively and without violence. It may be long before they are expressed in any written form: before vague conventions become precise rules, before common law becomes statute law, before, that is, a set of common *expectations* is established.

In international society these difficulties are even more obvious. There exists no central authority or accepted leadership to formulate the rules. Contact between the members may be only spasmodic. The need for common laws may not be generally accepted. There are no common values and assumptions, still less a common language, within which the rules can evolve. For this reason there has often been dispute or ambiguity about the content of the rules. The sanctions against breaking them (even the non-material sanctions) have always been weak and uncertain. Violations have been frequent. Indeed, it is arguable that it is the lack of a fully developed and fully accepted system of norms (rather than of more powerful institutions) which, above all, has prevented any genuine society of states, comparable to a domestic society, from coming into existence.

Despite these difficulties every international society has evolved rules of a sort. None has been genuinely anarchic. Most members have observed most of the rules most of the time.

In a certain sense there has been a progressive development. As communications have improved and contacts developed, ever more complex norms have been established. In the ancient Chinese society, though there were effective rules concerning diplomatic intercourse, rules in many other fields were ineffective or non-existent. The situation was little different among the Greek city-states, though religious taboos perhaps played a somewhat greater role there. During the last six centuries, though there have been periods of retrogression, an increasing range of detailed rules has gradually been established. Though these have not abolished conflict (and, as we have seen, there will always be conflict of some kind in every society), nor wholly abolished warfare (and questions of peace and war are by definition those where effective norms are hardest to establish, because they concern the questions on which people feel most passionately) they have done something to harmonise activities in many fields. These range from the law of space to the law of the sea, from the treatment of diplomats to the organisation of postal services, from trade rules to the validity and duration of treaties.

However, the range and effectiveness of norms is not the only factor which counts. The *type* of norms existing within each society is equally significant in determining its character. This is one of the elements which goes to make up the fabric of the international society as a whole. So in the age of dynasts the norms established are related to the rules of inheritance, chivalry and knightly combat; in the age of religions they are concerned with religious observance and the resolution of the conflicts occurring on that subject; in the age of sovereigns they relate to diplomatic precedence, the rules of war among states, the law of neutrality and similar questions; in the age of nationalism to finding accommodation among the major nations, distributing spheres of influence and defining the national principle; in the age of ideologies to laying down the ground rules for competitive coexistence; and so on. This relationship is not surprising. New norms must be adjusted to the type of conflicts encountered and the kind of behaviour which requires to be restrained. Today new rules have had to be formulated for outer space, satellite communications, biological weapons and so on, to take account of *technical* changes. But they are also needed in a more general way to order a world of ideological conflict, with relatively rigid frontiers and a high degree of interpersonal contact between states.

Because international society has always been a highly disorganised society it has inevitably been far harder than in smaller communities to establish the norms it requires. But the difficulty is not primarily the lack of a central authority. As we noted in the Introduction, it is not unusual among primitive societies for agreed principles to be established, and to be generally complied with, even though there exists no central authority having enforcement powers. The socialisation process to which all members are subjected has been able to create sufficient consensus among the society's members to secure compliance with the norms established and so to prevent excessive conflict without the use of coercive authority.

The main reason why international society has not yet been able to establish norms of conduct which would maintain a reasonable stable social existence is the lack of this kind of consensus. The problem is not the lack of agreement concerning domestic political systems. It is perfectly possible for states having totally different, even mutually conflicting, political systems none the less to live in peace together, provided there exists some consensus concerning the principles which should govern the *international* society. If every state maintained its own separate political existence within its own borders, and had contact with other states only for the purposes of trade, tourism and investment, undertaken according to agreed arrangements, a viable and peaceful international society could be established, however great the conflict betweeen their internal political systems. The reason that contemporary international society remains so unstable and beset by conflict is because of differences concerning *international*, not domestic society. It is because there is, as we have just seen, no agreement on the rules governing intervention in civil wars elsewhere, or on the right of a state to use armed force to protect its own nationals, and on the other points which we noted, that conflict and sometimes war is so frequent in the contemporary international society. Though there are now more, and more detailed, norms governing conduct in international society than at any earlier time, there continues to be disagreement about precisely those rules that are most necessary if a more peaceful society is to be created.

A condition for creating a more stable society is that more active efforts should be undertaken than at present to establish the norms that are required. Unless it is recognised that this is necessary, and unless a determined effort is made to arrive at understandings on the points in dispute, conflict, and sometimes war, will continue to occur. It is here that the lack of effective central institutions becomes more serious in its consequences. For the primitive society, without army or police force to punish or deter aggressors, will at least usually have a body of elders or a chief, or a high priest, able to pronounce on questions in dispute and to provide unchallengeable guidance concerning the law and customs of the people. In international society today no such authority exists. In a few cases the International Court of Justice is able to perform the function, though usually only on the less important matters in dispute (such as maritime boundaries). But it has never been given the role of pronouncing on the whole range of disputed questions relating to state behaviour. If a set of principles capable of sustaining a more viable international society is to be established, either the Court will need to be asked to make judgments on some of the controversial points at issue[19] – such as the obligations of outside states in cases of civil war, for example – or the UN General Assembly itself, perhaps through its committee on international law (the Sixth Committee) where governments are represented by international lawyers, will need to confront such questions more systematically.

If this is to influence the actions of states, however, public opinion generally would need to take a more concerned and more informed interest in such questions. In international society, as in others, the effectiveness of the principles which govern its operation is determined in the final resort by the degree to which they command the understanding and consent of ordinary people. Just as national governments, however great the power at their disposal, find it difficult to enforce a code of laws which is remote from the traditions and beliefs of the people as a whole, so in international society no code of international conduct that does not draw some support from individuals and groups within each state is likely to prove a viable one. In general it is the case that actions which governments undertake abroad, especially actions involving the use of armed force, are ultimately limited by what public opinion at home is willing to support (as the US found in Vietnam and the Soviet Union in Afghanistan). An effective code of international conduct, therefore, is unlikely to have effective influence on the actions of governments unless it is understood and accepted at least by the more educated and influential sections of the population in each state.

In international as in national societies, norms are a way of regulating and ordering society with the minimum encroachment on independence or free will. They induce conformity without imposing

19. The case the Court considered concerning US action towards Nicaragua is perhaps the closest it has yet come to considering such fundamental questions; but it is characteristic that in that case the judgment was rejected by the state against which it was directed (the US); as were its unfavourable judgments in other important cases, against Albania and Iceland.

it. Rules are always the ultimate rulers: they regulate society, as we saw earlier (p. 62), by securing *regularity* in behaviour and therefore making it more predictable. They have a special importance in international societies, where there exists no supreme authority able to secure conformity by coercive means. Within such societies, as our examples have shown, the norms evolve in response to a changing environment. They are moulded, as in narrower societies, by the prevailing preoccupations and needs of the society as a whole. But they secure their full effect only if accompanied by institutions capable of defining and enforcing them. And it is to the problem of establishing such institutions that we must now turn.

11 Authority

AUTHORITY IN DOMESTIC SOCIETY

Authority of a kind is exercised in almost all societies: a particular person, or a group of people, are widely recognised as having the right to reach decisions that others will regard as binding.

The basis for this authority is rarely, if ever, force alone. The recognised *right* to give commands, in other words, cannot be won by force (even if the *capacity* to do so may). In a few cases obedience may be imposed, for some or all of a society's members, for a time. But few if any societies can be maintained for long on the basis of coercion alone. For authority to be exercised successfully there must be a widespread recognition of its legitimacy.

Why do the members of a society recognise the legitimacy of a particular authority, for some or all purposes?

Political theories over the ages have found a variety of reasons why the citizens *should* obey authority: because rulers have been endowed by God with a divine right to rule, or with a mandate from heaven to do so; because the powers that be have acquired, by long possession, the prescriptive right to rule, acquired usually through inheritance, in the same way as a property-owner possesses rights to his own land; because of a theoretical contract between rulers and ruled, under which the former had the right to command obedience in return for affording protection and other benefits to those they ruled; because the rulers represented the general will of the population as a whole in the decisions they reached on government; or because they have been elected to do so by a majority of the population and so govern with their consent and according to their wishes.

Such theories, however, while they might be used to justify a particular form of government and the believed obligation of citizens to obey them, do not necessarily indicate the reasons why citizens do in fact obey authority. Sociologists have put forward a different set of theories to explain that fact.

Authority may be obeyed, they have suggested, because members of society recognise the *personal* qualities of the person who exercises it. They may respect *particular* people's judgment, bravery or leadership sufficiently to give them their unquestioning obedience. Such

227

obedience is given to the person and not to the position held; as French soldiers obeyed Joan of Arc, or Florentine citizens Savanarola, for example, though they held no office according them the right to command. This is the type of authority described by Max Weber as "charismatic".

In other cases, on the other hand, authority is obeyed, regardless of personal qualities of those that exercise it, only because of the *position* held by those people. So a soldier may obey his commanding officer, a priest his bishop, a government official his minister, without consideration of their character or abilities, but solely because of the office they hold. The person in a subordinate position accepts the tradition imposed by society that a duty of obedience to that authority exists and must not be questioned. This is the type of authority Weber named as "traditional".

But authority may also be obeyed for another reason: because the person who obeys rationally recognises the need for a system of authority, and so of obedience, if the society to which they belong is to function effectively. The need for order, for example, may be believed to create the need for an authority to maintain order, which must be obeyed. This obedience may not be unconditional. It may be given, for example, in a modern state, only if the authority is recognised as "constitutional"; or if it commands the "consent of the people"; or, in modern times, if it is based on a democratic election. This is the type of authority Weber recognises as "rational" or "legal". The claim to obedience, however, is not in essence different from that of "traditional" authorities: in both cases obedience is granted not to a person but to an authority which is recognised as properly constituted.

But these alternatives still do not necessarily describe the reasons why an authority is in fact obeyed in any society. They describe abstract categories: ideal types of authority. In many cases all three reasons for obedience may exist. The citizen may obey partly out of a rational recognition of the need for some type of authority and of the basis on which it rests; partly out of respect for tradition; partly out of personal regard for the qualities of those who exercise it. The three may be mixed in different proportions for different citizens. But others may obey authority for none of these reasons. The majority probably obey most of the time simply out of indifference or passive acquiescence: because in most situations it is simpler to obey than disobey. Nor do citizens even then give a general recognition of a government's authority. In real life they are willing to obey particular decisions in particular areas, because it is the simplest thing to do. But they reserve the right to disobey other particular commands that are unacceptable to them. Sometimes they knowingly break the speed limit, refuse to be vaccinated or decline to be conscripted. And they do this without rejecting the legitimacy of authority generally. In other words they recognise only a conditional, not an absolute authority. They will reject the right of authority to interfere in particular areas: for example their thoughts, feelings and considerable parts of their personal lives. They accept authority, that is, only for certain purposes and within certain limits.

Obedience is not only conditional. It is offered to different authorities for different reasons. In all societies authority is in practice *shared*: for example between central and local authorities; between secular and religious authorities; between official and unofficial organisations; and between different agencies operating in a variety of fields. Though a government may in theory reject all division of powers, and reserve to itself ultimate and overriding control in every field, in practice it is bound to delegate power to many other authorities and agencies which, on many detailed questions, reach individual decisions. For this reason too authority is never so simple and clear-cut as the questions of political philosophers debating political "obligation" might sometimes indicate. In practice authority is exercised not by a single all-powerful state or ruler, but on an *ad hoc* basis by innumerable lesser rulers; and obedience is accorded on an *ad hoc* basis in return.

It is true that in the highly centralised unitary state the presumption is made that the higher authority can, in the final resort, override a lower one, including unofficial agencies (such as a church). But which is the highest authority of all? When citizens rarely if ever stepped outside their own country and had few contacts with members of other societies, it was reasonable to suggest that they were ultimately subject to the "highest authority in the land", the sovereign power. Today that situation no longer holds true. There exist, besides a multitude of authorities and agencies with various responsibilities within each state, an almost equally wide range of such agencies that are international. Are their commands less binding on the citizen? Or do they have an authority that, on the contrary, transcends that of the national state? Is the UN the ultimate authority of world society, to which every inhabitant of the earth now unchallengeably belongs and to which all should give allegiance? And if so, how should that authority be exercised, in a world where power is still mainly vested in the hands of individual national states?

Authority is always ultimately a subjective factor. It exists only where it is believed to exist. The authority which governments, or individuals, in practice enjoy is that which is attributed to them by the populations they claim to rule. This does not depend solely on power. A government with little power may be recognised as the legitimate authority by most, and command their obedience. And one with great power may have little authority. In international society, while power is vested mainly in national governments, authority remains widely distributed. It is exercised by a wide range of agencies, both within states and among them. It is the balance of authority *between* these various agencies that will determine the character of world society at any one time.

AUTHORITY IN INTERNATIONAL SOCIETY

In international society the relationship between authority and power is still more tenuous than elsewhere. Here even more than in national society authority is ultimately a subjective factor; even more than in that case the authority international bodies can exercise is that which is attributed to them by the states they claim to influence; even more than in that case the obedience that states grant is conditional (so that they may obey UN resolutions most of the time but reserve the right to flout those they disagree with).

By tradition individual states have recognised no power above them. The independence which each above all demanded has made them recalcitrant to all attempts to create a superior authority which could exercise coercive power, or even a dominant influence, over them. The doctrine of "sovereignty" developed in the writings of Bodin, Hobbes and other writers, created the belief that each such state could decide for itself how much or how little account it would take of any proposal or demands coming from elsewhere. The parallel doctrine of "positivism", under which states held themselves to be bound only by those provisions of international law to which they had given positive assent, reflected a similar belief. As a consequence the disputes which arose in international society between one state and another have ultimately been settled on the basis of power alone.

These two doctrines reflected the distribution of power in international society during recent times. That society has always been one in which power was highly decentralised. Individual states have kept in their own hands sufficient armed power to defend themselves against other states; and this has been sufficient to enable them to maintain their independence also against attempts to establish an international authority which might constrain them. On this at least they have had a common viewpoint and a common interest. Whatever else they might disagree about, states, through most of international history, have been at one in seeking to maintain their independence of action – that is, their sovereignty – against any attempt to subordinate that power to a common authority or to joint decision-making. Many proposals have been made, from the earliest days of the state system, for the establishment of some such authority. Even in the highly competitive Chinese system successive hegemons sought to re-establish the traditional authority of the Chou dynasty, and there were even occasional efforts to establish a disarmed world. In ancient Greece the religious Amphictyonies, besides safeguarding shrines and regulating pilgrim traffic, sought to deal with political conflicts among the city states; and for a short time there existed a league of city-states, to which almost every city belonged, which was able to reach joint decisions especially on matters of defence. In medieval Europe there were proposals for the establishment of a league of Christian states, which might serve to resolve conflicts among such states (even if mainly to enable them to fight more effectively against the Turks). Later, William Penn, the Abbe St Pierre, Kant, Bentham and many other visionaries drew up plans for European institutions designed to resolve conflicts among the states of the continent through discussion in representative councils or through arbitration.

Such ideas were rarely taken seriously by the statesmen of the day. The proposals represented such a radical departure from the state system with which these were familiar that they did not appear to be remotely realisable to practical men of affairs. Because they interfered with the tradition of national autonomy which such statesmen valued above all else (and because they often appeared particularly unfavourable to the most powerful states, which benefited most from unfettered independence), they were not even discussed with any seriousness by governments. The closest these came to setting up any such system before the present century was in arranging – as in the concert of Europe – regular conferences to find solutions to the international crises of the day; establishing a system for regular mediation and arbitration of disputes by foreign sovereigns; and by establishing a framework for co-operation in particular practical tasks, as in the international commissions set up to manage the Rhine, Elbe and Danube rivers, and the international unions set up to establish agreed principles for running international posts and telegraphs in the course of the nineteenth century.

There are a number of reasons, apart from the tradition of national independence so powerfully established, why it has proved difficult to create an effective international authority within the society of states. Such an authority can be established on a number of different principles. One way in which it might come about would be if a single state could so extend its own power that it came to exercise a virtually universal authority over a very wide area. This is what occurred when the state of Ch'in established a unified empire in China on her conquest of the other states in 200 BC, and when Rome ruled a large part of the Mediterranean world a little later. In more recent times it has proved impossible for any single power to establish its authority in this way. For whenever any particular state has appeared to harbour that intention other states have combined to prevent it from succeeding. So when Charles V appeared close to securing the universal empire which his minister Gattinara aspired to, the alliance of France with the Protestant states of Germany proved sufficient to prevent this; just as the same combination, nearly a century later, was able to prevent the two great Hapsburg powers from winning a similar pre-eminence. Sixty years later Louis XIV was prevented from acquiring a dominant position in Europe by a combination of most of the other states; and a century later in Napoleon's day French hegemony was prevented by a similar combination. So too in the first half of this century Germany was twice prevented from securing domination of the continent by a combination of other powers; while in more recent times the US and the Soviet Union with their allies are each able to prevent the other winning for itself the world domination each is sometimes accused of desiring. This pattern is likely to be repeated indefinitely. Thus even if China were at some future time to be of a power that could win domination of the world, a new combination (even one bringing together the US and Soviet union) would undoubtedly come about to prevent that outcome occurring.

Nor is a diarchy of two powers any more likely to secure domination of world affairs. Where two major centres of power arise – like Athens and Sparta in ancient Greece, Spain and France in medieval Europe, the US and the Soviet Union today – they normally become more concerned to resist the power available to the other than to bind together to dominate the smaller states. Lesser powers tend to gravitate into the protective embrace of one or other of them so that a bi-polar world results. Somewhat more viable is an oligarchic system, in which five or six major powers together manage the affairs of the world in such a way as to ensure that in the settlement of every issue which arises something like a balance of advantage between them is achieved. Something like this occurred at the time of the Concert of Europe during the nineteenth century. But though such a system may secure settlements of lesser matters (as the Concert did on the question of Greek, Belgian, Egyptian, Romanian and Bulgarian independence, neutralisation of Belgium and Luxumburg, the navigation of great European rivers), it is usually unable to resolve the more fundamental differences between the great powers themselves. It may too prove increasingly unacceptable to the middle-sized and smaller powers, which are not themselves part of the oligarchy and are therefore unable to influence the decisions reached even if closely affected by them. Above all, there exists often insufficient unity among the great powers to impose agreed settlements.

Because of these problems and because of increasing concern over the scale and destructiveness of war, over the last eighty years an attempt has been made to establish a more democratic type of international authority, in which states are represented on a more equal basis. This was the nature of the system established both in the League of Nations and in the United Nations. In neither has there been strict equality among the membership. Both provided for special representation of the largest powers in their Council; and in the latter case accorded them the important privilege of a veto over important decisions. But membership was open to all states, and they enjoyed an equal *voice* on most of the questions discussed, regardless of huge disparities of size and power. This system, while it may have been more acceptable to the mass of the members of the international community, was inevitably far less so to the great powers. The latter became less and less inclined to submit themselves to the pressures from the weak which could be mobilised there; and they were increasingly tempted to reach private accommodations, outside the confines of any international organisation and regardless of its wishes. In other words the "democratic" structure of the organisations in the long run ran the risk of reducing, rather than enhancing their authority.

Nor was this the only difficulty. The organisations suffered from the fundamental weakness that they were unable to impose their authority when a government was determined to resist this. The power available to them has always been much less than that available to national states. They were never able, as national governments had been, to assert their authority by armed force in the final resort. This need not in itself have been fatal to their effectiveness had they sought to build up their authority by other means (p. 241 below). But in default of this, the deficiency of power was highly damaging in its effect. Peace-keeping forces, which some hoped might have been able to function effectively by dint of the "moral authority" they were said to enjoy, in practice had great difficulty in doing so in any state where a national army (such as the Israeli army in South Lebanon) chose to ignore their existence. The respect of the membership which might, as in other societies, have been the main basis for authority, even in default of powerful sanctions, was not sufficient to compensate for the lack of brute power available to buttress it.

This problem in turn reflected a more fundamental one. Different members of international society had differing interests in the creation of an effective international authority. In general, as in smaller societies, it was the smaller and weaker members which had the greatest interest in a strong central authority: to reduce the instabilities and uncertainties of a free-for-all, to contain the pretensions of the mighty, even to bring about some redistribution of power and wealth from strong to weak. But the strongest states had an opposite interest. They were concerned to prevent international bodies from acquiring any such power as might encroach on their own independence of action. And because they were the more powerful they were the more able to ensure that their wishes were fulfilled. Even weaker states were often more concerned to defend their own sovereignty from excessive intervention than to help create a more effective international authority. While within states the establishment of effective power at the centre usually reflected the interests of rulers seeking to reduce the pretensions of over-mighty citizens, as well as that of less powerful citizens who shared that aim, there was no similar focus of power in international society concerned to reduce the authority available to national states and increase that available to world bodies.

For the most part, therefore, within international society a central authority has been established only where a common interest has been manifest. For many functional purposes that common interest has brought about the creation of a wide range of multilateral institutions: for regulating international posts and telegraphs, sea and air transport, for maintaining joint meteorological services, for promoting common labour standards, organising cultural and scientific exchanges, providing development assistance of many kinds, regulating trade and payments among states. These were the kinds of organisation which were least controversial in their activities and their area of authority.

Joint legal institutions also began to emerge. For centuries heads of state had been asked to mediate and arbitrate the disputes of other states. That practice was now extended and strengthened. Already in 1856 a Protocol to the Treaty of Paris expressed the hope that "states . . . should, before appealing to arms, have recourse, so far as circumstances allow, to the good offices of a friendly power". An increasing number of bilateral treaties providing for arbitration were agreed. In 1873 an Institute for International Law was established to formulate rules for arbitration. In 1899 at the first Hague Conference a convention for the peaceful settlement of international disputes was drawn up, providing for mediation, conciliation and arbitration of international disputes. A permanent Court of Arbitration was established. And at the end of the First World War a Permanent Court of International Justice was established which, it was hoped, would settle disputes between states on legal questions.

The *political* institutions of international society were, not surprisingly, the last to emerge and the slowest to develop. It was here above all that states were most reluctant to accord effective powers to any international authority. States would agree to meet together to discuss their problems. They would even accept resolutions passed by such organisations when it was in their interests to do so. But they had no difficulty in finding reasons to flout all those resolutions believed contrary to national interests. On the questions of peace and war above all, where it was most desirable for international organisations to acquire effective authority, states were especially reluctant to grant it. World bodies could implore, demand and exhort. But they were able to do little to influence the use or threat of force by one state against another. In the very area where international authority was most required it proved in practice to be weakest.

AUTHORITY IN CONTEMPORARY INTERNATIONAL SOCIETY

Within the contemporary society the need for more effective international institutions is probably more widely recognised than ever before. But the difficulties of establishing them on a mutually acceptable basis remain formidable.

There are conflicting tendencies at work. The creation of more powerful institutions, or even of a more firmly established system of co-operation, can come about only by the voluntary decision of member-states. But there are many reasons why these may not be forthcoming. Power at present is concentrated in 160 or so national governments, conditioned to value their independence and sovereignty. But the divergences of attitude which inhibit co-operation are greater than ever. What is required is no longer an authority among a relatively small number of European states, of similar traditions and systems of government, as in the nineteenth century. It is one that is acceptable to 160 or more governments, of widely varying size, power, standard of living, tradition, culture and political belief. Acute ideological divisions prevent the development of the consensus, of values and principles, that is widely considered the necessary condition for creating even a *modus vivendi*, let alone for establishing viable common institutions. Perhaps most fundamental of all are the huge differences of interest between rich countries and poor, large and small, strong and weak.

Yet the need for more effective international institutions is greater than ever. With increasing economic interdependence (so that, for example, inflation, growth and interest rates in one country determine the level of economic activity in many others), there is increasing need for more effective international economic institutions. With the diminishing distance and rapid technological change, an increasing range of functional tasks can only be effectively carried out at the world level: the protection of the international environment, the safeguarding of patents, the regulation of trans-national corporations, the care of refugees, the control of trade in narcotic drugs, the regulation of satellite communications, the management of sea-bed mineral production and many others. Above all, the continued intensity of political conflict, the growth of intervention by some powers, often the most powerful, in the affairs of other states, the ever-increasing power of modern weapons brings a greater need than ever for effective international action to maintain world peace. In other words the very divisions – between ideologies, religions, races and continents – which makes international co-operation more difficult, also makes it more necessary.

Some new international bodies have been established to meet these needs. A wide range of international agencies, commisions and programmes have been established, which, within the constraints of their budgets, seek to perform a number of specialised functions. But their usefulness is inhibited by persistent disputes concerning the size and direction of their programmes. In some cases this has led to major states withholding funds or leaving organisations altogether. Sometimes more effective co-operation has been developed outside the ambit of official organisations. The regular economic "summits" which take place among the heads of government of developed states are held without reference to the UN or the great majority of its member-states. The superpowers meet and negotiate bilaterally on many aspects of their relations, including disarmament, outside the UN framework. Regional bodies, in Europe and elsewhere, establish a far closer degree of co-operation with neighbouring states than occurs at the world level. Professional organisations, non-governmental bodies, meetings of industrialists and trade unions, reach understandings in a number of areas. In this way a network of international co-operation, a least on lesser matters, is established among and between states.

But there are many weaknesses in this process. In general the more important the area in which an international body works, the weaker its authority. While it has been possible to set up organisations to operate effectively in the field of patents or the notification of infectious diseases, it has proved far harder to do so in the area of peace and war, where the need for an effective authority is greatest. Decisions of the Security Council in that field are frequently vetoed by one or other of the permanent members; and the more important the question being discussed the more likely it is that a permanent member, usually a superpower, feels it necessary to use the veto. Even where a veto is not employed the majority of resolutions have little effect. The mandatory decisions which the organisation is competent to reach have almost never been taken; and where they have been (as over Rhodesian sanctions), they have still been flouted by important states. Other Council resolutions and all Assembly resolutions are only recommendations; and governments have little hesitation in defying them when it is in their interest to do so. In general international authority has been almost entirely without effect in preventing or even deterring war.

Even in functional fields, where the benefits of co-operation are most apparent and its costs are lowest, the development of international authority has been slow and hesitant. It has not proved the case, as was once forecast, that functional bodies could be insulated from political conflict. There have been widespread differences of view, between east and west or north and south, especially on questions of membership, programmes, funding and "politicisation". Above all, there is continual conflict about the size of budgets, and especially about their rates of growth. Such disputes have led, in extreme cases, to the withdrawal of important members from such organisations. The Soviet Union withdrew from nearly all the agencies for a few years in the early fifties, while the US withdrew from the ILO in the late seventies and from UNESCO in the mid-eighties. Though there is a general recognition that such bodies have some role to play, there has been increasing pressure in the richer countries to halt their growth, even to reduce their role. They are represented as having fallen under the control of a majority of small, poor and irresponsible states. It is therefore suggested by some that rich countries would do better to look after their own interests entirely independently of world bodies.

Thus there are a number of obstacles to the development of international authority at this time. First there are the deficiencies of many of these bodies themselves. It is not difficult for those so inclined to show that they are less effective than they should be; that some of their programmes are diffuse or ill-conceived; that some of their organs spend much time in ill-tempered and ill-organised debate; that extraneous political disputes are sometimes injected into their proceedings; and that administration is bureaucratic and sometimes less than efficient. The fact that exactly the same charges could be made about most national administrations does not reduce their attractiveness to those already predisposed to criticise international organisations. And the fact that some of the work of those organisations, especially in the field of peace and security, has been unsuccessful (mainly *because* of the actions of national governments) has given further ammunition to such critics and further reason for disillusion and censure. A vicious circle is at work. The obstructions placed by national governments reduce effectiveness. And reduced effectiveness stimulates further opposition.

Second, and related to this, is the lack of deeply based political support for such bodies. To ordinary citizens in most countries international organisations are almost infinitely boring. They are remote and inaccessible. Their activities are largely unknown. And if the citizen has any view at all it is more likely to be resentment at their interference or inefficiency, than appreciation of their achievements. Thus if it is hard enough for the citizen to identify with national governments it is even harder to do so with distant international bodies with which they have almost no direct contact. They are more aware of the failures of such organisations than of their successes, since the former secure widespread publicity and the latter win little attention. It is not therefore possible for international authority to appeal over the heads of governments to a broader constituency of support outside. The mass of the public is usually even less enthusiastic about the performance of these organisations than are the governments which raise the money for them. International institutions, in other words, even more than national governments, lack the basis of public support which could alone give them legitimacy.

Third, there does not exist, even among governments, any consensus concerning the purposes and principles which should underlie the activities of international institutions. For authority of this kind such a consensus is particularly necessary. Where a powerful central authority, wielding superior power, can impose its will, such consensus may not be required. But in a society which is dependent on voluntary co-operation, it becomes essential. In earlier international societies, for example in Europe in the eighteenth and nineteenth centuries, whatever the differences between states and however much they might from time to time enter into conflict with each other, there was a considerable degree of mutual understanding among them about the way in which relations should be conducted and the principles that should underlie their co-existence. In the contemporary international society even this degree of consensus has largely been lacking. Differences of viewpoint, between east and west, north and south, are such that there is no agreement even on the basic principles governing the society: whether or when revolution is legitimate, when it can or should be assisted from outside, when the use of force against another state is permissible, on the desirability of a new international economic order and so on.

Finally, and most fundamentally of all, behind this lack of consensus lies a fundamental division of *interest* between different states within the society. The most fundamental is that between the strong and the weak. In general the strong have an interest in a free-for-all, and a minimum of international authority, whether in the political or the economic field. The weak, on the contrary, have an interest in strong world institutions which are capable of placing restraints on the actions of the strong, and so of defending the weak from the effects of those actions. There is a corresponding division of interest between the rich and the poor. Rich states, whether strong or weak, have an interest in the minimum degree of intervention by international bodies, in low levels of spending and so in the minimum redistribution from themselves to the poor. The poor, on the other hand, have an interest in more effective international institutions which may be more capable of bringing about such a redistribution. Even when states have a similar view about the *degree* of international authority which is desirable, they may have very different ideas about the *type* of authority: about how it is to be constituted and controlled, and in which areas it should be most active. And once again, in a society where authority can only be strengthened by the voluntary commitments of all states, such differences of viewpoint are especially limiting in their effect. Though there are a few areas in which most states have a common interest in joint action, there are many others where one group or another is opposed to any strengthening of authority and is in a position to prevent it.

There are therefore many reasons why international institutions have developed more slowly and more hesitantly than many had believed and hoped. As a result, international society, though undoubtedly a society of a sort, remains a fragmentary one. Authority of the kind wielded in states, resting on a concentration of power at the centre, cannot exist. Authority of other kinds, because of the lack of consensus, remains weak. If it is to become eventually a more integrated society, authority of a different kind may need to be called into play.

CONCLUSIONS

In common parlance today, and even in much political theory, "authority" is often identified with the authority of a central power, seen as alien and external, capable of imposing its will on unwilling citizens. Yet authority need not have that meaning. In many simple societies authority does not necessarily imply constraint, and certainly not the constraint of overriding physical power. Authority need not be associated with power at all. The authority of father, teacher, leader, rests on the respect in which they are held, not on the power which is available to them. In many societies the authority that is most revered is that of custom – customary belief and customary rule – and these may be seen as the property of society as a whole, in which all share: so that authority is internal rather than external, voluntary not compulsory. Thus the village elders, the high priests or public opinion generally, in laying down a particular interpretation of jointly-shared customs, are felt to guide and influence, not to coerce. And because authority in that form is willingly accepted, those who exercise it do not need coercive power to secure conformity.

International society has far more in common with a simple society of this sort than with a centralised modern state. Thus, within the foreseeable future, international authority is likely to be of a similar kind. It is improbable that there will exist any central authority holding coercive power within that society. The tradition of sovereignty encourages member-states to oppose the transfer of power to central institutions, whether through forcible conquest by a single power, or through a voluntary ceding of power by each state individually. At present national states see the maintenance of their sovereign independence as a safeguard of their ability to sustain their own way of life according to their own individual values. They would not sacrifice this safeguard unless there existed some consensus concerning the basic principles on which a wider international society should be based (in other words unless supreme power at the centre was no longer necessary). Individuals and groups in international society in general share the same view: they would probably fear the encroachment of an interfering world authority at least as much as do their governments.

But this does not mean that a greater degree of authority of other kinds could not be established. If effective authority does not depend on the availability of superior power, it is of little importance that superior power is not available. International bodies might acquire for themselves the international authority they seek if they devoted themselves to the more difficult but more fundamental task of winning influence rather than power. There are a number of ways in which authority of this type might be created.

First, it could be based in part at least, like authority in many smaller societies, on *tradition*. Certain traditions commanding authority have already been established in international society. These are seen, for example, in the conventions that have developed concerning the conduct of diplomatic relations, consular affairs, maritime law, the law of treaties and many other aspects of day-to-day relations among states. In some cases these are accepted, by states and by lawyers, as representing "customary international law". In others they have been incorporated in formal international conventions. In others again UN Declarations, formal statements of basic principles, often passed unanimously, or with very few dissentients, can be seen as extending the scope of this consensus. Judgments of the International Court of Justice are similar in effect. Taken together these come to represent a body of tradition which is increasingly difficult for individual states to ignore, or even to flout without substantial cost in terms of loss of international good will. They can defy that tradition in particular cases: they cannot unmake it.

A second possible basis for international authority, again comparable to that established in many primitive societies, is the development of more firmly established *procedures* for dealing with conflicts and crises. The use of such methods is seen in the traditions and ceremonies employed in simple societies in dealing with disputes among members and families; or in the complex sets of procedures established for dealing with industrial disputes in modern Western society (another case where authority cannot be imposed by force, if only because it is impossible to lock up thousands of striking workers). In each of these cases the procedures laid down establish a known pattern of events which influence expectations, and so responses, each time a dispute occurs. If international society were likewise to establish equally consistent procedures, equally firm expectations could be created, and the responses of those involved in disputes would eventually be similarly influenced. Where disputes arose, the contestants, instead of instinctively reaching for their guns, would look to their lawyers. At present no such procedures are sufficiently firmly established within international society. Some disputes are taken up by the Security Council, but many are not (in general only those are considered which are raised by the disputants themselves, even though the Charter clearly lays down that any member can raise any dispute). Even when a conflict is discussed, the responses of the Council can range from almost total inactivity, reference to a regional organisation, proposals for mediation or the dispatch of the Secretary-General. If a consistent course of action was adopted, if every dispute was considered at an early stage, if a commission of inquiry was habitually appointed to examine the facts and propose a settlement, the expectations of those involved would be more strongly influenced. The knowledge that a particular type of inquiry would be instituted, and particular forms of international pressures therefore brought to bear, could serve to deter, marginally at least, resort to force and the attempt to seek unilateral settlements immune from public scrutiny.

Third, in the same way appropriate *institutions* can become, as in other societies, the means of enhancing international authority. As we have seen, the condition of effective authority is that it commands respect. To win respect, international institutions must be seen to be visibly representative of the world as a whole: that means that large states should neither be over-dominant (as in the Concert system of the nineteenth century) or under-represented (as in the UN today). Permanent membership would need to be redistributed in accordance with the realities of power and size, while a new category of semi-permanent members might ensure adequate representation of other large powers. But to win respect, international institutions also need to be seen to be responsible and impartial; which means that they must cease to be demeaned by the political squabbling and national rivalries so often seen in UN bodies today. To bring this about its meetings would need to cease to be public, creating an open invitation to propaganda and abuse, and become confidential acts of judgment, in which a sense of co-responsibility and collegiality among the members could be established. So long as international bodies appear essentially political and partial in their approach, it remains easy for states that have no wish to comply with their judgments to ignore them. Only if they can appear disinterested and objective will they secure the respect which is the condition of effective authority.

For the same reason international bodies will win the authority they seek only if they are seen to be implementing consistent *principles*. So long as they react in an *ad hoc* way to each new crisis which occurs, so long as they decide on one course in one case and something totally different in another, they will no more be able to win influence over their members than could priests or elders if they issued judgments that were prejudiced, arbitrary and inconsistent, or than could parents secure discipline if they applied one rule to one child and a different one to another. As we saw in the last chapter, it is generally accepted principles of international conduct, which are most visibly lacking in international society today. National states in many cases are able to justify the use of armed force – for example in intervening in civil conflicts elsewhere, in defending their own nationals in another state or restoring law and order in a neighbouring territory – precisely because the principles which govern that conduct are at present ill-defined. Only if international bodies could, by consisten practice and regular precept, establish a recognised code of conduct such as operates within most smaller societies will peaceful co-existence among states be established, and the authority which international bodies claim appear to be based on a rational set of principles.

Finally, if international authority is to be strengthened, it may be necessary to enhance the personal role of individual figures within these institutions. At present the UN Secretary-General and his opposite numbers in other international organisations are inclined to cloak themselves in the grey anonymity of faceless civil servants. This reflects an understandable desire to protect themselves from the charge of overreaching their authority, or challenging the policies laid down by the intergovernmental bodies. But it may also reduce the authority that international organisations might otherwise acquire. Their authority can never be genuinely charismatic, that is based on their personal qualities rather than their office (though Dag Hammarskjöld came close to enjoying such prestige): since they must always be servants of their organisation, and of majority feeling within them, there will always be strict limits to their freedom of expression and action. But if allowed to play a more personalised and public role than they do today (as Hammarskjöld was in his own day), they could do much to humanise international authority and rescue it from the remote impersonality by which it is obscured today. In the same way, greater publicity for the myths and symbols which surround the organisation – blue berets, UN flags, international ceremonies – as well as for its main achievements – in peace-keeping, disaster relief, the care of refugees and other fields – would do much to enhance its standing. Since authority is, as we have seen, ultimately a subjective factor, and rests in the minds of those who are subjected to it rather than on those who exercise it, such public relations efforts, as national rulers have long realised, are of profound political importance. For international authority, which cannot be buttressed by armed force, these intangible means of influencing opinion are especially vital.

In all these ways international authority may be enhanced even without any enhancement of international power. It has never been the case that the conditon of order in any society is the submission of its members to the superior power of a central authority. The condition of order is the adoption by all members of society of behaviour which is compatible with the freedom and independence of fellow-members. In international society, as in other societies, that behaviour may be encouraged by peaceful means as much as by force. Effective international authority, therefore, is likely to be created by securing conformity without coercion; restraint without constraint; influence without power.

12 Conclusions

THE NATURE OF INTERNATIONAL SOCIETY

What conclusions can be drawn, on the basis of this survey, about the character of international society?

The first and most obvious feature which distinguishes it from other societies is its *complexity*. It comprehends a vast range of subordinate societies, each themselves subdivided in complicated ways. It not only contains many different national states, with their component regions, counties, cities and villages, but countless organisations, enterprises, groups and individuals, organised in many different ways for many different purposes, both within and across the principal political boundaries. Each different kind of actor, individual and collective, is related in many different ways with other actors. There are no clear lines of authority, nor clear hierarchies, linking one to another in predictable ways. Above all, there is no overall authority in a position to determine, either directly or indirectly, what happens at lower levels and so to establish order within international society generally.

A second and related feature is its *diversity*. Not only is there no clear political or administrative structure. The individual units – national states, economic organisations, associations of many kinds – vary widely. There is no common value-system, no common culture, no common beliefs, no common way of life, of the types that often exist within smaller societies. Still less is there any deeply established common loyalty or common purpose to link the disparate units. Though in each of these respects the divergences are probably diminishing, and are certainly far less than the differences which existed a hundred or so years ago, they remain considerable. And though there also exist, as we saw in the Introduction, very wide divergencies in values, culture, beliefs and way of life within national states, those differences clearly condition the extent to which – in either case – an integrated social structure can be created.

Third, both of these features partly result from the fact that it is a highly *decentralised* society. Power at the centre, that is in the hands of international organisations, remains extremely weak; as it is also at the periphery, among groups and individuals. Against this power at the mid-point – in the 160 or so national governments – is very strong. For the most dramatic development within international society over the last century or so is not the increase in international authority which has occurred there. As we saw in the last chapter, such an increase in the authority of international bodies has occurred, especially in a number of functional fields. But it has been outweighed by the even more dramatic increase in national power which has taken place during the same period. National governments have not only for the first time established, in most cases, unchallenged military power in their territories. The resoures of which they dispose, measured in national budgets, have over that period multiplied very many times. Through the use of those resources, and of the authority they can command, they have extended their control over a vast range of activities, and reduced the independence of action of the lesser centres of power which previously operated largely autonomously. This increase in state power has counteracted, and partly nullified, the increase in international authority which has occurred. Strengthened by the power which they have acquired at home national governments have been careful to place strict limits on the degree of authority or power which international bodies are able to wield. The more powerful states particularly, as such bodies have increasingly fallen under the control of a majority of very small, very poor states, often seeking to operate them to their own advantage, have been increasingly unwilling to concede any effective authority to, or even to play a positive and constructive role within them. Only in a small number of areas where there exists a manifest common interest in the development of effective international bodies – for example in a few technical fields – and within some regional institutions, has any significant degree of influence been transferred from the national to the international level.

Fourth, despite this concentration of power in a number of national centres, contemporary international society is characterised by a large flow of trans-national movements of many kinds. The rapid development of communications over recent decades has made possible a huge increase in contact across national boundaries. People and ideas, trade and investment, cultural contacts and political influences, flow across frontiers in a way that has never been seen before. To some extent these flows have an assimilating effect. Differences in culture, thought and way of life in different parts of the world are rapidly reduced. A common basis of ideas, a common culture, common political institutions, even to some extent a common way of life, begin to be established all over the world. Increasingly the most striking differences which exist in each of these respects are no longer, as in the past, those to be seen between different states and different regions: for example between the patterns of thought of Greco-Judaic civilisations in Europe and of Confucian ways of thinking in China or Hindu ways of thinking in India, between the Christian cultures of Europe and the Buddhist culture of the East, between the political ideas of the Western world and the traditional political concepts of other civilisations, between the way of life of an African village or of a European city. Today the main differences exist *within* each country: between the urban civilisation of the great cities and that of the remote agricultural village, between the culture of teenagers and that of the elderly, between the way of life of the wealthy surburbanites and that of the unemployed slum-dweller. Culture, way of life and way of thinking are similar for the privileged classes of the world; as they are for the unemployed masses all over the world. It is between the two that the main differences now exist.

This leads to the final characteristic of contemporary international society. It is one that contains very large *inequalities*: not only in standard of living but in levels of education, technology, culture and amenities generally. Though there always have been substantial differences in every society, above all between the rulers and the great magnates on the one hand and most of the rest of society on the other, they have perhaps never been as great as in the modern world: for example between the oil tycoons of Texas and the illiterate peasant of Bihar; between the large landowner of a Latin-American state and the shanty-dweller at the edges of its big cities. The capacity to increase wealth which modern technology provides produces huge advances in standard of living for a significant section of the population in most countries, but none at all for the most deprived sections which, with increasing unemployment, become, even in developed states, a larger and larger proportion of the total. Moreover these substantial differences between individuals in every state are intensified by the increasing inequalities between entire countries. In previous ages, while there were large differences between the richest and poorest in every country, the difference between the standard of living in entire states was far less. Today, though there are some rich and some poor in every country (and the very rich in poor countries are often almost as rich as the very rich in rich countries – sometimes richer), there are hugh variations in the *average* standard of living available in each. And though the average rate of growth in poor

cONCLUSIONS

countries is no less than rich ones, and sometimes greater, because of the different starting-points the differences become in absolute terms greater all the time. A growth rate of 3 per cent in a poor country may give an increase in average income of US$3 a head; while the same growth rate in a rich country will give an increase fifty times as much. As a result the large differences which already exist in incomes – and so in educational and cultural standards, in technical attainment, in public services and amenities of many kinds – become steadily greater.

It is therefore not only a society of great inequalities, but of *increasing* inequality. Even within a single state the rapid increase in income and standard of living of managerial, financial, professional classes co-exists with an almost stationary level of income for a substantial under-class, the workless, the homeless, the elderly and the fatherless family. Increasingly the latter may appear to have more in common with the dispossessed of other countries than they do with the privileged of their own. At the same time, differences in wealth of different countries to a large extent determine their influence on international society generally. The ideas, culture and institutions which increasingly become the common world norm are overwhelmingly those derived from the more developed countries of Europe and North America which are progressively adopted among most poorer countries of the world. As power shifts to new centres such as Japan, China and the Soviet Union, new sources of culture and ideas may emerge. But it will remain the case that the character of society as a whole will be strongly influenced by the distribution of economic, and so of political, power within it.

Each of the factors we have identified – the complexity of international society, its diversity, its decentralised character, the profusion of trans-national influences and the great and growing inequalities among peoples and states – helps to determine its character. The first three are all factors which make it more difficult to establish a more integrated international society. Even the trans-national forces, which might be expected to have the opposite effect, are only marginal in influence: they are themselves to a large extent under the control of national governments which can determine how much movement – of people, of goods, of ideas and culture – they will permit to and from their own state. Because of the size and fragmented character of this world it might be questioned whether an international "society" can be said to exist at all. In the absence of a common culture (as, for example, the Greek city-states or medieval Christendom possessed), of similar political institutions and ways of thought (as existed in nineteenth-century Europe), can there be said to exist anything which could reasonably be described as a society?

The common assumptions and understandings which an international society requires are quite different from those required within a domestic political system. Even within states a well-ordered society, and a viable political system, can exist without any unanimity of views on political principles or even a common "value-system". The fact that there are wide divergencies between conservatives, liberals and socialists, or even between communists and non-communists, need not prevent the working of such a system provided all accept the necessity for peaceful change within society and do not seek to impose their own views by force on other members. In international society too differences of view whether on domestic issues or on desirable international relationships can be sustained provided, here too, there exists a commitment to peaceful change only, and no attempt by one or more states to press their views on others by force. In theory at least it might be possible for a number of states of diametrically different political systems and political ideology to co-exist peacefully with each other, provided only that they were agreed on the principles which should govern relationships among themselves.

In practice, however, international society does not consist and has not for a century or so consisted of a series of totally self-contained and separate political systems of this kind, requiring only some mutually accepted principles of peaceful co-existence. Increasingly there exists not a series of separate political communities but a single interrelated international society. And the problems of establishing a system of order within such a society become not less but greater as a result.

There are two main difficulties. The first is that the development of modern communications makes it more difficult for states, and groups and individuals within them, to maintain the degree of indifference to events in other states which a system of live-and-let-live requires. They are increasingly concerned over the situation of fellow human-beings, even though they live in different states and under different flags. The memory of the abominations committed, largely ignored by the outside world, in Germany during the Nazi period, not to speak of mass slaughters on a somewhat lesser scale in Cambodia, Uganda and Equatorial Guinea in more recent times, means that the governments of one country are no longer willing to leave to the governments of other countries total discretion as to how they treat their own populations. Equally significant as an influence on state actions is the fact that concern over national security increasingly extends far beyond the borders of each state, so that the character of the governments in power in neighbouring territories is seen as a vital interest, especially within the more powerful countries. In the eighteenth century, when distances were greater, and knowledge of events elsewhere therefore less, governments were often willing to avert their eyes from domestic developments in neighbouring states. By the nineteenth century intervention had already become more common, usually to assist national revolution in neighbouring states. Today, with all the modern means of communication which exist, and the far greater knowledge and concern about events elsewhere which results, states are less willing than ever to remain indifferent to internal events elsewhere.

The second difficulty is that international society is not exclusively a society of states. It is a society of groups and individuals as well. Even if *states* were willing to accept a simple doctrine of peaceful coexistence – live and let live – groups and individuals would not. Revolutionary movements emerge which operate simultaneously in a large number of states all over the world; environmental movements challenge the actions of governments elsewhere in undertaking nuclear tests, building reprocessing plants or exploiting the Antarctic; international trade unions co-operate together to contest the actions of employers in foreign states. The problem of creating a mutually acceptable international order is therefore not simply one of securing the agreement of 160 governments, difficult enough though that may be. It becomes one of securing understanding among a multiplicity of individuals, groups, associations, political parties, trade unions and others about the legitimacy of actions taken by governments, enterprises and authorities of many kinds throughout the world.

Such conflicts arise because of the conflicting interests of individuals, groups and states concerning events which may occur anywhere throughout the world. It is these conflicting interests which present the main dynamic for change, in international society as within other societies.

INTERESTS IN INTERNATIONAL SOCIETY

Within every society the actions which the members take depend largely on their conceptions of their interests.

These interests are of a number of kinds: individual and collective, material and non-material, short term and long term. While individuals will find that in some respects their interests coincide with those of other members, in certain respects they discover that their interests conflict. This divergence of interests may stem from differences in occupation, wealth, power, abilities or opportunities.

In international society too the actions taken – by states, groups and individuals – depend on the way they conceive their interests. These interests too may be individual or collective, material or non-material, short term or long term. In this case too interests will coincide in some respects and conflict in others. Finally here too the conflict of interests stems from differences in starting positions, measured in terms of wealth, capacities and opportunities.

Thus, for example, a state may be concerned about its individual interest in improving its balance of payments or defending its territory against a neighbour; or about its collective interest as a member of the Group of 77 or of an ideological alliance. It may be concerned with material interests, such as winning a contract abroad or negotiating a loan from the IMF; or with non-material interests, such as winning a seat on the Security Council or some other mark of international status. It may be concerned with its short-term interest in solving an immediate financial crisis, or in strengthening its air defences, or with its long-term interest in winning lasting prosperity and security for its people. A trading company may be concerned about its individual interest in increasing its share of a particular foreign market, or its collective interest in securing better access to that market for trading companies generally. It may be concerned with its material interest in increasing its world-wide profitability, and its non-material interest in winning a reputation for fair dealing; with its short-term interest in increasing sales this year, and its long-term interest in expanding its activities over the next decade or two. Finally, individuals may be concerned about their personal interest in a successful career in a foreign country, or their collective interest in improving the conditions of work of all workers in their industry in many countries; with their material interest in being allowed to inherit property in a foreign country, and their non-material interest in securing the right to marry there; with their short-term interest in being able to travel to a foreign country, and their long-term interest in being able to settle permanently there.

States, groups and individuals each become aware that these interests are in conflict, in one respect or another, with the interests of others. The interests of a rich state in access to a market may conflict with that of a poor state in protecting an infant industry or conserving foreign exchange; the interest of an international trade union in raising its members' wages and conditions of work conflict with that of international employers in higher profits; the interest of the individual of one country who has taken a job in another may conflict with the interests of an individual elsewhere who might otherwise have held the job. Conflicts of interest are not always between entities of the same kind. The interest of a state in a strong balance of payments may conflict with that of a foreign company in selling its production to that country; the interest of an individual who has taken a job in another country may conflict with that of a trade union in protecting jobs for its members. And so on.

In international society, as in other societies, it is *consciousness* of interests which is the decisive factor. It could almost be said that interests exist only in the mind, or at least become effective only when thought about. It is not possible to establish incontrovertibly what are the interests of a particular individual or group: any such statement will be influenced by preconceptions concerning what those individuals and groups should seek and how they should seek it. To state that their *true* interests are of a particular kind is only to give a subjective opinion, based on particular preconceptions, of what their interests are or ought to be seen to be. When therefore, Marxists seek to raise the "consciousness" of a sleeping proletariat, or denounce its "false consciousness", they seek merely to persuade that proletariat to accept the assessment of their interests which they have made themselves: to substitute one subjective judgement for another. Whatever judgement may be made by others concerning the interest of an individual, group or state, the only assessment which is socially significant, that will affect outcomes over the long term, is that which is made by those individuals, groups or states themselves.

These assessments will be based in the first place on their conceptions of their own situation in relation to that of others. If it appears unfavourable, they will be disposed to seek change; and the more unfavourable it appears the more strenuously they are likely to seek to bring about such changes. In modern international society, because of the decline in distance, the changes they seek will not necessarily be within their own state alone but within that society generally. So the revolutionary Cuban will seek to bring about revolution not only in Cuba but in Bolivia and other parts of Latin America, and will join with others of like mind to do so. The Islamic fundamentalist group will seek to establish an Islamic state not only in Iran but in Iraq and Lebanon and many other states as well. The disadvantaged African state will seek to bring about change not only within its own economy, but in the international economy as a whole, and will join with other like-minded states, groups and individuals to do so. With the shrinking size of the world, a single state is insufficient space to contain the political and economic ambitions which are now widely held. The changes that matter are not those that take place within a single state but within the world as a whole. Conflicts of interest are thus increasingly seen in a world-wide perspective, and must be fought out in a world-wide struggle.

Are there, therefore, today international "classes", replacing the purely national social classes of earlier times? Will international history increasingly become the history of an international class struggle transforming international society in the way that domestic societies have been transformed by the domestic class struggle? There are many who assert that this is so. But though such a struggle may ultimately occur, there is little evidence that it has begun as yet.

Interests, as we have seen, become an effective political force only when they are perceived. Today there is little *consciousness* of international class interests, or the need for international class solidarity, of the kind which some have demanded. The industrial workers of Britain enjoy a material standard of living so different from that of the industrial workers of India or Colombia that it is almost impossible for them to perceive a common class interest. Moreover, if they are aware of the latter at all, they may see them as a *threat* to their own interests as producers of goods which could compete with those which they produce. Even the workers of Colombia and India, though sharing a comparable standard of living, and a common situation and a common need to secure access to the markets of rich countries, have little *sense* of that common interest, still less a disposition to participate in common actions to promote that interest. Even trade unions in different countries, which represent such workers and which might be expected to have some consciousness of a long-term common interest, and a need for common action against common opponents (such as the multinational companies often active in both their countries) have, with rare exceptions, few contacts with each other and rarely consider even the possibility of common action; and such action, on the very few occasions when it has occurred,[1] has rarely succeeded.

Neither individuals nor groups, therefore, at present are normally sufficiently conscious of a common interest with those sharing a similar situation in other countries, to organise for common action, to make themselves an international "class", and as such a significant force for change. For it is not only power which has become increasingly concentrated in a small number of centres – national states – within international society, but loyalties as well. What has occurred has been the *collectivisation* of interests. Increasingly the interests of groups and individuals are seen as incorporated in those of their state. The material betterment they can secure, their relative situation compared with other individuals, their status and sense of achievement, all of these appear to depend on the relative success of their own states – in securing high growth rates, in establishing lavish public services and amenities, in winning power and prestige abroad – rather than on their own capacity to win these for themselves, still less on the success in joining with those in similar occupations in other states to improve their relative situation in all simultaneously. It is *national* accumulation and *national* production, rather than that of individuals or enterprises, which increasingly determines individual standards of living; and increasingly therefore it is *national* interest, rather than the interest of classes, groups or individuals which becomes the principal focus of concern and activity within international society.

Individuals and groups conceive of their own interests in terms of state interests at present partly because states are more capable of promoting their interests than they are themselves. The ability of individuals to promote their own interests in international society, alone and unaided, is limited. Even in domestic society there is little that most can do, by individual endeavour, to increase their own status or standard of living. They are able to do so mainly through their membership of an enterprise, trade union, political party or other collective body. Unless they are enterprisers of unusual drive or good fortune, or political leaders of special charismatic power, they are rarely able, through their own independent activities, to bring about significant changes, even in domestic society, to their own advantage. In international society their ability to do so is still more limited. The size amd amorphous character of that society

---

1. For example, among international seamen, or among Ford workers in different countries.

makes it particularly resistant to change by isolated individuals. Groups – economic enterprises or organised pressure groups and associations – are marginally better equipped to bring about the changes they demand, not only in one country but in many simultaneously. But they too are constrained in what they can do by the power that is available to states to restrict and control their activities. The changes they can institute are essentially only those which states can be persuaded to make. In general, to secure their own success within international society, both individuals and groups are dependent on the assistance of their own governments. What they are able to achieve will depend on how far their own government can defend or promote their national interest in dealing with other states: whether it can secure an increase in foreign loans, a reduction in world interest-rates, a lifting of foreign protectionist barriers, a larger programme of aid from abroad. Whether they are able to emigrate to a foreign country, to acquire property in that country, the conditions on which they can marry or educate their children there, all of these depend on the agreements undertaken by their governments with other governments elsewhere.

It is mainly the actions of states therefore which can promote the interests of those groups and individuals which live within their borders. How far the interests of the latter are adequately promoted depends therefore in the first place on the relative success of states in achieving their objectives. And it is the conflict among states, each seeking to promote the objectives of the state as a whole, including that of their individual inhabitants, which represents the main dynamic of change within international society.

But clearly the interests of individuals and groups within states are not uniform. Not all will benefit in the same way by any particular action which a state may take. Some may not benefit at all. In seeking to promote the "national interest", therefore, states – that is their governments – are continually needing to make choices between the benefit of one group or another (in other words to define the national interest in a particular way). And individuals and groups are mainly able to promote their own interests in international society, not through any independent actions which they may take there, but through their differential influence on the policies which their own government undertakes. It is the relative success of each in this respect which will determine the kind of changes which ultimately occur in international society.

CHANGE IN INTERNATIONAL SOCIETY

What are the most important types of change which may be brought about in international society? How and why do such changes occur?

The most obvious forms of change are those that take place in the structure of power. Since most international power is in the hands of states, the structure of power in international society is changed principally through changes in the relative power of states. Some states may increase in power through the success of their armed forces, or because of rapid economic or population growth, while others decline because of defeat in war, social instability or economic failure. The relative position of the leading states may change, so that the hegemony of one state or group of states is displaced by the hegemony of another, leading to a kind of circulation of élites of the kind discussed by Pareto. The number of states may increase (as over the last forty years), leading to a reduction in relative power of previously dominant states and a wider distribution of power generally. Or, conversely, the absorption of small states by larger ones can lead to a reduction in a total number of states, having the opposite effect. Changes of this kind affect the character of the international society as a whole. A society of many states of equal power will be different from one dominated by a few; one in which differences of size and power are very great will differ from one in which the members are more nearly equal; one in which there are two dominant powers (bi-polar) will be different from one in which there are three, four, five or more. Moreover particular powers may be associated with a particular view about international society and relations within it, so that an increase in its relative position may affect the way in which inter-state relations are in practice conceived and conducted (as US dominance, for example, largely determined the kind of society established in 1945). And so on.

Next, there may be changes in the character of the principal units, affecting their relations with each other. A society of states ruled by dynasts will be different from one ruled by powerful chief ministers, and from one ruled by democratically elected governments. A society of states concerned above all with economic growth at home or other domestic preoccupations will be different from one where governments are mainly concerned with the acquisition of territory abroad. The coming to power of highly nationalistic governments within states will affect their capacity to co-operate with one another for common purposes. The coming to power of governments deeply concerned about ideological questions will affect their willingness to accept drastic political change in neighbouring states. The main international consequence of a change in the internal structure of a state results from changes in its motives. And, as we saw in Chapter 6, the character of an international society is strongly influenced by the character of the dominant motives of its member-states.

Next, changes in technology, and especially those which affect communications between states, will affect the general character of an international society. The most obvious effect of developments in communications is to bring states closer together, and so to affect the geographical size of the international community. They will also determine the degree of interdependence among states especially economic interdependence, and as a result the vulnerability of each to developments which occur elsewhere. Industrialisation affects the kind of demands which states make on each other: their desire for markets, raw materials or opportunities for investment in other countries. The need of funds to finance industrialisation among very poor countries can bring about the establishment of new relationships, whether based on aid-giving and aid-receiving, or on inward investment and a dominant role for trans-national companies. The development of international investment may lead to large-scale transfers of funds from one state to another and to the creation of a new kind of relationship between creditors and debtors. The development of a capacity to exploit the minerals of the sea-bed or the Antarctic area can lead to new international conflicts concerning rights to the resources of those areas. Changes in military technology, creating the capacity to transmit vast destructive power over many thousands of miles within a period of minutes, transforms strategic relationships and the relative vulnerability of different states, while the cost of acquiring such capabilities equally transforms the relative power available to states at different levels of economic development.

Another type of change results from changes in the *institutions* established within international society. The development of diplomacy affects the knowledge which each state possesses of the intentions and capabilities of other states and so the rationality of their own actions. The growth of regular consultation among leading governments, as in the Concert of Europe, increases mutual knowledge and understanding and the capacity to secure accommodations on issues in dispute. The development of world-wide institutions, such as the League of Nations and the United Nations, increases the influence which small and powerless states can exert on the international environment and the necessity for more powerful states to explain and justify their policies. The development of procedures for conciliation, mediation and arbitration may affect the willingness of states to accept a peaceful resolution of disputes, rather than to determine them by recourse to armed force. The development of functional organisations of various kinds increases the scope and volume of co-operation among states, including states of widely conflicting political beliefs, and so may influence attitudes concerning the potential for co-operation in other areas. The development of trans-national associations and contacts of many kinds influences personal attitudes among races and nationalities and reduces hostility resulting from ignorance and traditional national stereotypes.

More important, perhaps, than any of these are the changes which occur, less perceptibly, in the ideas that are widely held about international relationships: in other words in the international *ideology*. Such changes reflect developments occurring *within* national states. As we have sought to show elsewhere,[2] and in Chapter 5 above, changes in the ideology of an international society result primarily from the emergence of new élites or ruling groups within states. This leads to changes in the motives of states corresponding to the interests and desires of these groups. These changes in the motives of states bring about fundamental changes in the character of international society generally. So a society in which the dominant motive of rulers is the acquisition of crowns in neighbouring states is wholly different from one in which the dominant motive is to determine the type of religion which is practised in neighbouring states; a society in which the dominant motive is to defend the sovereign independence and promote the power of existing states is wholly different from one in which the dominant motive is the creation of new states on the basis of national sentiment, or one in which the dominant motive is to secure victory for one ideological viewpoint or defeat for another.

Though the most important changes in international society are changes in the actions of states, these themselves stem from the actions of groups and individuals. It is the latter that are ultimately decisive, in this as in all other societies. Because of the power that is wielded by states, individuals and groups act at present to promote

---

2. Evan Luard, *Types of International Society* (London, 1976) chaps 5 and 6, and *Economic Relationships among States* (London, 1984) chaps 1 and 2.

their interests, or to bring about the changes they desire, primarily through seeking to influence the actions of their own states, or, very occasionally, the actions of states generally.

They do this partly by seeking to influence the *particular* actions of a state or states: by calling for the protection of their own industry or for the right to emigrate. But they do it ultimately through the influence which they are able to have on the ideology of the society as a whole. Thus the Dutch and English merchant classes, with the aid of the theories of de la Court and Adam Smith, succeeded in changing the thinking and policies, first of their own governments, then of many others as well. The monarchs of Europe, with the aid of such ideologists as Bodin, Machiavelli and Hobbes, succeeded in establishing the principles of sovereignty which reflected their own interests and ultimately prevailed throughout the world. The leaders of nationalist movements, first in Europe and later in other parts of the world, were able, with the aid of the writings of Mazzini, Fichte and others, to secure the acceptance of the national principle and "self-determination" as the basis of the world order established after 1918 and after 1945. It was the leaders of ideologically motivated governments, in east and west alike, with the aid of writings of Bentham, Mill, Lenin and Trotsky, who were able to establish ideological concerns as the dominant motivation of states in the most recent period.

Traditionally groups and individuals have sought to promote their interests through securing changes within *domestic* society, local or national. Today, increasingly, that situation has changed. The rapid decline of distance, the extension of political and economic relations across frontiers, the close interdependence of states and their peoples, have the effect that many of the changes which are most important today are not those that occur within states but in the wider international society. The standard of living individuals can secure, the price of the products they can buy in the shops, the quality of the environment in which they live, whether or not they will survive the next armed conflict, all these depend not on what happens within their own states but on events and decisions taken in the world beyond. Their welfare depends not only on the rate of growth in their own country but on the rate of growth of the world economy as a whole, the level of interest-rates established in New York, the level of oil prices established in Vienna, the trade policies adopted by Japan and the EEC. Social and cultural developments in one state are influenced by the social and cultural developments in others.

Thus the search for change is internationalised. And in consequence the most fundamental cause of the search for change, the demand for justice, is likewise transformed and internationalised. The justice which matters in the modern world, and the justice which is mainly sought, is no longer justice within the domestic society alone: it is justice in international society as a whole.

JUSTICE IN INTERNATIONAL SOCIETY

Justice is always ultimately a subjective concept. Even within the same society at the same time, among similar groups and individuals, opinions on what represents justice will differ: what seems just to some will seem unjust to others.

But judgements concerning what is just vary not only from individual to individual and group to group in this way. They vary equally from age to age according to changing philosophical, social and political ideas. However strenuously it may be believed and asserted that a particular idea of justice is based on absolute principles – based, for example, on natural law, the fundamental character of human nature, utilitarian philosophy or the principles of logic – no such arguments will prove equally convincing to all. And any arguments that may be put forward on the basis of one set of criteria (for example the need to treat those who are "essentially" like according to like principles) can always be countered by counter-arguments based on other criteria (for example that likeness is always relative and that there are always some differences which can be found to justify unlike treatment). So long as the judgements of reasonable people continue to diverge on questions of valuation, there will continue to be disputes on what is just. These differences will reflect differences in judgement and differences of interest alike. Though such differences may be narrowed by rational arguments, they can never be totally removed.

If it is impossible to secure agreement even among similar people within the same society on such matters, it is clearly still harder to do so within international society as a whole. Here too judgements about what is just will vary, from individual to individual, group to group, and state to state. And here too there will be equally wide variations from age to age, according to changing attitudes, beliefs and preconceptions. Each of the international "ideologies" we described earlier, for example, presuppose or imply differing ideas of justice. These too reflect differing judgements, which are themselves often influenced by differing interests.

Because of the complexity of modern international society the differences which exist there concerning questions of justice are themselves particularly complex. For the concept of justice in international society comprehends justice of various kinds. It includes justice between states, justice between groups and justice between individuals. Measures that bring about a greater degree of justice between states do not necessarily bring greater justice between individuals. Arrangements might be made, for example, which effectively secured the independence and integrity of individual states all over the world, while groups and individuals within those states continued to suffer the grossest abuse of human rights. Institutions could be created which brought about a substantial degree of redistribution from rich states to poor states all over the world without securing any redistribution of income within each state. The average income a head might be made identical within every state in the world, without in the least reducing the differences in incomes between individuals in each of those states.

Similarly justice between groups may fail to procure justice for individuals or states. A world economic system could be established which permitted totally free trade and investment in every part of the world on a basis that was totally non-discriminatory between companies, banks and other economic enterprises, yet failed to secure justice between states seeking to promote the development of new companies, banks and other enterprises among their own nationals; nor between individuals in different states, affected in various ways by the economic activities of groups which resulted. A world political system that was just between rival political parties, by allowing equal opportunity for each in every state, would not necessarily secure justice between states, if it enabled large states to dominate small ones; nor between individuals, if it meant that the rights of minorities were ignored.

The demand for justice (which everybody supports in theory) may be taken to imply either stability or change. Those who have an interest in the existing order will be inclined to believe that it is already a just one (for example, they may argue that the inequalities which it contains are only those necessary to secure greater efficiency, and so, by benefiting all, promote greater justice). Those who are dissatisfied with the existing order will claim that the inequalities which exist within it are *un*just, and that the changes they demand are necessary to remedy those injustices. While both will claim to believe in the establishment of a just order, they will not invoke the principle of justice equally. The former group, because they hold that justice already exists, will be less inclined to invoke that concept, and more inclined to maintain the need to resist disruptive demands for change in the interests of "order". The latter will, on the other hand, make frequent use of arguments relating to justice, and will accord them a higher priority than those based on the need for order. In other words, it is those who demand change who most frequently speak of justice. Or, to put it differently, it is those who are most satisfied with the justice of the existing order who find it least necessary to concern themselves with questions of justice generally: they already have the justice that they demand.

Those who demand justice, in the international as in any other society, call for a greater degree of equality in one form or another. They do not normally, there as in other cases, call for total equality in any respect. But they believe that under the existing order they suffer from *undue* disadvantage in one respect or another. The demand for greater justice comes primarily from those who feel that the existing distribution of power, wealth, trade, technology or other assets is unfair and should be remedied in their favour. Among states this demand is reflected in the call for a "new international economic order" that would bring about an irreversible shift of power and wealth from rich countries to poor. Among groups it can be seen in the demands of international trade unions or international environmentalists that policies should be adopted which provide better protection of labour rights, or of the world environment, than they do at present. Among individuals it may be seen in the demands of radical political parties and development groups that the aid policies of international agencies should be such as to benefit disadvantaged groups in the receiving country, regardless of the policies or will of their own governments.

Such claims for a greater degree of equality may be resisted, in international society as in other societies, on a number of grounds. The demand for justice can be said to call for greater inequality as well as greater equality. This may be based on the argument that, as Aristotle stated, it is as unjust to treat unequals equally (including those unequal in ability) as to treat equals unequally.[3] It may be held

3. It was on these grounds, for example, that in a civil rights case in the US it was held that the establishment of quotas for blacks among university entrants discriminated against qualified white applicants.

that a state (or a company or an individual) which has become wealthier than other states or companies or individuals *deserves* to have done so, by reason of the industry of its population, or the wisdom of its policies, and should not be penalised by measures designed to redistribute wealth in favour of the poor. Or the arguments in favour of greater equality may be resisted on the basis of different criteria altogether. It may be held, even by those who claim to believe in justice, that it is a value which must be balanced against other desirable objectives. Thus it may be said that the international status quo – territorial, economic, ideological and other – should be maintained, however unjust, because any attempt to change it will be resisted, and will thus give rise to conflict on a scale that would outweigh any benefits likely to be obtained (and which might lead not to a more just order but only to one in which the powerful were still more dominant). In the same way the demand for justice may be resisted in the interests of greater diversity. Total justice at the world level, it may be held, can be brought about only by the establishment of a world state, dedicated to organise world affairs in such a way as to eliminate injustice and reduce inequality; but this could only come about at the expense of the existing sovereignty of states, and so of the diversity, in culture, political systems and way of life, which at present result from it.

But the principle most commonly brought into play against the demands for greater equality is that of freedom. So in domestic societies it is held that redistributive taxation should be resisted, even if it does promote "justice", on the grounds that it violates individual liberty. At the international level this freedom is symbolised by the idea of sovereignty, embodying the independence of action of each individual state. Thus measures to bring about a redistribution of resources in favour of poorer states and individuals through the activities of international institutions, securing their revenues by levies imposed on wealthier states, will be resisted on the grounds that they infringe the "sovereignty" of each state: so that even the richest states will be willing to offer only voluntary (and therefore minimal) contributions for that purpose. Measures designed to bring certain resources – such as the minerals of the sea-bed or Antarctica – under international control and to use them to benefit poorer countries will be resisted on the grounds that this violates the freedom of states and their companies or nationals to secure "free" access to any part of the globe and to exploit the minerals they find there on the basis of their technological capabilities. Proposals to make patent rights more freely available are resisted on the grounds that this violates the rights of those groups and individuals which have developed the products in the first place, and the states from which they come, to draw the principal benefits from them. Demands for freer access for the products of manufacturing industries in poor countries to the markets of rich states may be resisted on the basis of the right of every state to control the conditions of trade in its markets and to protect the interests of its workers. (Yet, paradoxically, the very same states which make use of the concept of sovereignty to resist redistribution by such means often denounce the same concept when it is used in ways which they believe contrary to their own interests. Thus when poor states, on the basis of their own claim to sovereignty, nationalise raw materials production, or join in combinations with other producers of particular commodities such as oil, they are denounced on the grounds that they deny by such measures the right of "free access to resources". When, on the basis of the same claim to sovereignty, poor countries impose measures which restrict the right of their companies to trade or invest, in order to preserve foreign exchange or to reserve opportunities for their own infant industries, this is held to be an abuse of sovereignty and a denial of free economic competition.)

Differences concerning what represents "justice" in the international society occur not only in the economic field. They occur equally on political questions. The main difference here concerns the limits of the action one state is justified in undertaking to bring about "justice" elsewhere. Again the conflict is between the requirement of justice and those of freedom or "sovereignty". This difference of principle occurs most obviously where one government pursues policies held by other governments to violate the basic "rights" of their population. There exist wide differences of view concerning what type of conduct by governments within their own states towards their own populations is totally unacceptable, and what kind of action may therefore be taken by other states to reverse it. But there is increasing acceptance that, if the injustices being committed are great enough, and outside opinion sufficiently unanimous, action may be taken, at least by peaceful means, such as trade boycotts and other measures, to bring about the changes in policy demanded (as is now generally accepted in the case of South Africa).

The choice made in these cases between respect for sovereignty and the remedying of injustice – that is, between the values of order and justice – has varied from one case to another in a highly inconsistent way. Gross violations of human rights in one country – Cambodia or Equatorial Guinea – are ignored, while lesser violations in another are passionately condemned. Nor is the conflict that arises confined to serious violations of human rights of this kind. There remain legitimate differences of view as to what policies by governments towards their own populations represent "injustice", which must be universally condemned, and which are merely a legitimate exercise of sovereignty. Measures undertaken by governments to restrict immigration by their citizens are denounced as iniquitous by some but defended equally strenuously by others; just as restraints on emigration were equally denounced and defended only fifty or so years ago. There is no consensus concerning the duty of governments to allow freedom of the press, to form political parties, an indepent judiciary, the right to legal representation and a speedy trial after arrest, the right to a minimum standard of living or to work if willing to do so and many other issues. In a world of conflicting ideologies, governments of one persuasion denounce governments of another for the iniquities of their policies of different kinds. Western states denounce communist states for the political inequalities of their system, while communist states denounce Western countries for the economic inequalities of theirs. Some will believe that the injustices they denounce in their opponents are sufficient to justify intervention in those cases; yet will bitterly resist it if undertaken against themselves. In practice most states from time to time resort to unilateral action to secure the "justice" they favour, intervening in the civil conflicts of other states to save them from "totalitarianism" or from "imperialist exploitation".

In smaller societies the principal way in which changes designed to secure greater justice are brought about is by changes in the law. The immediate objective of those seeking change is therefore to win control of the law-making process – through political activity and the winning of elections, through influence over governments, or through revolution, civil war and *coups d'état* – so that the desired changes can be introduced. In international society this means of bringing about change is not available. No process of legislation takes place there comparable to that occurring within states. The UN General Assmebly can pass resolutions, Declarations or even draft Conventions (having legal force for those states which ratify them). But in each case their effect in each state depends on the voluntary assent of its own government. That assent is in practice in the hands of the government alone.[4] which may or may not be representative of populations.

In consequence the "international law" which states at present claim to respect in practice embodies only those principles and "customs" acknowledged by governments themselves. Because it has developed over centuries, and because there exists no simple procedure for amending it with changing circumstances, it reflects the attitudes and assumptions of states in the past as much as those of the present. It therefore reflects the traditional concern of states with stability rather than change; with order rather than justice. Demands for justice in international society, which like all demands for justice normally imply a demand for change, are thus often in direct conflict with the principles of traditional international law. For justice is not the primary concern of that law.

As we have seen it is those who most wish for change who most frequently appeal to justice. Always there will be some states that will be more concerned than others to secure change, more likely than others to proclaim the requirements of "justice". This may be those which feel that the territorial order unjustly denies their aspirations (as for example Somalia today may reasonably feel that the frontiers inherited from the colonial past unjustly deny her legitimate aspirations for a national state embracing all her peoples). It may be those that feel that the traditional legal order denies legitimate claims to sovereignty (as Panana and Egypt have long felt that the treaties governing their canal zones, even if freely entered into at the time, unjustly denied them full sovereignty over important facilities within their territories). It may be those which feel that "unequal treaties" inherited from the past deny them their full rights (as China and Argentina today claim, like Turkey, Persia and Egypt in the past, that they have been compelled to accept an unjust diminution of their territorial and other rights by being compelled to submit in years gone by to the superior power available to European states). It may be those states which find large parts of their mineral wealth under the control of foreign enterprises, inhibiting their right to exercise full control over them or derive the benefits these would otherwise afford to them (as in recent times the countries producing oil, copper, tin and other minerals have demanded the right to

4. Formally international conventions are ratified by parliaments but they may not be submitted for ratification if they are unacceptable to governments.

nationalise or otherwise acquire control of those resources). But the demand for justice, and therefore for change, comes above all in the modern world from poor countries demanding a greater degree of economic justice: a redistribution of resources, technology, managerial skills and other assets from rich countries to poor. As within states, it is today economic injustice – a denial of economic rights, rather than of legal or political rights as in the past – which has become the principal stimulus to demands for change in international society: for a new "international economic order".

Such demands do not come only from governments. Ultimately all demands for justice, within states or between them, come from individuals. In some cases the demands put forward by individuals and groups are transmitted by governments, seeking to influence the policies of other governments. In other cases those demands are expressed directly: they are addressed equally to all governments and are not reflected in the policy of any. So revolutionary groups may call for a fundamental change in the political or economic systems of all states simultaneously. Disarmament groups may call for the abandonment of nuclear weapons and the destruction of all stocks of such weapons by all states. Environmental groups all over the world may call for the abandonment of atomic power, the abolition of whaling and a ban on all economic development in the Antarctic. Autonomist movements may call for the granting of independence to Basques, Corsicans, Kurds, Eritreans, West Papuans, West Saharis and other groups throughout the world, without any support from governments. Often it is demands for justice of this kind, directed against established authority all over the world, which arouse the deepest feelings and the strongest commitment. And it is they which may ultimately, though only after long struggle, produce changes within international society more profound than any which are called for by states directing their demands at other states. For often they challenge the basis of the existing order: the authority of governments.

Because conceptions of justice are subjective, no society – domestic or international – can establish an order universally accepted as a just one. Always there will be some demanding further change in the name of justice. What each society needs, if those demands are to be contained without excessive violence, is procedures by which the demands can secure proper attention, and the changes, if accepted, be implemented. It is such procedures which international society at present lacks. Yet, in a rapidly shrinking world, it is changes in international society and institutions, rather than those within single states, which now matter most, since it is they which can most affect people's lives. And it is adequate procedures to effect such changes that are today therefore most urgently required.

Without them justice in international society will appear a dream even more distant than justice in domestic societies: a dream which, even more than there, may provoke desperate remedies. The demand for justice, if sufficiently widely felt, can never be persuasively countered by asserting the need for order. However deeply felt the demand for order in international society, it can never obliterate the demand for justice, since a system which denies justice cannot for long be orderly. The demand for order must for that reason imply ultimately an equal concern for justice. And international society, however complex, diffuse and ill-organised, can no more insulate itself from that concern than can any other society. It too can become more orderly only in becoming less unjust.

Index